APERTURE

Cultures in Transition: The World's Reality

Increasingly a sense of interdependence has come to characterize relations between cultures—a sense of shared problems and concerns; of multivalent exchanges, whether political, economic, or artistic. This new sense of connectedness can be found not only among industrialized nations, as political barriers in force since World War II fall, but also in relations between industrialized and developing nations. Lands and peoples once considered exotic and therefore "Other" now come into contact on a daily basis, undermining old assumptions and stereotypes. The legacy of European colonialism remains an important factor in cross-cultural relations, but this sad heritage is now accompanied by an awareness of the changed terms of cultural interaction.

Within countries, too, there is an increased recognition of the need to find new ways to mediate the assumptions and aspirations of distinct groups. Tribal peoples, in particular—under continuing pressure from the outside—seek to use industrialization for their own ends while retaining their cultural traditions. Meanwhile, many in the industrialized world continue to project a false "primitiveness" on tribal cultures, even as they maintain patterns of economic and political domination. Others, though, actively question the familiar terms of cultural exchange, seeking to foster more equitable relations between peoples.

The photographers in this issue focus on these complex issues, and especially on the ways photography represents people both to others and to themselves. Operating in the space between anthropological and documentary photography, and questioning the assumptions of both, these photographers explore new ways to depict cultures and peoples in an interdependent world.

This issue grows out of a special symposium entitled "The World's Reality"—organized by Aperture, hosted by the Esalen Institute, and supported in part by the National Endowment for the Arts and the Paul Strand Fund for the Aperture Foundation—held in February 1988. During the course of this four-day gathering, photographers, anthropologists, filmmakers, and others discussed issues involved in depicting cultures in a changing world. Several essays in this issue highlight topics that were central to the symposium's debates: In any photographic exchange, who decides what will be depicted, and how it will be shown? Who are the pictures being made for? In studying another culture, does the observer—whether photographer or anthropologist—have a responsibility beyond simply making a record, to attempt to influence or arrest the change?

Questions of this sort reach to the heart of the ethics of photography. In this issue we strive not for resolution but for discussion, presenting images and essays that demonstrate a range of approaches to these concerns. These photographers and writers attempt to adjust familiar but no longer adequate equations that continue to define the terms of cultural exchange, and to acknowledge the importance of retaining cultural diversity in an increasingly homogenized world.

THE EDITORS

The Unveiled: Algerian Women, 1960

By Carole Naggar

What are you trying to pacify? The walls?
—A Muslim to a young draftee

Virtually forgotten today, the Algerian War (1954–1962) was for France somewhat like what the Vietnam War was for the United States: a painful era, woven with errors and official denial, unconsciously repressed so that even today, French people find it difficult to confront directly. In 1960, when Marc Garanger, a twenty-five-year-old draftee, started taking photographs, it had been lingering for six years. For two years before, it had been on the front page of all the French dailies, at the heart of all conversations. France was split into two factions that drifted further apart every day. On one side, the supporters of *Algérie française*; on the other, a growing part of French youth, and intellectuals such as Jean-Paul Sartre, Simone de Beauvoir, and Francis Jeanson, a founder of a support network for the National Liberation Front (FLN), *Jeune Resistance*. In February 1960, several members of the network were arrested, and Jeanson, wanted by the police, held a clandestine press conference: "We must break the cycle of the abominable complicity that has allowed forty-five million French people to accept the slaughter and torture, through intermediaries, of ten million Algerians."

The Algerian War has scarcely been documented in France. One could even describe the French response to the war as one of collective amnesia, so rare have testimonies about it been, at least until the last few years. Garanger's two books (*Femmes Algériennes,* 1982, and *La Guerre d'Algérie,* 1983) are notable exceptions to this willful forgetting. In fact, Garanger is to date the only photographer to have published even a single monograph on the war.

In 1960, Garanger landed in Kabylia, in the small village of Ain Terzine, about seventy-five miles south of Algiers. Like many politically conscious young men, he had put off his departure for the army as long as possible, hoping that the war would come to an end before he would have to go. In a recent interview he recalled this time: "War was a heartbreak, photography a mode of survival. My life had already started: I left a wife and a daughter behind me." Though a primary school teacher by training, Garanger had been photographing professionally since 1950. When he went into the Army he was soon selected as his regiment's photographer.

But while French opinion progressively evolved towards the acceptance of Algerian independence, the French army, already frustrated by its defeat in Indochina, could resign itself to losing face and leaving. At stake for the army was a symbolic victory: the crusade of the free world against international Communism, French Algeria being to them the last remnant of France's past grandeur.

By then the war was almost over. At the head of the army, General Maurice Challes attacked the center of FLN support. Perched in the mountains like eagles' nests, the villages were occupied by approximately two million people who had joined the FLN since 1954. To deprive the rebels of their contacts with the village people, Challes decided to transfer the population. Says Garanger: "The French army had adopted 'pacification' as a strategy: they demolished the farms and isolated villages, they knocked down everything, they pulled down the roofs." Once the houses had been leveled, the civilian population was forced to build their own "regroupment villages" around the military outposts. "They were concentration camps really," Garanger recalls, "encircled with barbed wire, closed at night, and supervised from observation posts." This brings to mind similar operations described by Philip Jones Griffiths in his 1971 book on the Vietnam War, *Vietnam, Inc.*

At certain hours it was possible to go out of the camp. Garanger always went around to the same five or six villages where he had met the local civilians: "They were the only ones who interested me: how could they survive under the conditions that they had been given? It was to survive and to express my disagreement that I took photographs.

"One day the camp major decreed that the inhabitants of the villages must all have identity cards. Naturally, he asked the military photographer to make these cards. Either I refused and went to prison, or I accepted. I understood my luck: it was to be a witness, to make pictures of what I saw that mirrored my

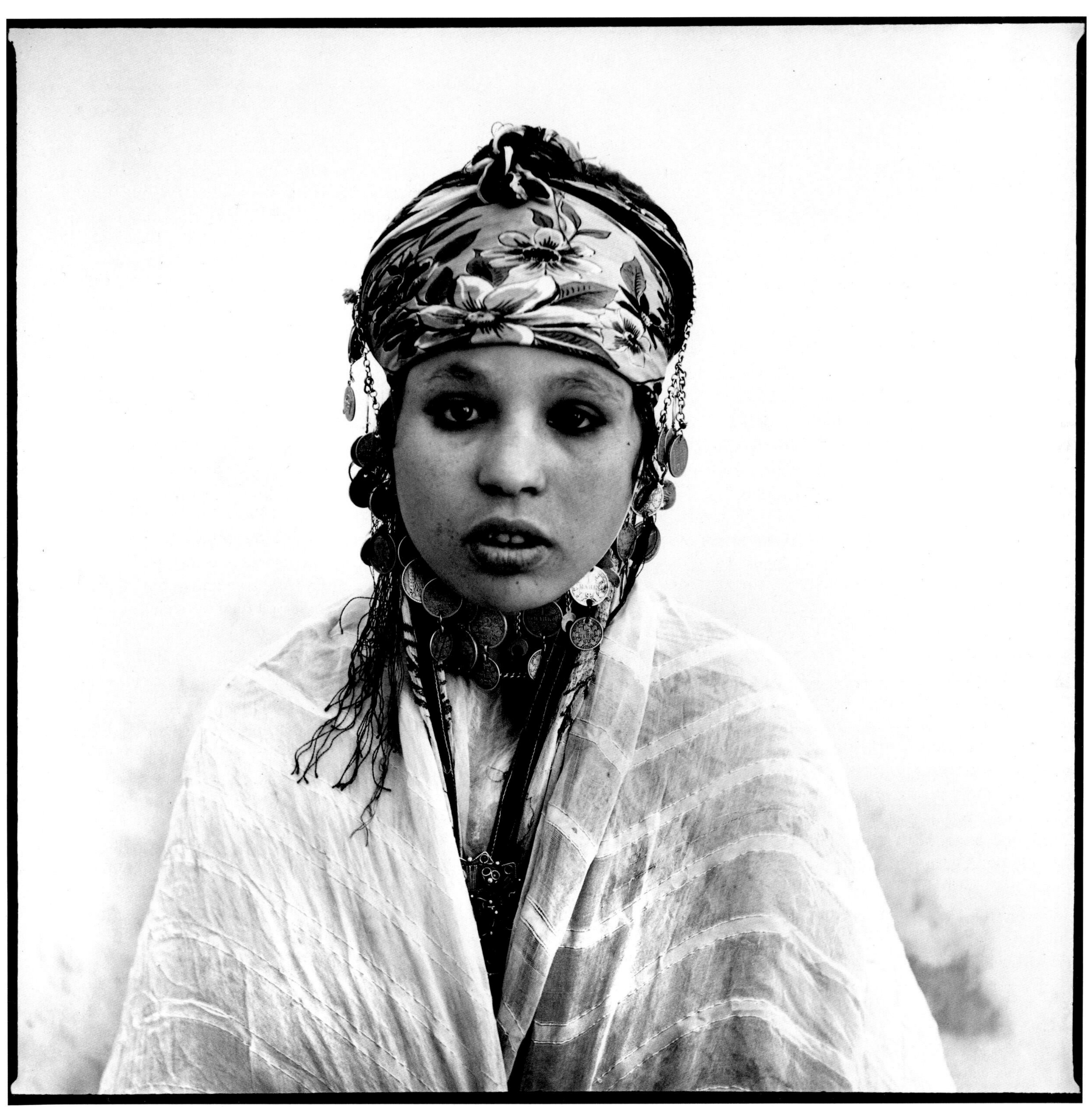

Photographs by Marc Garanger, from *Femmes Algériennes 1960*

opposition to the war. I saw that I could use what I was forced to do, and have the pictures tell the opposite of what the authorities wanted them to tell.

"Berber or Muslim, the women came from the neighboring villages: Ain Terzine, Bordj Okhriss, the Mezdour, the Meghine, Souk el Kremis. They had had no contact with Europeans whatsoever. People who live there are half-nomadic shepherds. The climate in those parts is very hot and dry in the daytime, cold at night, with snow in winter. The people have a very hard life; it shows in their faces.

"When I arrived for the sittings, there would be a detachment of armed men with machine guns across their shoulders, an interpreter, and the commander. The women would be lining up. Each in turn would sit on a stool outdoors, in front of the whitewashed wall of the house—the *mechta*. I would come to within three feet of them. They would be unveiled. In a period of ten days, I made two thousand portraits, two hundred a day, mostly of women. They were from fourteen years old to no age. They had no choice in the matter. Their only way of protesting was through their look.

"It is this immediate look that matters. When one discharges a condenser, a spark comes out: to me, photography involves seizing just that instant of discharge. In these sessions I felt a completely crazy emotion. It was an overwhelming experience, with lightning in each image. I held up for the world a mirror, which reflected this lightning look that the women cast at me.

"Only one woman refused to sit down. She shouted insults at all the French who were there. She was a very old woman. The officer asked the interpreter: 'What did she say?' He covered for her: 'Don't worry, she's nuts.' This was the only time I ever saw the women. My photographs were used for the identity cards for a year and a half."

At one point Garanger's major "started screaming, stirred up the staff: 'Come and see these macaques, they look like monkeys!' " Their identity defied him completely—or else he would not have used Garanger's pictures. But "even the stupidity of officers has limits," says Garanger, who also recalls how the colonel had asked him to photograph Bencherif, an FLN leader, after he had been arrested. This photo was to be printed on the back of flyers that were to be dropped by parachute in a French campaign to bring the FLN into disrepute with the Algerian population. But Bencherif's dignity when handcuffed, the defiance of his look, would not have helped the colonel's scheme. He knew this, and as a result the flyer was printed and distributed without a picture.

The major's perspective on the portraits was obscene, a kind of rape. This rape was not the first that the Algerian women had to suffer: the first rape was the unveiling itself. The veil—in Arabic *hijab*, "what separates two things"—has complex meanings in Islam. Al Hallaj, a commentator on the Koran, writes that it is "a screen interposed between the searcher and his aim, the probationer and his desire, the archer and his target. . . . It is not God that wears a veil, but His creatures. God has clothed the creatures with the veil of their name" because "if He were to uncover reality for them, they would die." God's face itself is said to be veiled by "seventy thousand curtains of light and darkness." To the woman, a symbol of divine beauty in Islamic poetry, one does not talk except through a veil.

In the Western world, a veil is only for hiding; in North Africa and the Middle East, men are used to deciphering the face of a veiled woman through her veil. Where a Westerner would see only a sketch, Arabs can guess the minutest details of a face and can say honestly of a veiled woman who passed in the street how beautiful she was. For an Algerian woman, the veil is inseparable from the face. It may be taken off within the secrecy of the walls, among women or between husband and wife, but never publicly in front of a stranger, particularly if he is an infidel. The veil is like a second skin, and the unveiling does more than lay the face bare: it flays it. The humiliation of having one's face uncovered is to an Algerian woman as great as imposed nudity would be for a prisoner in a concentration camp. On that level Garanger's portraits symbolize the collision of two civilizations, Islamic and Western.

There is another rape in this confrontation, and it is photography's. In Islam, representation is forbidden. A portrait is *ha-*

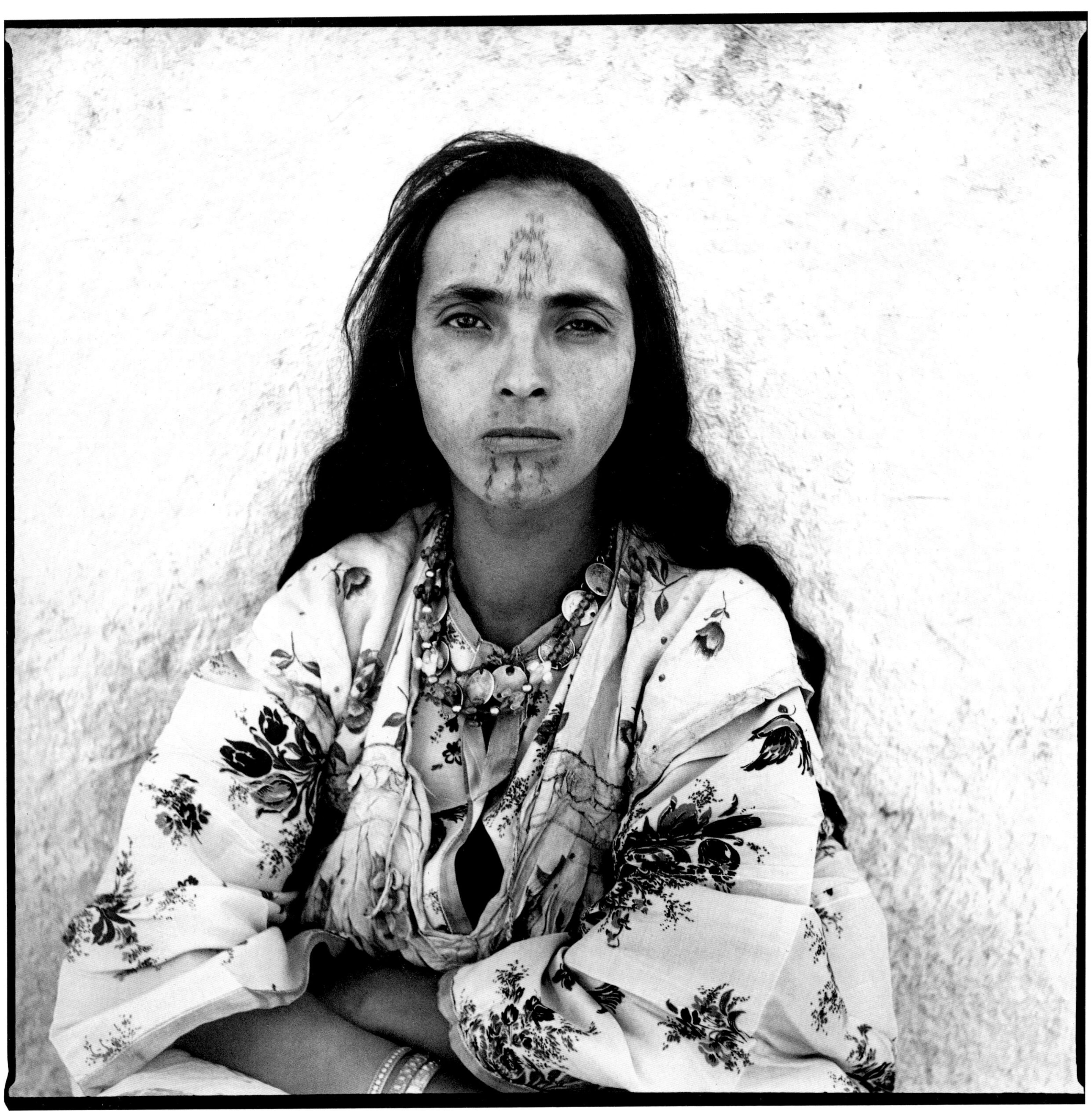

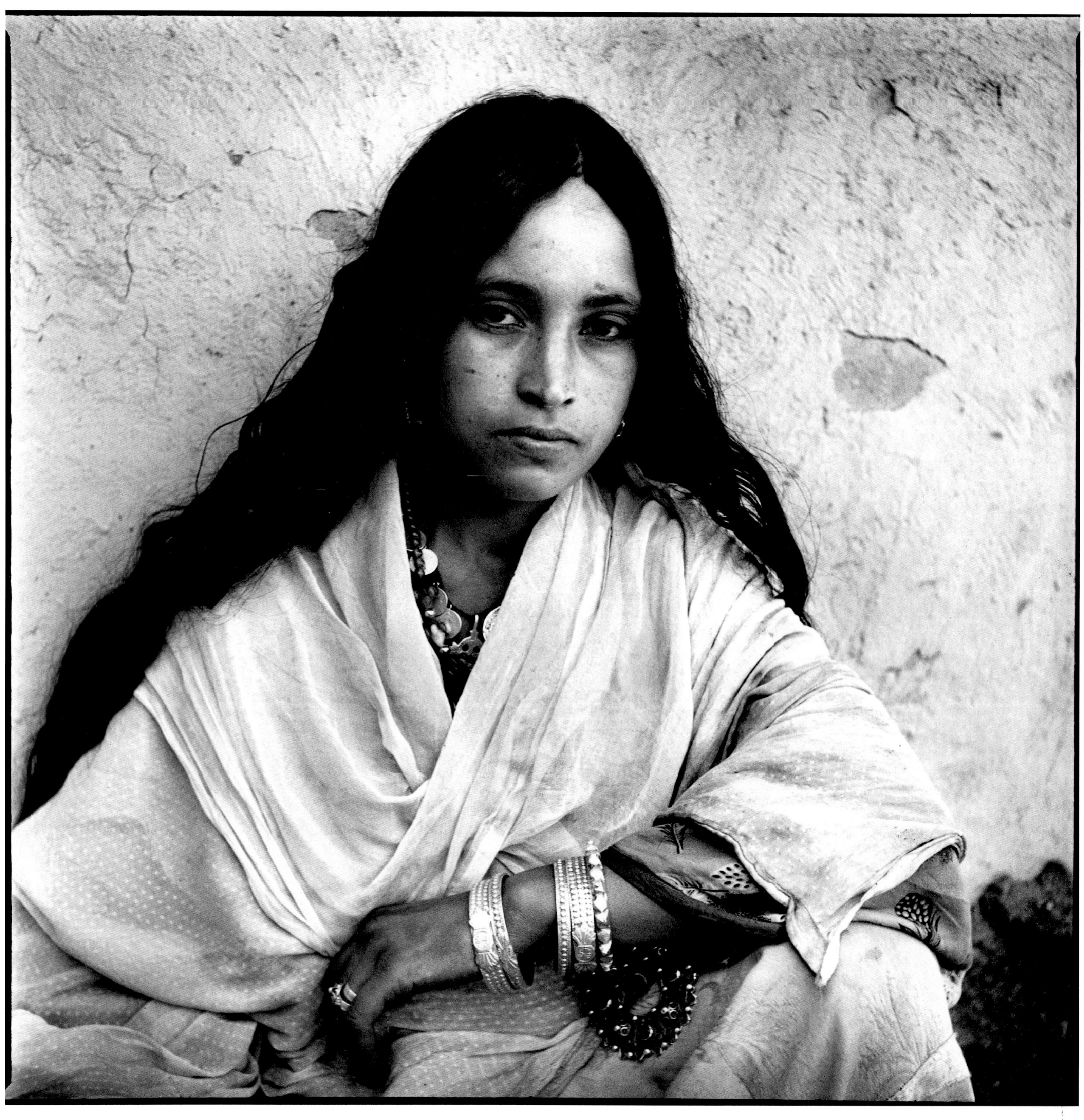

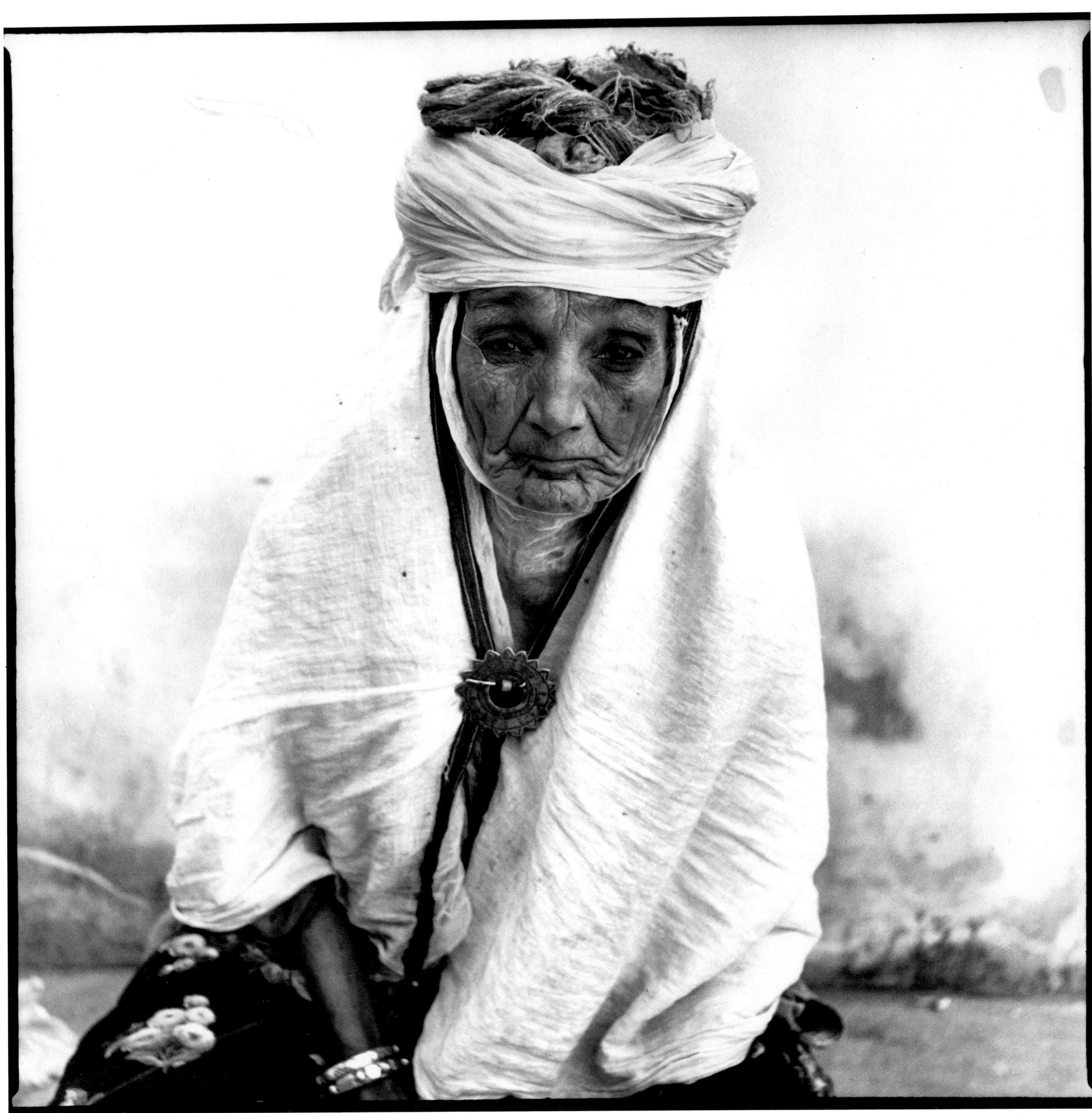

suma, shameful. For these women only their husbands, their siblings, their children, their friends and the woman who tattooed the blue marks against the evil eye on their chin, nose, and forehead, had known their face before. But in front of Garanger's camera all at once the taboo is destroyed. The veil is pulled down on their shoulders. Under their black, heavy, dishevelled hair, here are their feverish cheeks, the fire of their insulted gaze. The protective tattoos are exposed. Maybe as a challenge, the women wear their best ceremonial dress, their silver jewelry. The white wall they stand in front of, guarded by a soldier, is a kind of execution wall, the camera a weapon through which a murder is performed: exposing them to everyone's look, stealing from them their freedom that was linked to secrecy.

Pushed from behind, they enter the twentieth century in its most frightening aspect: they are identified so they can be controlled, supervised, repressed. This was also the case in 1848 when Eugène Appert, in Versailles prison, made hundreds of portraits of Communards that were then put into the file of the military police, or when Alphonse Bertillon invented his descriptive files (front and profile) in 1887 for the archive of the Service of Judicial Identity. Out of these early examples grew the idea that a photographic record of the identities of a complete population might be useful. In October 1940 the Vichy regime finally carried out this idea, making everybody submit to a control that until then had been applied only to "dangerous minorities."

Looking at Garanger's photographs we may think of this history of identity photographs and especially of those identity cards on which in 1942 the word "Jewish" was imposed. Thus the portraits become an image of a more general suffering. Behind them I also see in a watermark all the violence of the Algeria War: beatings, tortures, imprisonments, humiliations.

So why is it that, being victims, the Algerian women do not appear to be such? It seems to me that, paradoxically, a space of freedom is enacted in these portraits. They are the contrary of what has been called "modern" in photography: although they were taken in an instant, they are not snapshots. The models are fully conscious. The Algerian women, never photographed before and probably never to be photographed again, recall in the stiffness of their pose and the intensity of their look the beginnings of photography. So upsetting are these portraits that we think of the first daguerreotypes: some viewers, thinking that the images could return their gaze, were afraid of these minuscule faces. But, where the sitters in daguerreotypes had a strong desire to be photographed, what we read here is a refusal. Saying no, the women seem to add: "Even if you have photographed us, we remain uncontrollable."

A few months later, in December of 1960, the U.N. declared the right of the Algerians to independence. In March 1962 this right became a fact. What happened to the identity cards? Says Garanger, "I had the list of the women's names [but lost it]. As for the identity cards, they must have been torn up when independence arrived."

In the twentieth century the image of war has changed drastically, becoming at once broader and more precise. Since the Spanish Civil War, photographs have shown us not only armies confronting each other, but the wider repercussions of broader, more diffuse conflicts: lines of refugees, prisoners in camps, hungry children, torture. Modern war is documented as much by suggested violence as by violence seen directly. An example of this is a photograph made by Shomei Tomatsu, in Hiroshima, of a beer can that the atomic explosion has bent and squashed into an unrecognizable form, like a flayed body by Chaim Soutine. Similarly, Garanger's pictures, of civilians rather than soldiers, depicting psychological rather than physical violence, tell us more about the Algerian War than photos of torture or lynching would.

Looking like the landscapes of Little Kabylia, of smooth or furrowed sand, the women's faces tell us about the difficulties of their lives, but they also tell us that they will not yield. Their angry look is the "evil eye" that they cast to protect themselves and to curse their enemies. These defiant looks tell us of France's coming defeat and shame. Though we do not know the names or ages of these women, these glaring gazes alone guarantee their real identities. We are as if tattooed by them, and the burn persists.

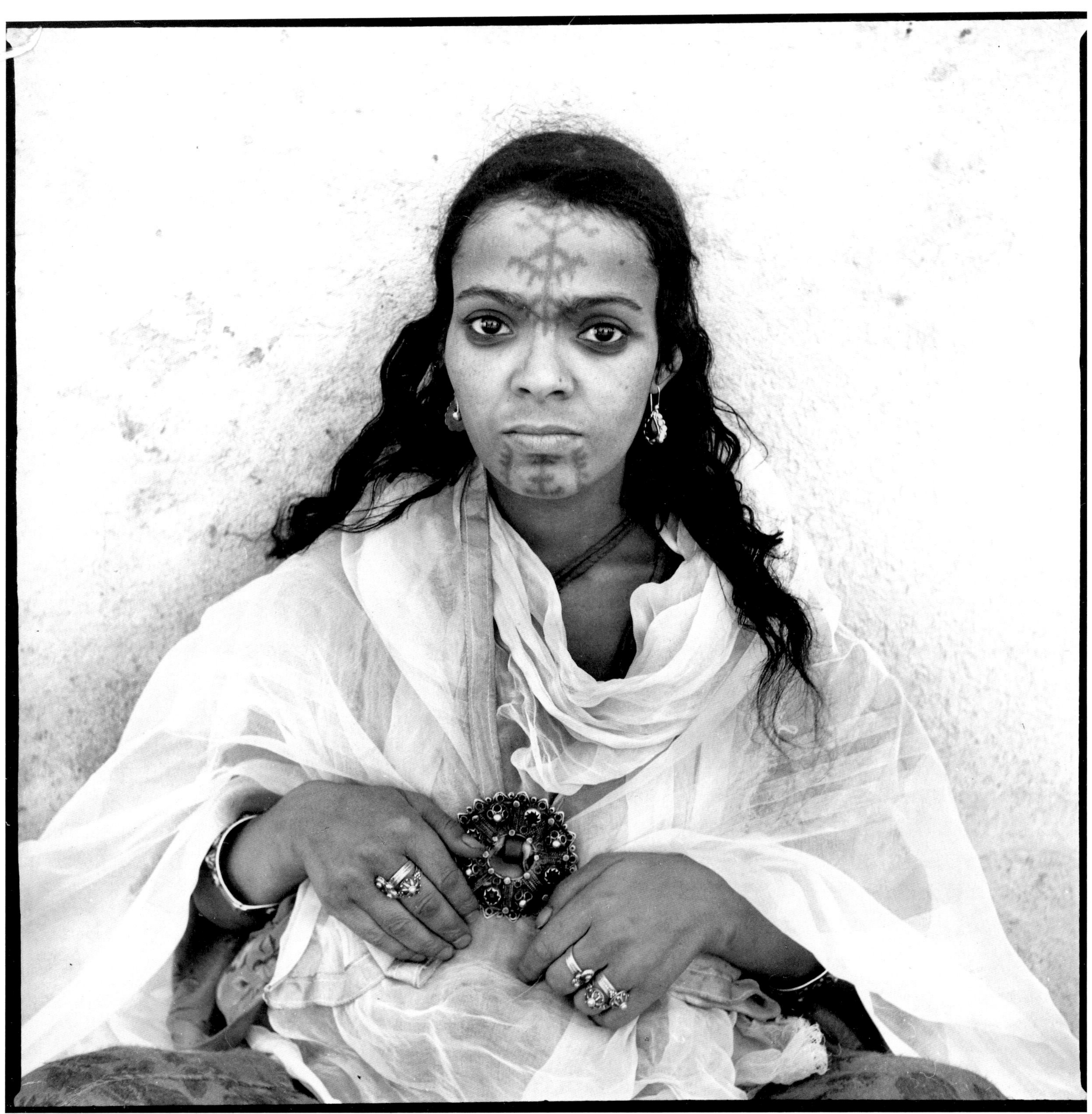

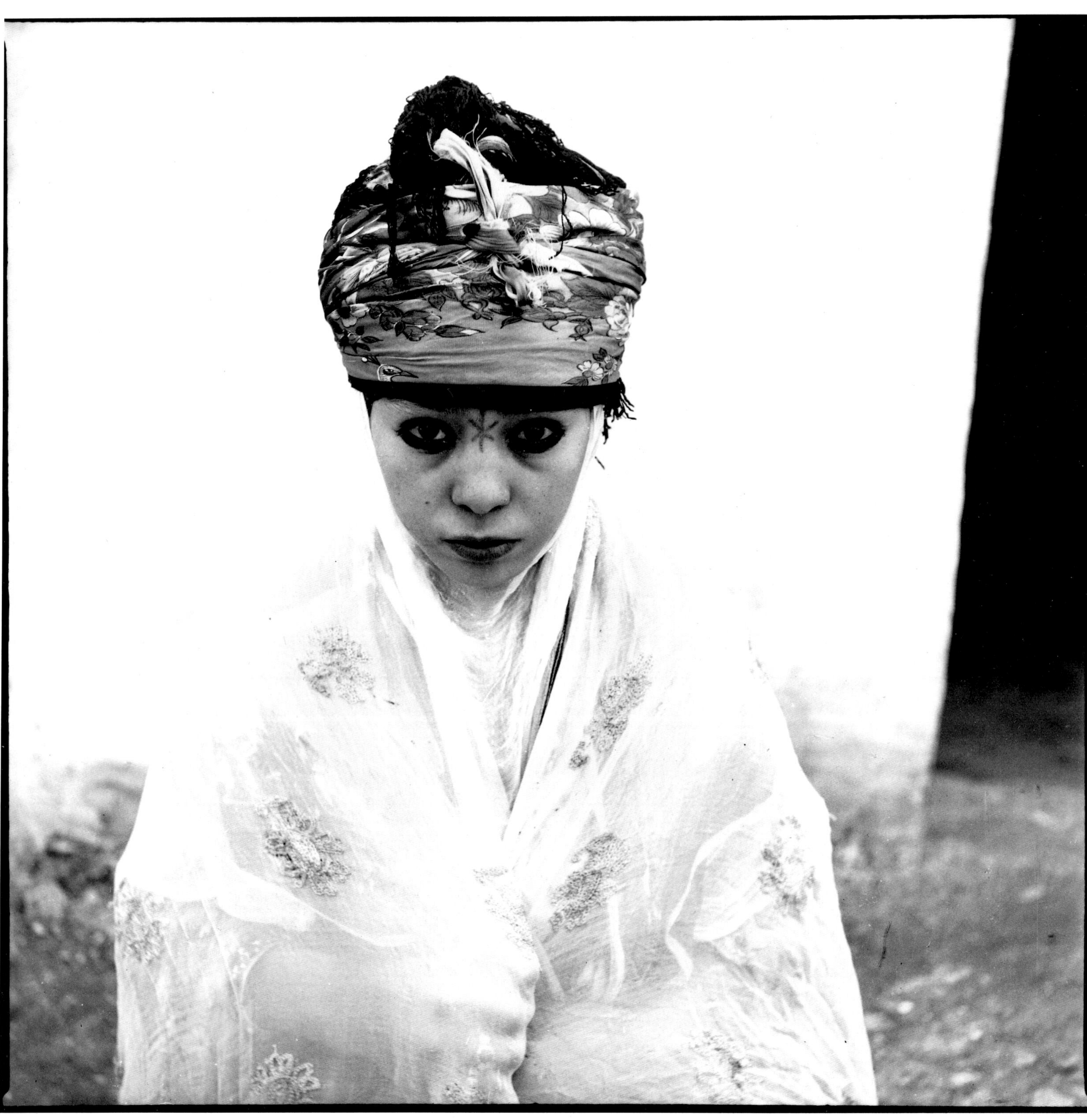

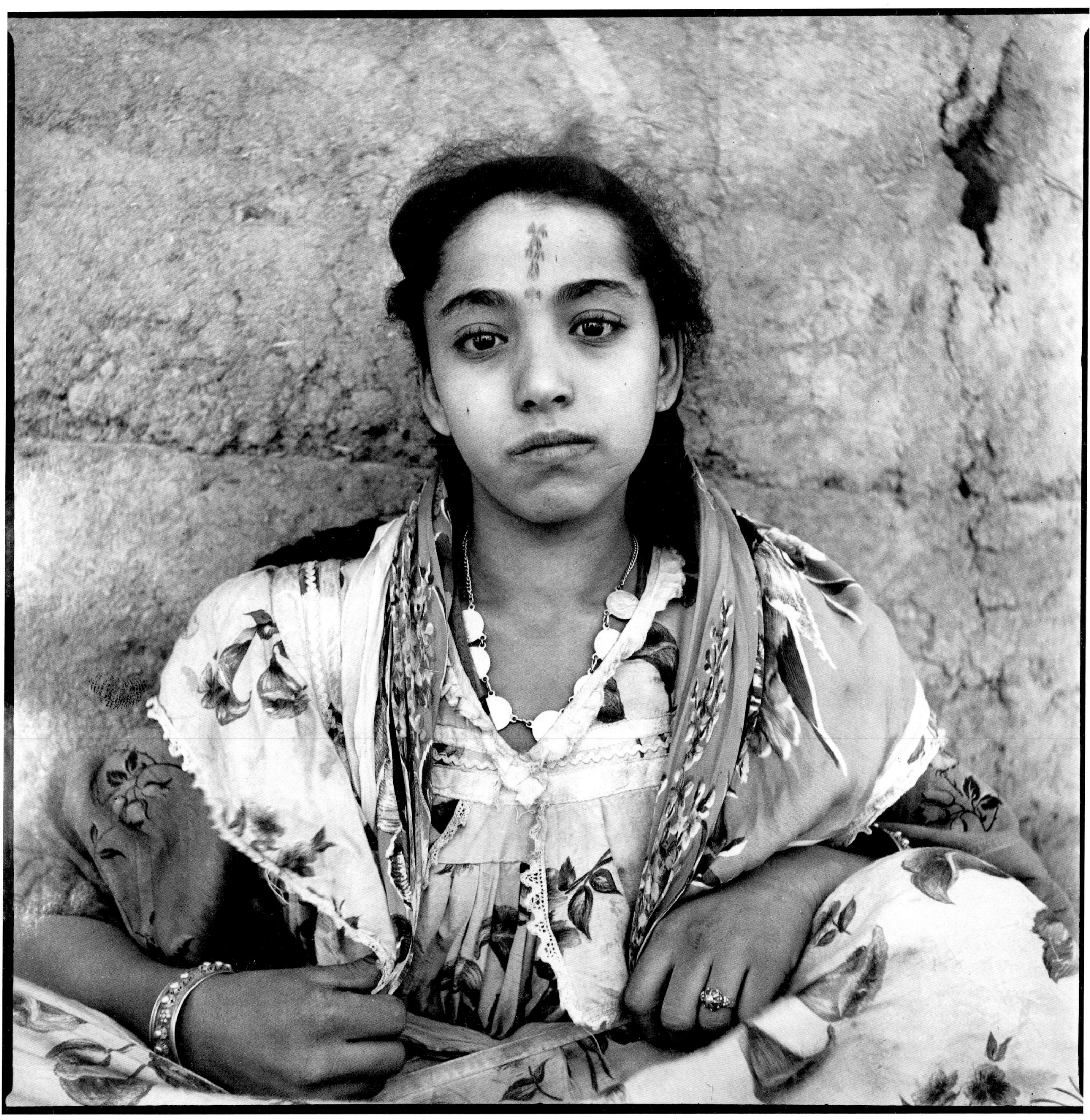

A House Divided: South Africa's Hostels

By David Lewis

Hostel life is the quintessential apartheid experience for millions of black South Africans. It is the mortar and brick representation of the recently scrapped pass laws. Men—and, less frequently, women—denied the right to settle permanently in the towns where they were forced to seek work, and denied the right to be accompanied by their families, spent eleven months of each year in one or another hostel complex, often returning for decades on end to the same dormitory, even the same bed.

Go to the "Kirk" hostel complex in Gugulethu, one of Cape Town's black townships, on a Saturday afternoon and some of you might even romanticize it. Vendors ply their trade in the sand; clumps of men sit on makeshift benches, usually at burial society meetings; young men drink beer and brandy while mpaqanga—the popular reggae-type music of the African townships—blares from speakers placed on the hostel roofs.

However appealing it might seem, that picture reflects an indomitable will to survive with dignity. The material reality is unremittingly grim. A 1988 government survey found that in the hostels of Langa, Nyanga, and Gugulethu—three of Cape Town's African townships—82,565 people shared 25,701 beds. What can you expect of the ventilation, light, toilets, and water, when there are more than three people per bed?

This adversity breeds resistance. Stepping out on a Saturday afternoon in a neatly ironed shirt is an act of resistance; surrounding half of a double bunk with curtaining to provide a husband and wife a modicum of privacy is an act of resistance.

In the 1970s and early '80s the hostel dwellers in the townships were the backbone of the union movement. While they remain a numerically important component of union membership, as the union movement has become more sophisticated, more urbane, more youthful, the

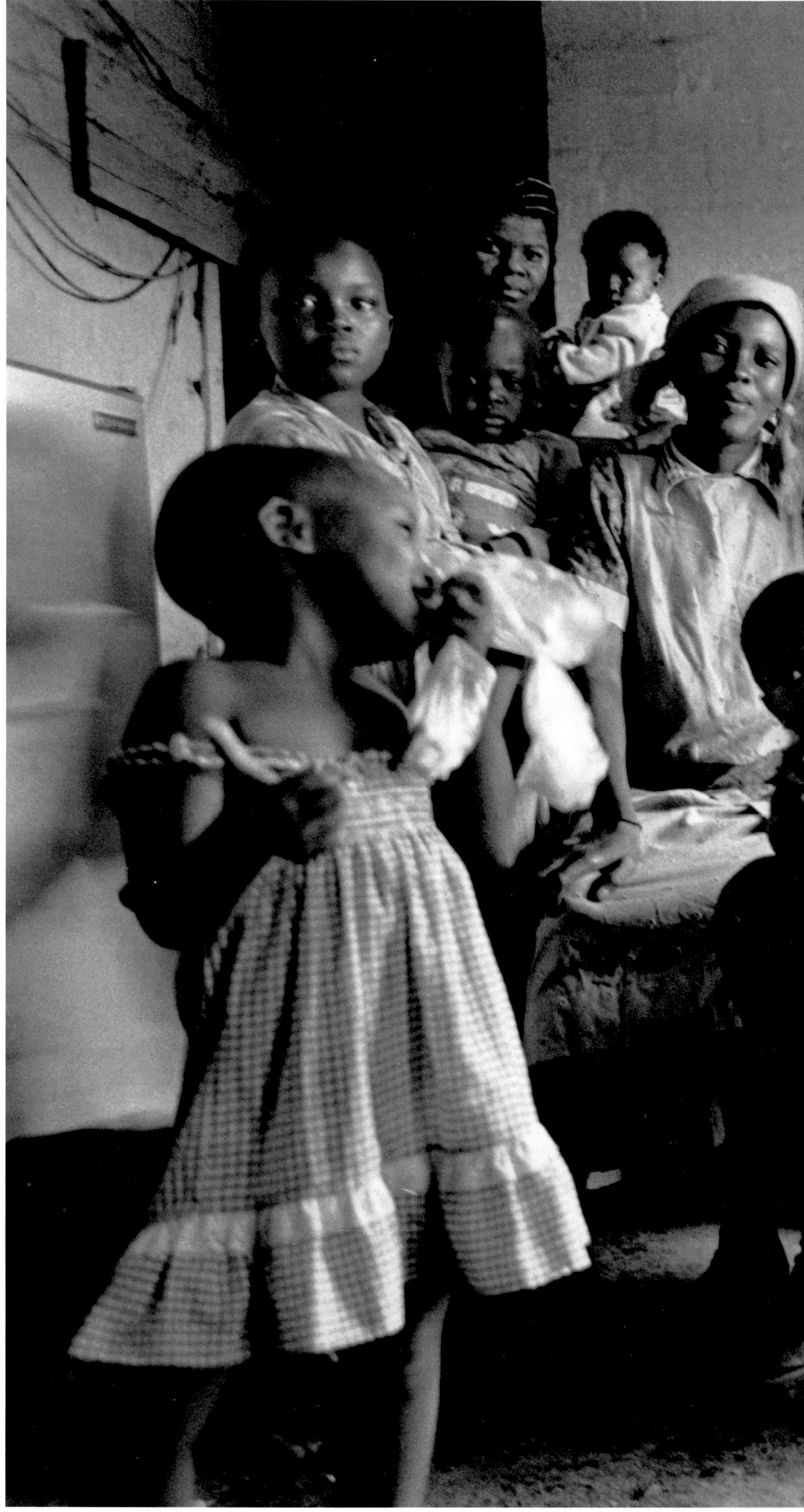

Roger Meintjies, *Women and children, Khiki,* 1987–89

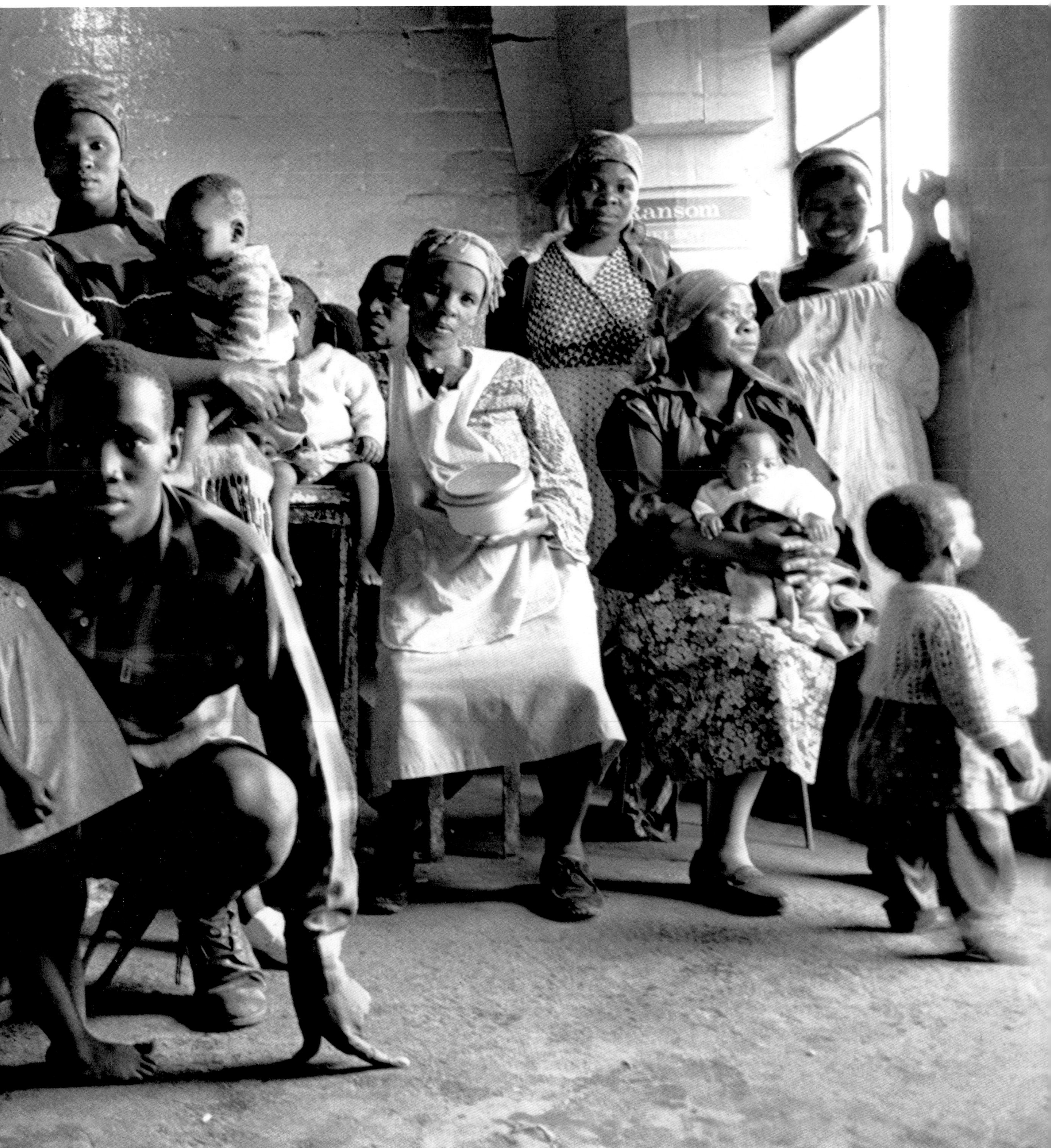
Ransom

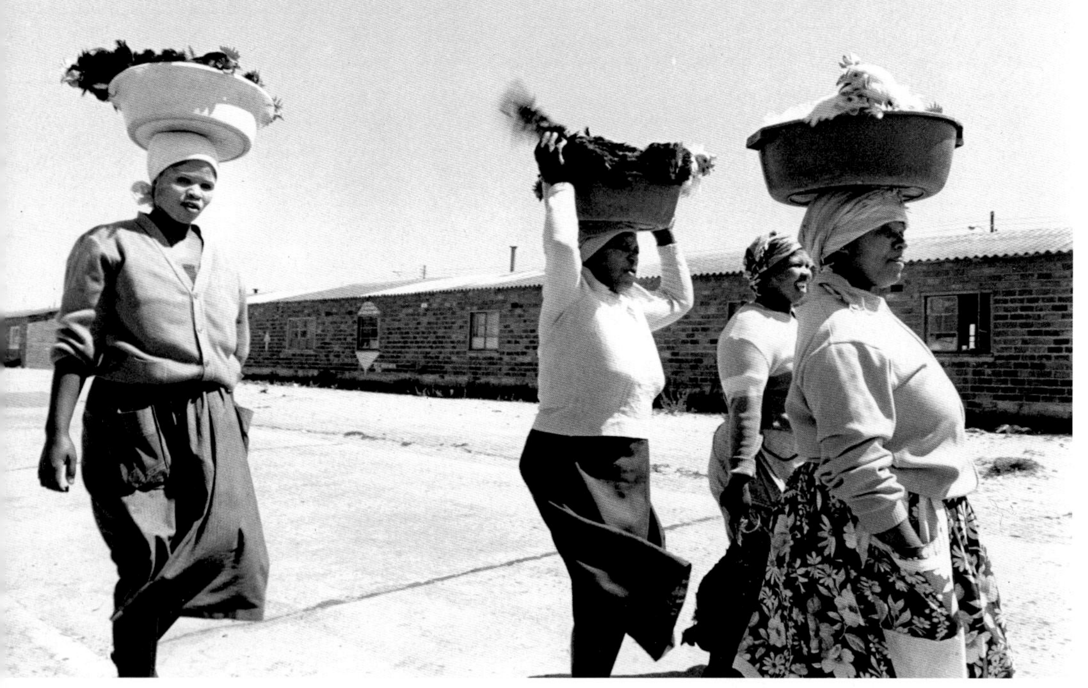

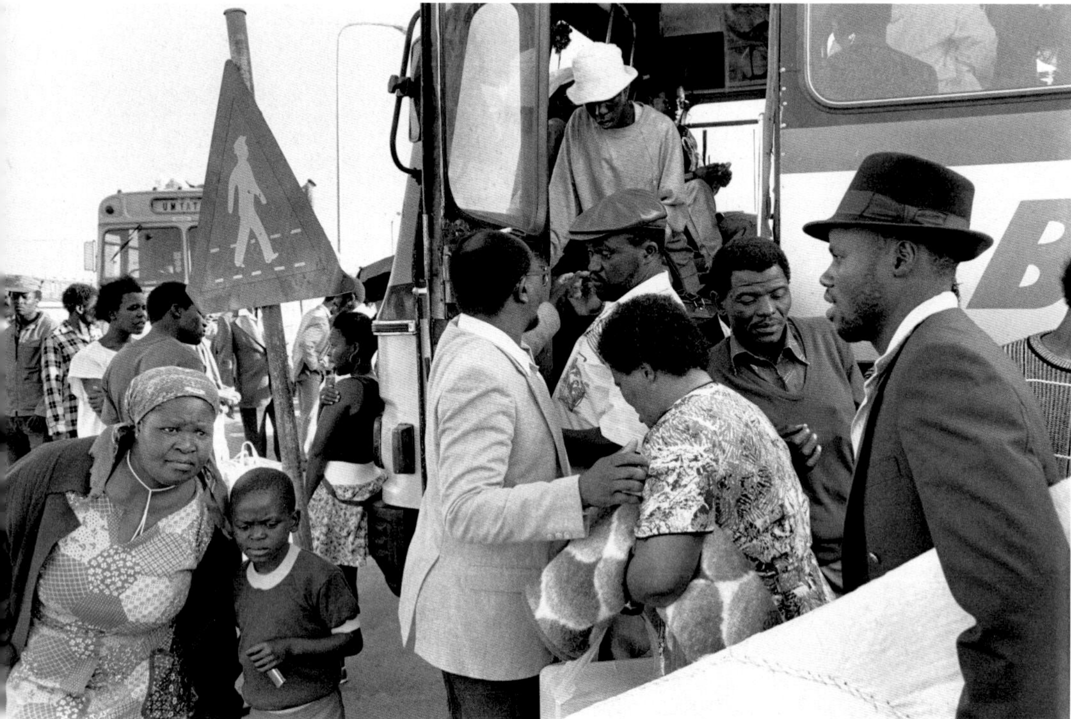

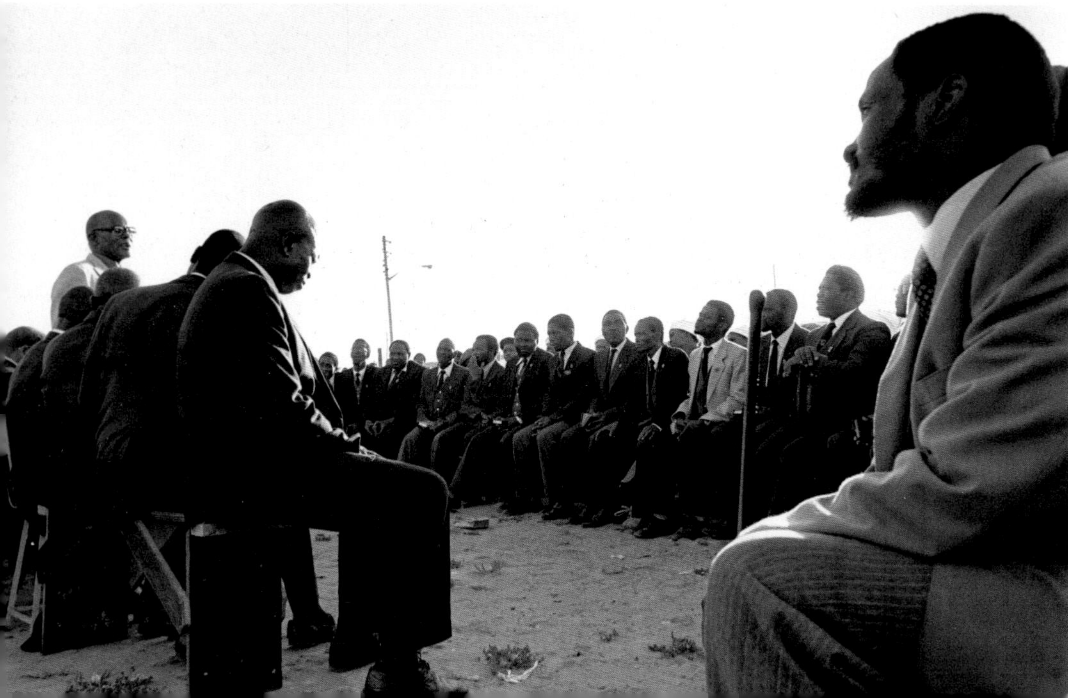

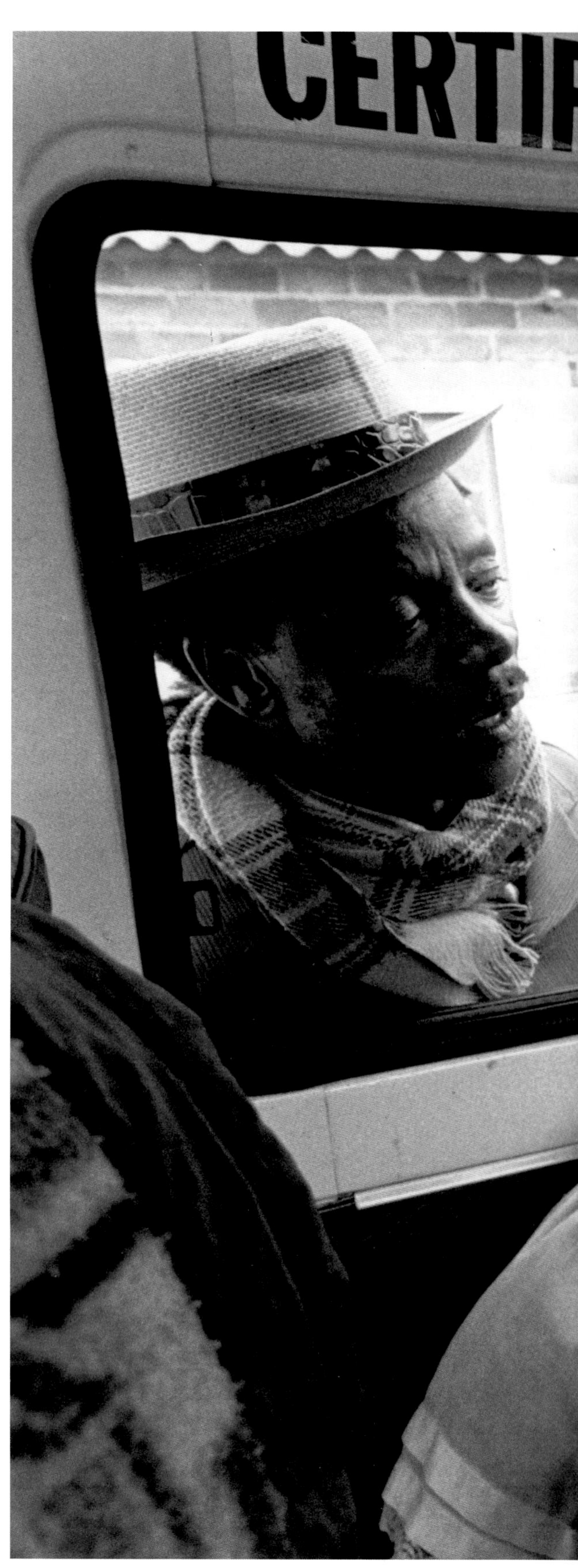

Left, top: Roger Meintjies, *Women return from a nearby farm with chickens to slaughter and sell at the market*; middle: *Bus stop, Khiki*; bottom: *Funeral service for a young hostel dweller killed in a fight over his girlfriend*; all 1987–89.

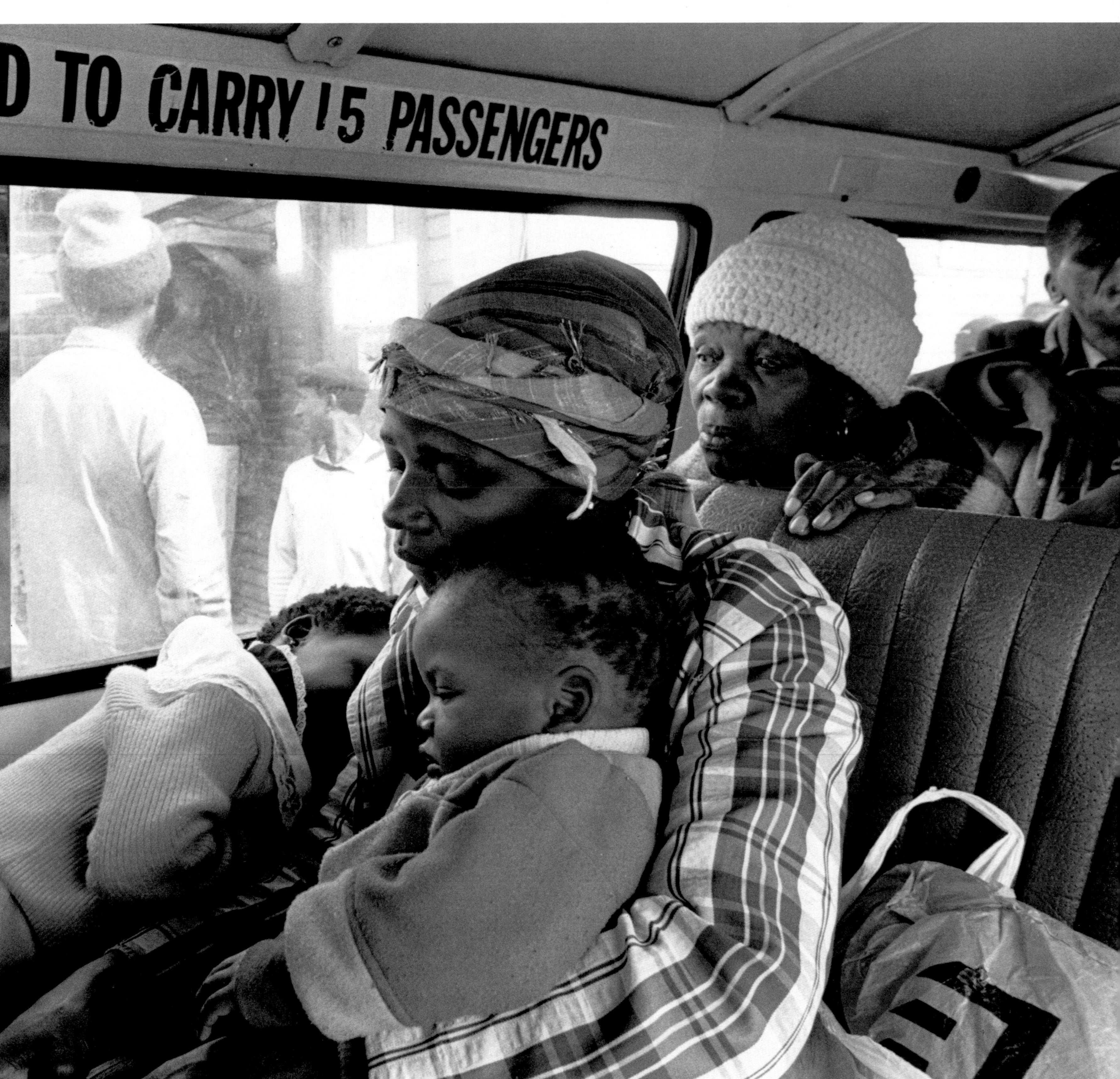

Bidding farewell to relatives on their way back to the Transkei.

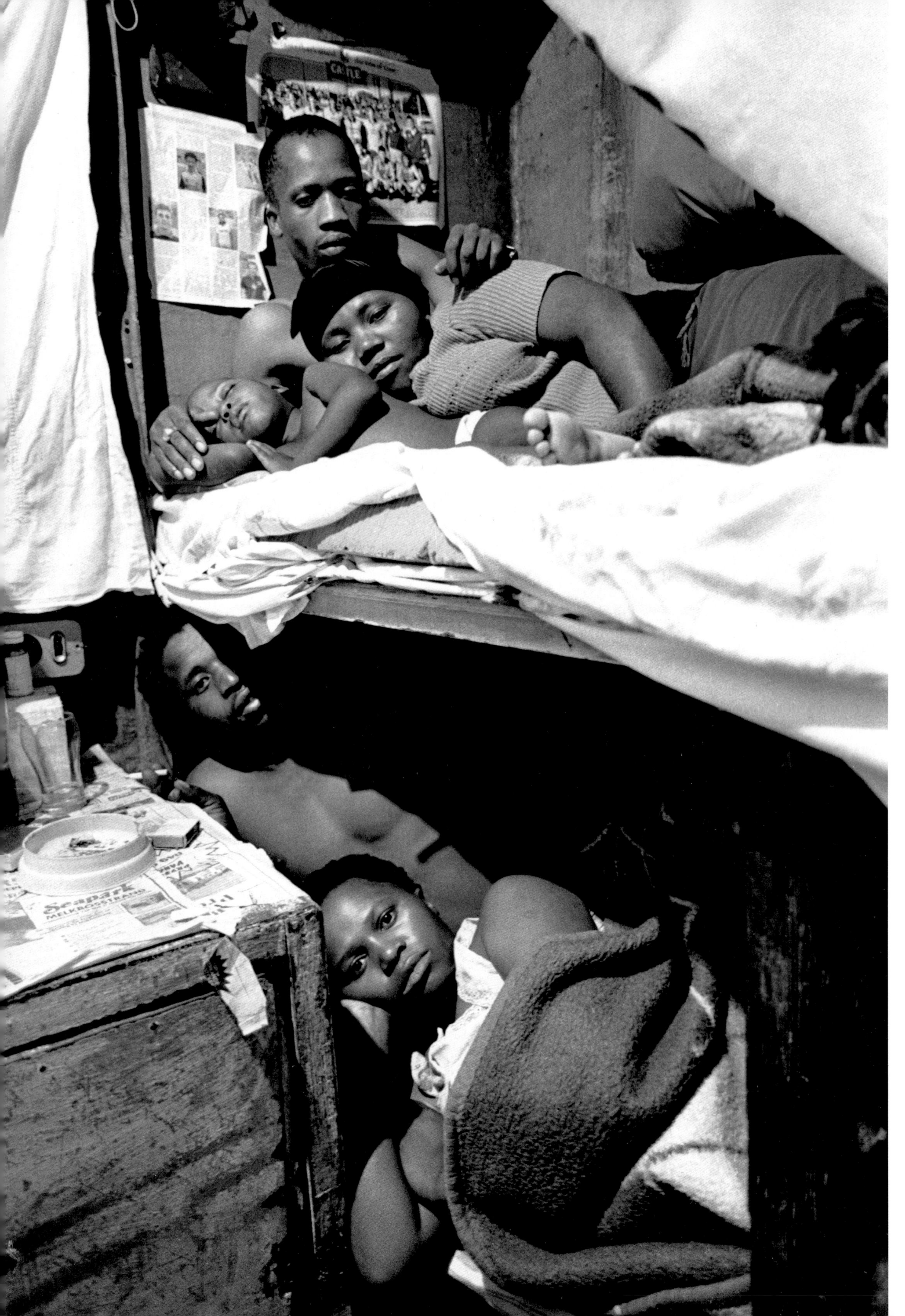
Seapark
MELKBOSSTRAND

participation of hostel dwellers in its leadership has diminished. The recent Congress of the National Union of Metalworkers of South Africa—one of the largest black unions in the country—committed the union to drawing hostel dwellers back into active participation in the unions.

In several areas the hostel dwellers have organized themselves in their residential areas. One of the most effective of these is the Western Cape-based Hostel Dwellers Association. Tapping into the formal and informal networks that stretch back into the various Bantustans, and acutely sensitive to the peculiar needs and style of its constituency, the Hostel Dwellers Association boasts some 14,000 members.

The pass laws have been repealed for three years now. Women and children have flooded into the cities. Single beds house entire families. The major effect on the hostels has been even greater neglect at the hands of the state. The state has converted several hostels into family accommodations, moving hostel dwellers out, replacing them from the long waiting lists for housing from the townships. The Hostel Dwellers Association is involved in an ambitious scheme to provide accommodations to the hostel residents and their families. However, the state's preferred mode of accommodating those on the bottom rungs of the economic ladder has shifted from hostels to the squatter camps—"informal settlements," in current officialese—springing up on the peripheries of the major cities.

But migrancy and the hostels will not go away in the near future. And so the struggle of the hostel residents will continue. For many hostel dwellers there remain strong social and economic ties to the rural area; many cannot move with their family to the squatter camps in the cities. Many don't want to move. I once asked one of the leaders of the Hostel Dwellers Association how he saw his role in a liberated South Africa. "In the South African parliament, of course," he replied; "MP for Idutywa, Transkei."

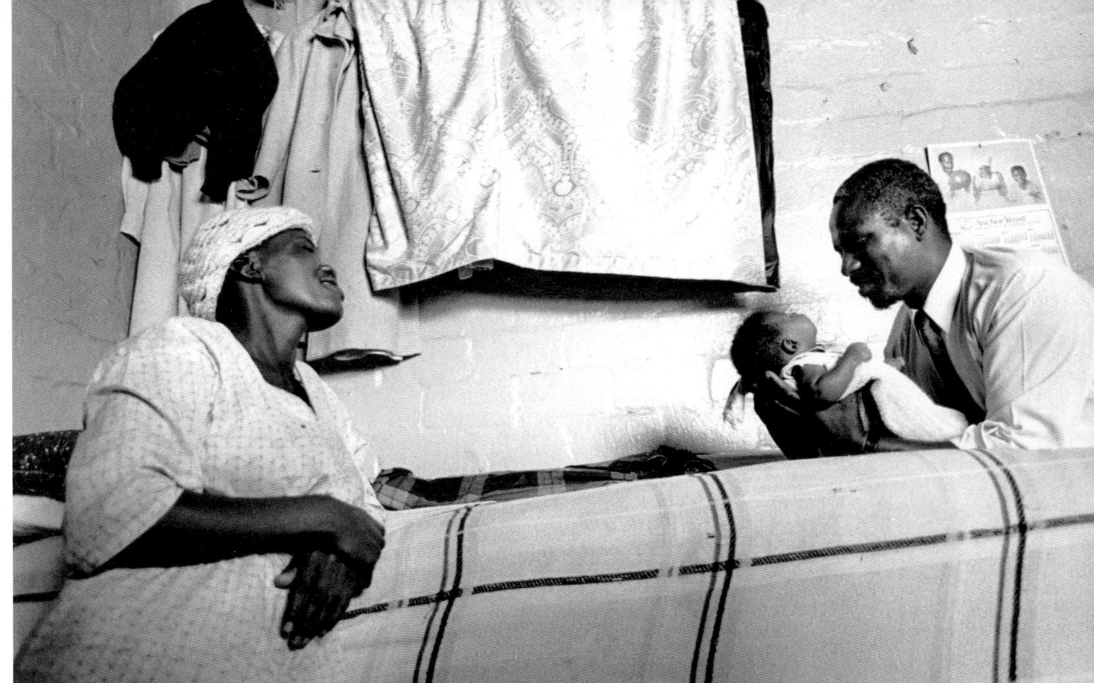

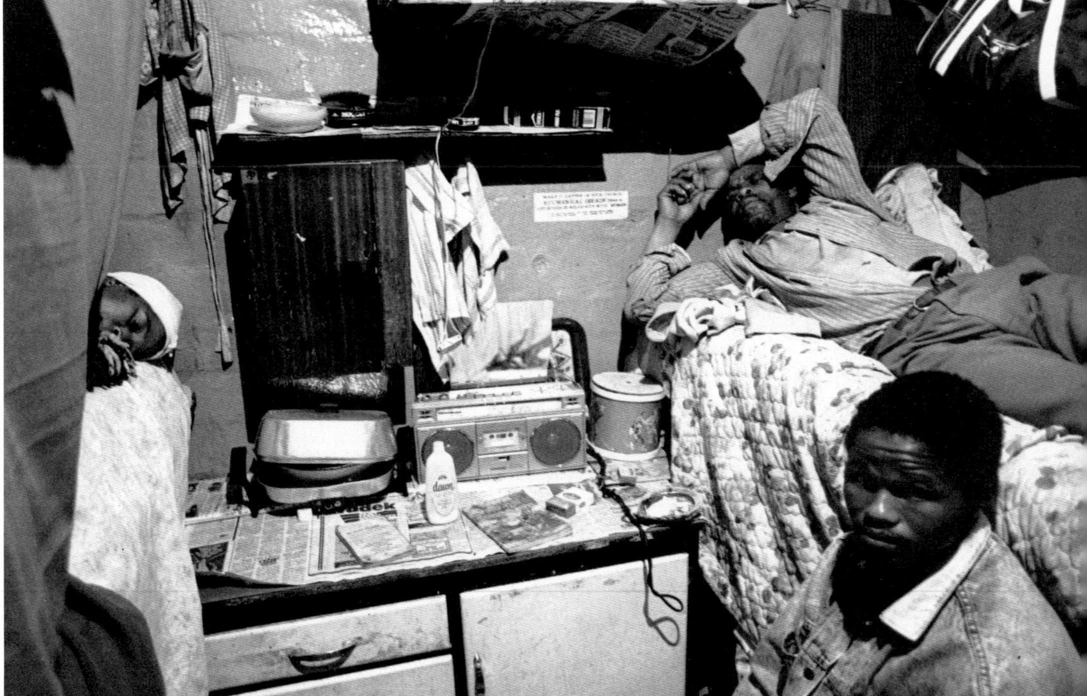

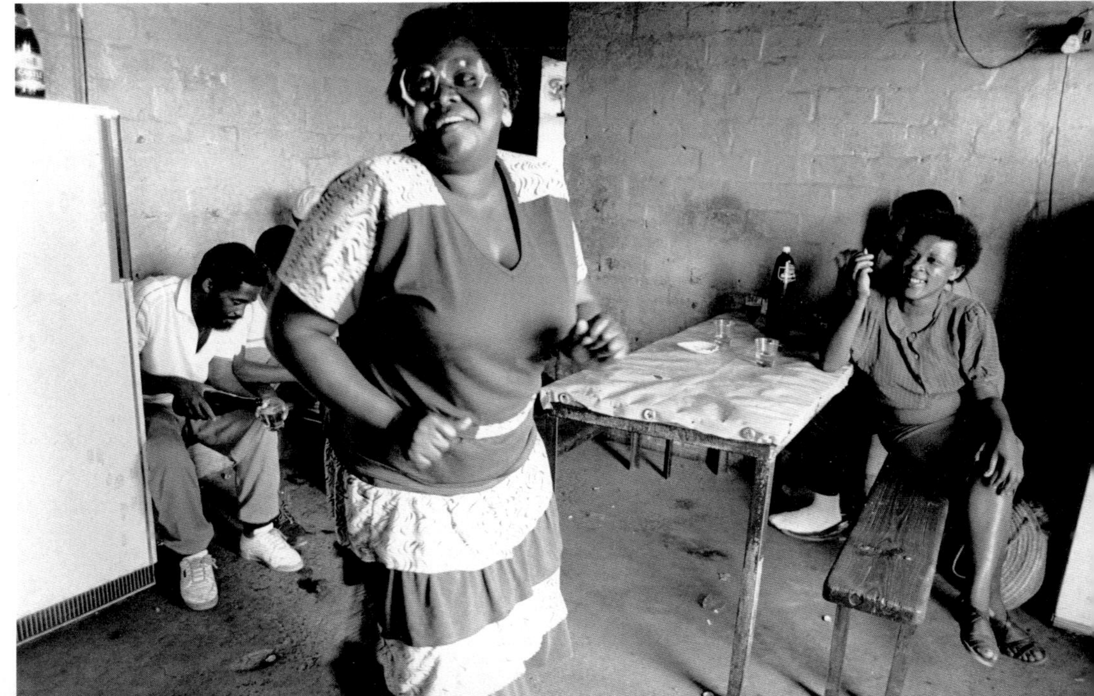

Opposite page: Roger Meintjies, *Hostel dwellers, Khiki*; this page, top: *Family, Khiki hostel*; middle: *Nighttime, Khiki*; bottom: *Friday evening in a shabeen, a township speakeasy*. Following page: *Mr. Nosam and Bongani Maruluba in their room on a Sunday afternoon*; all 1987–89.

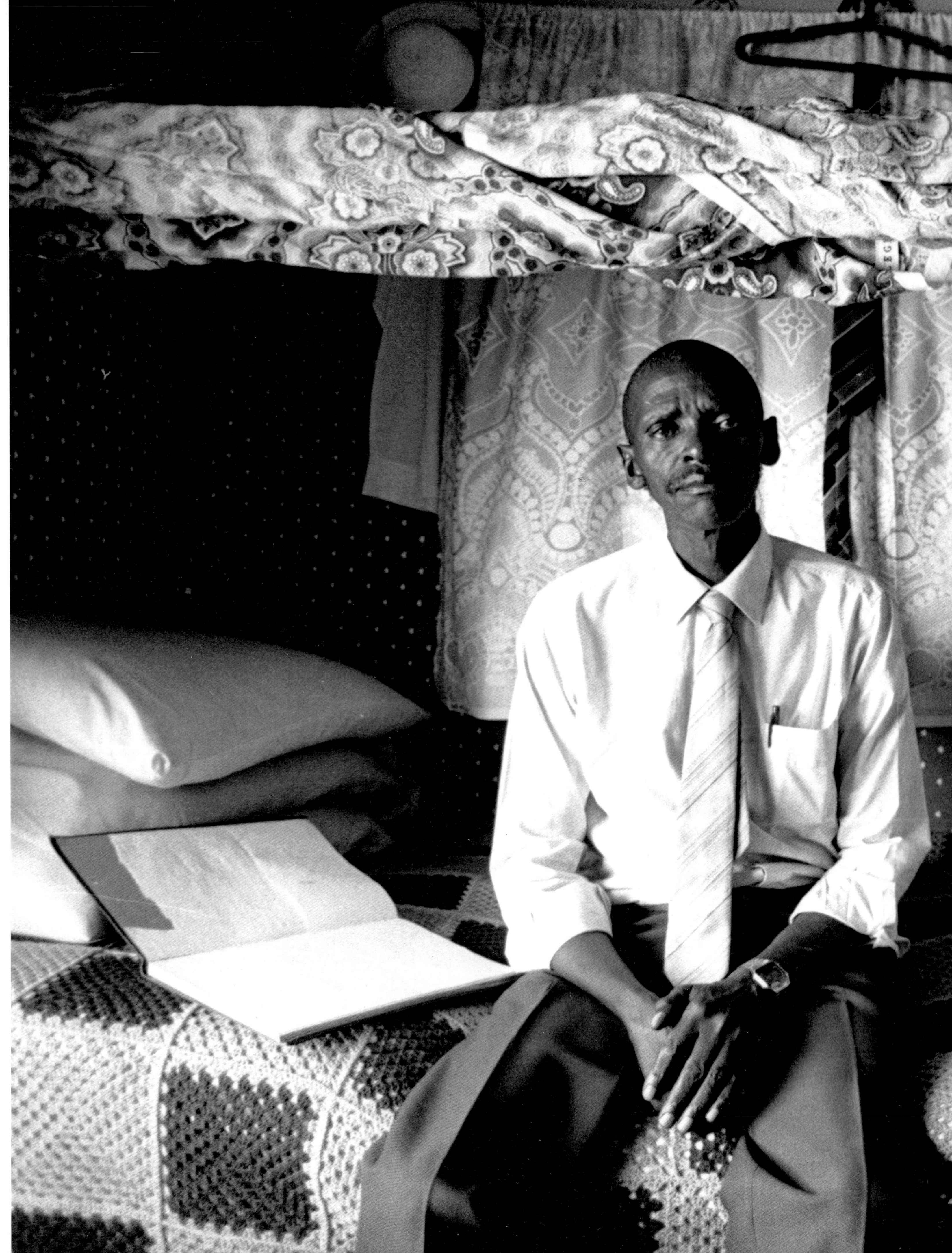

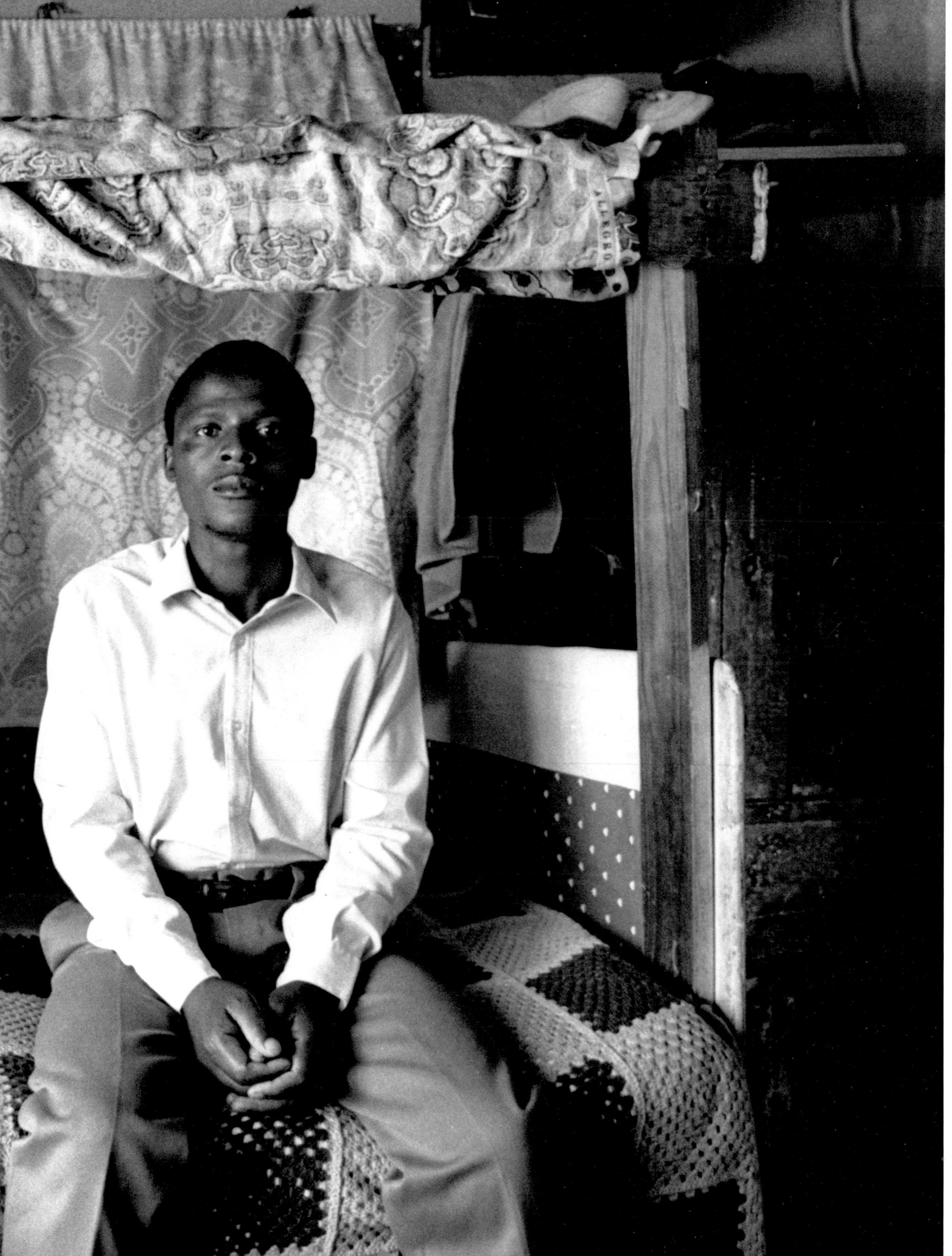

Retrato de un Pueblo

By Wendy Ewald

In 1981 I received a Fulbright fellowship to work in Colombia. I settled in Ráquira, a small village on the western spine of the Andes. Set in the wide-open, gentle mountains, everything in the village looks diminutive: from the adobe huts made by children from the mud after a rain, to the horses, cows, pigs, and cane fields—all like toys in a farm set. The campesinos divide their fields by piling stones to make fences. At dusk, when the sky darkens and light comes through the gaps where the rounded stones don't touch, the fences look like stone lace sewn to the contour of the mountains.

Though only four hours by bus from Bogotá, Ráquira has kept many of its pre-Columbian traditions, particularly pottery making. The people say that Bochica, a divine messenger and master of crafts, was sent to teach them how to make pots. It was Bochica who named the place Ráquira, town of potters. When the Spanish arrived in 1573 they found a region populated by ceramicists and farmers. The Indians carried wood, water, and food for the conquerors, cultivated their land, built their houses, and sold pots to pay their tithes. Some died of European diseases, some married Spaniards. By 1810 the indigenous people were no longer Indians but mestizos.

Long ago Ráquira was a fertile valley where avocados, oranges, and many kinds of potatoes were grown. But sometime in the last century, no one knows why, the rains began to come less often and the temperature dropped. The avocado and orange trees died. The peasants cut more and more of the trees and shrubs to make cooking and kiln fires. The land turned arid. When I arrived Ráquira was a patchwork of desert and clumps of dark green trees. You could see in one glance the evolution of the landscape from the lush valley the Spaniards found to the dust and cacti of today.

I met Luz Marina Bautista the day I arrived in Ráquira. She had come to town to see the dentist who attended patients once a week in the village. She watched me cross the town square to my rented room. When she found out from my landlady, Dona America, that I was some kind of a teacher, she marched up to me, introduced herself, and said she'd like to take me to her home in the mountains to meet her mother. The friendship among the three of us became deep and complicated. Luz Marina and her mother, Monica, were shunned and feared as witches.

Ráquira is losing its young people, Luz Marina Bautista among them, to the city. The children and the old people are left to be educated and nurtured by nature. Left alone, the old women, like Luz Marina's mother, seem to grow back down into the earth. They wrap themselves in layers of long, dark clothes; they no longer have a shape of their own; only their eyes and part of their mouths are visible. Dirt is everywhere—on their shoeless feet and hands, on their dirt floors, their mud houses, their crops, in their labor in the clay ("mud," as they call it), and in their meals cooked and eaten from mud pots. Maybe the city is an escape from dirt.

For a year and a half I photographed in Ráquira while teaching in the tiny village school. My students were fifth graders, the oldest of the primary school, attending their last year of school. Most of them lived in the mountains above the town.

Luis Arturo Gonzalez woke every morning before dawn; fed and milked the cows, chopped wood, made a fire, and cooked breakfast. Then he walked two hours to the village with the milk, sold it, bought supplies, and was at school by 7:30. A year later he would be a shepherd, guarding the flocks for weeks at a time without seeing another human being. He might visit the village once a year.

I shared the last year of what might be called the students' childhood. The regular fifth-grade teacher was a drinker with a habit of nodding out in class and calling his students savage Indians. He was happy to let me take them several times a week.

The children learned to shoot, develop, and enlarge their own photographs. I lent them 126 Instamatic cameras and gave them assignments to write about and photograph themselves, their families, their animals, and their fantasies.

At first they didn't understand how to look through the viewfinder of the camera. Instead of framing someone's face as they intended, they might frame his knees. I realized that since they had no windows in the mountain huts where they slept, and since they had never seen television, the idea of "framing" was utterly foreign to them: they had never seen their surroundings *through* anything. I asked them to carry a piece of paper with a hole in it and look through it at everything they came upon. Within a couple of weeks the problem was solved.

They brought their exposed film to school and developed it in the little darkroom I built in a room of a colonial house in the village. They never damaged a roll of film. They had been making pots since they were five years old; they knew the importance of craftsmanship.

For me, teaching is like having accomplices in a secret game. My students were as passionate about describing the village with their cameras as I was. Instinctively, they knew that sometimes you have to trick adults into letting them do what you want. Moreover, children develop their own innocent fascination for images that adults often censor. After my first class, Javier came up to me and said, "Guess what? I am going to take a photograph of my uncle. He is coming to visit this afternoon." He smiled and whispered, "He doesn't have any hands."

Though more than half of the people in the world are peasants, few contemporary visual artists have described rural com-

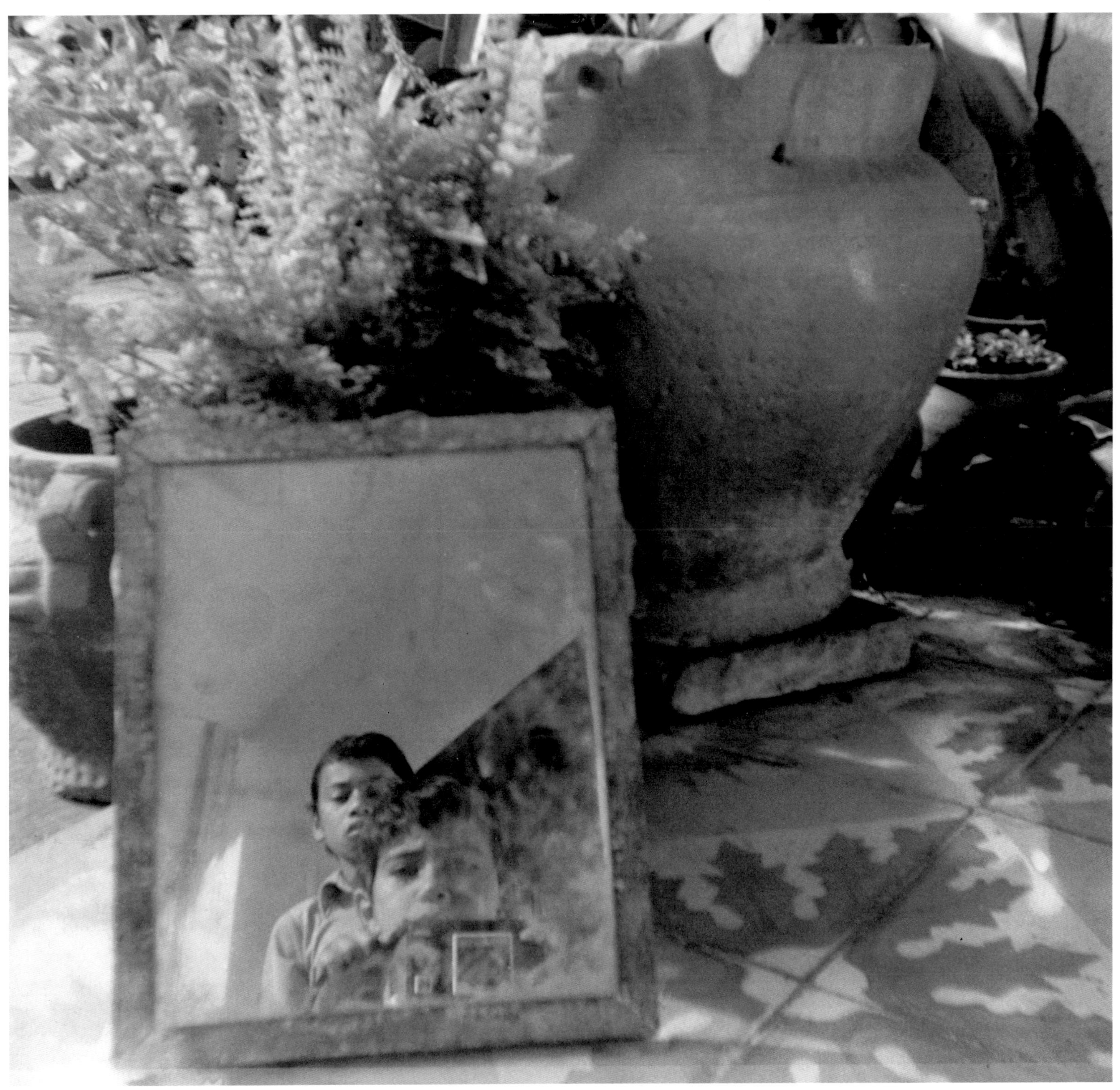

Javier Reyes, *My brother and I in a self-portrait*, 1982

I like to take photographs of my family so their memories will remain after they die. In twenty years when I look at the photographs I might think, "Oh, what a different life that was. What a hard time I had."

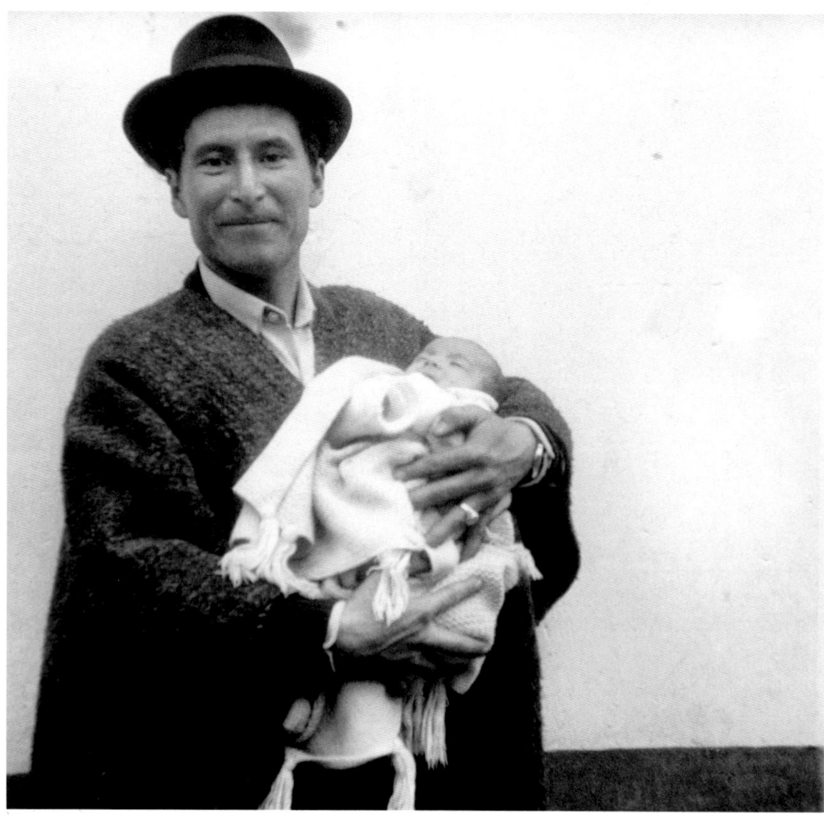

Alirio Casas, *A friend carrying my little brother, Orlando*, 1983

munities in terms of their own values, successes, and failures. In order to bring myself closer to my subjects and to capture the rhythm of their environment, I have developed two separate but complementary ways of working: making photographs that narrate the daily life of the villagers (almost always women with whom I feel a spiritual tie), and teaching elementary school children to take photographs of what they feel closest to. In this way, I try to avoid the coldness which can result from a technical medium that sometimes devalues the passion and subtlety of individual lives.

LUZ MARINA BAUTISTA

I was born in the hospital at Chiquinquira on the sixth of January, I don't know what year. I was born right after my Mama got frightened by an old man named Rudy. She felt me flip in her belly. "Help me," she said to her neighbor, but the neighbor didn't come and Mama went to the village by herself. She left at eleven at night and arrived at five in the morning. She suffered the whole journey, the way women do when they're in labor. When she got to the village she tried to find a car to take her to the hospital ten miles away, but no car would take her, so she walked.

She took her time, but when she got to the river, her water broke. "This is as far as I go," she said to herself, but she got up and kept going. She got to the hospital at five that afternoon and they took her right into the delivery room. I was born at five the next morning, feet first. They pulled me out by one paw and gave me three spanks on the tail.

I was born anxious. I've always liked to tease, make a fuss, hide myself, and laugh. When I was three Mama started going off to work. She'd leave me locked in the house with a ball, a stick, something to write with, and a few sheets of paper. When I got bigger, she left me outside with a big gourd full of cornmeal. I liked it because when I was alone I could play with the dogs, the cattle, the turkeys. I didn't have brothers or sisters. Animals are better. You can play with them without fighting.

I started working when I was six. Imagine six years old—and tending livestock on a strange farm. A bull gored me. All I remember is, he threw me unconscious against a rock and I broke three ribs. Mama caught the bull and took me home and bathed me. Then she tied me to her back with a sheet and carried me to the hospital. I stayed there for a year, but I still have pain. Sometimes when I'm tired and have to work, I say, "Why didn't you let me die, Mama, when the bull gored me?"

Mama says they raised her like they were trying to kill a snake; one day they broke six sticks on her. She raised me the same way. When I did something wrong, I ran to Grandma as fast as my feet would go. Mama couldn't hit me then, but sometimes I didn't make it. Mama hit me with a leather strap with four knots tied in it. Sometimes I want to drown myself or throw myself off the mountain because my life has been so

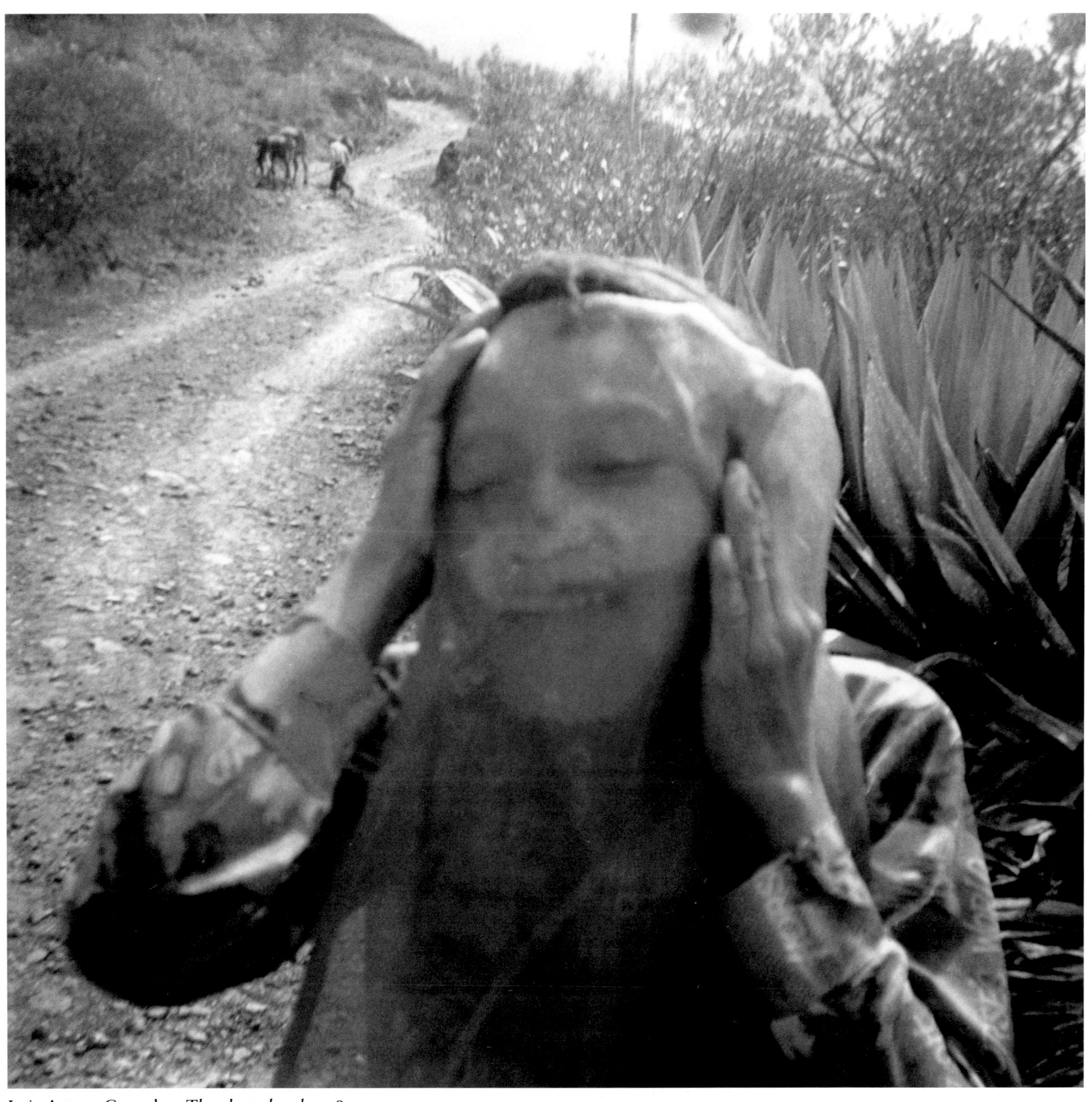

Luis Arturo Gonzalez, *The sleepyhead*, 1982

Some people worry that I'll use a picture of them to cast a spell. We all believe that in one way or another. I've heard it said that you should never give a photograph of yourself away. Someone might stick a pin in it in the middle of the night and you'll feel a prick in your middle finger and then get sick. Sometimes they cut the photograph in half and put it in the smoke between two candles and they curse you. It's dangerous. That's what we believe.

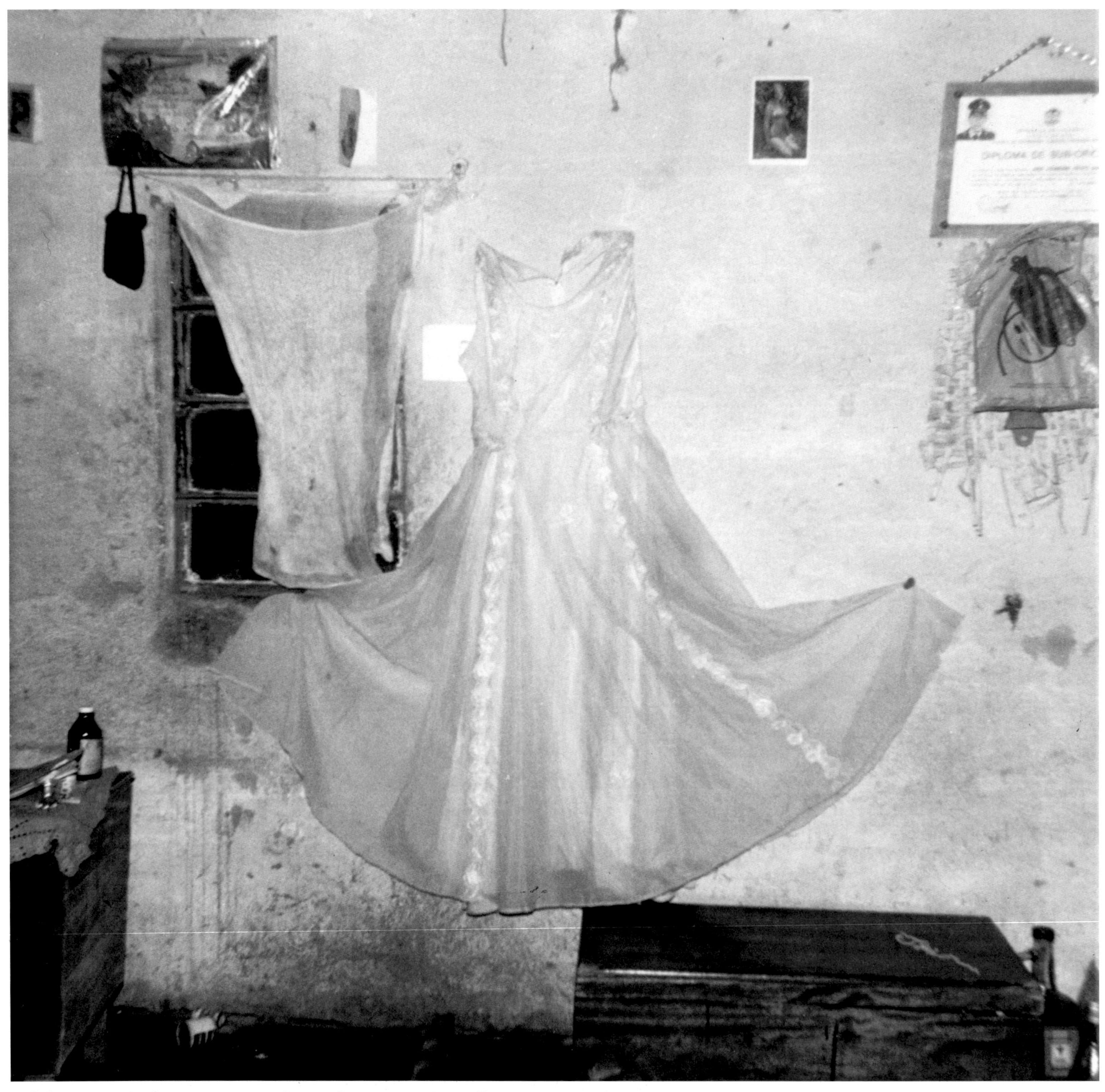

Dalida Reyes, *My first communion dress is hanging on the wall*, 1982

I'm glad that you people outside our village can see these photographs because you'll learn a lot about us—if we're rich or poor, if we have a car or animals, if our village is clean or disorganized or if we're happy. Don't praise us; we're nothing special, just ordinary country children, but we're grateful.

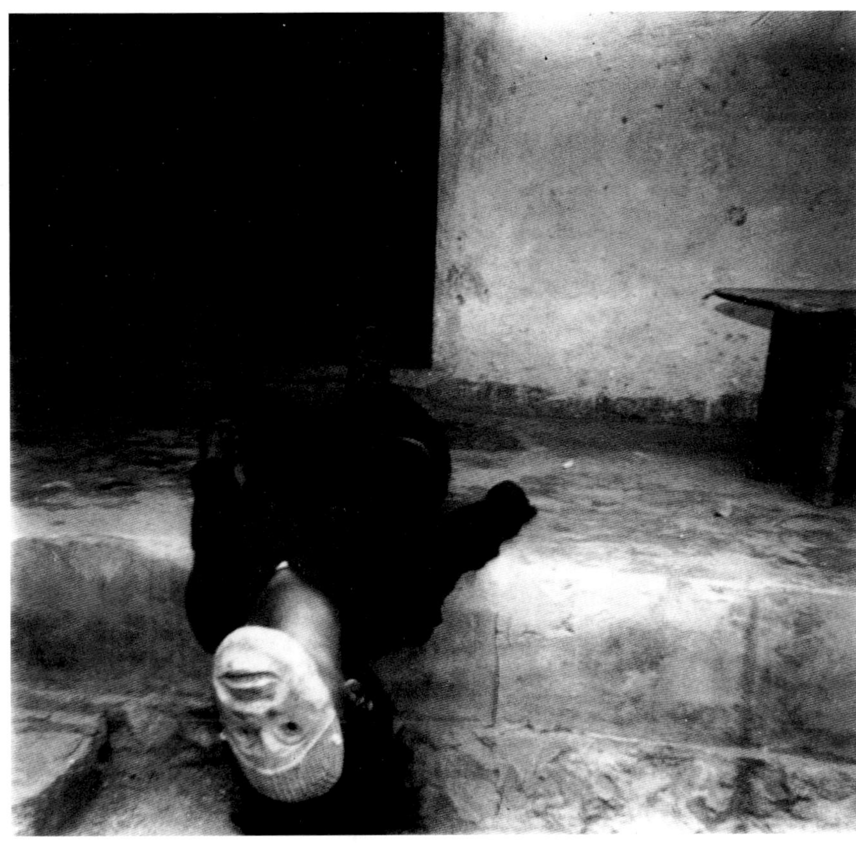

Diamel Vargas, *The ghost named Sunday fallen from fright*, 1982

tough. But with all that she's done to me, I love my Mama. And I will keep all the memories of what's happened to us in life.

We divide the work. Mama cooks the meals and I watch the animals. We bathe. She tells me jokes and riddles, and stories about her childhood. At night we listen to Mass on the radio. After dinner we go to sleep in our bed. Mama hugs and kisses me, and I snuggle into her breast to sleep. The next morning we turn on the radio to hear Mass and then we get to work.

I don't feel poor now that we have a table. I have my clothes and shoes. That's enough. I feel rich when I have shoes. I feel sad, though, when we don't have food. It makes me ashamed to bring people to our little house. I think they'll be revolted by our cooking and the blackened pots. Mama's old-fashioned; she doesn't scrub the vegetables.

When we fight, I hate her. I hide from her in the trees until my anger passes. I have a temper like Papa's. They say the war affected him. When I feel like that, I can't feel anything—only my rage. Cut me, hit me with a big stick—I can't feel it.

Sometimes I dream that Garbanzo the bull has gored me. Almost all my dreams are like that. Maybe it's because I haven't made my First Communion. They say you end up in hell for that, and you burn and burn until all your sins are burned away. When you die, if you're lucky, you won't suffer much and you'll find everything that was taken from you like our sheep, the radio, and the turkeys. Don't worry, the Padre says; all the hairs on your head are numbered. Who knows what God and the Virgin have in store for me?

I want to make progress and show the people. I study day and night. I want to be a doctor, but I'd have to study for twelve more years. It's late for that. But I know the Virgin will give me the brains to study. If God and the Virgin let me be a professional, when I have my big house, I'll invite poor people in and give them what I can. When I'm rich I'll take vacations and go back to the farm and do what I used to do: make baskets, swing the machete, dig furrows—like now. Because that's me, I'm a country girl.

Luz Marina is 20 now. She works as a maid in Bogotá and studies in an elementary school on weekends. "I'm resigned to my new life, but everyday my soul is in the country. When I'm working, I think about Mama, the things we did and where we walked. She's with me in the city, I carry her in my mind. I wake up with her every morning."

I left Colombia five years ago. Except for visits when I see Luz Marina briefly, our only communication is by letter. Luz Marina writes, "I've lived a lot since I saw you—with new experiences, deceptions, sadnesses, and of course, the most agreeable, happinesses. Two years ago I met a man who has become part of my life. I will tell you everything, but you must promise to come to Colombia soon. I want to invite you to eat and dance with me all night long."

Other Viewpoints, Other Dimensions

By Susan Morgan

My curiosity about alien cultures was avid and obsessive. I had a placid belief that it was good for me to live in the midst of people whose motives I did not understand. —Paul Bowles

A traveler's curiosity courts a variety of uncertainties: unanticipated pleasures, tragic realizations, happy accidents. Elaine Reichek's work takes possession of that curiosity, orchestrating cultural questions through images. In the reclusive atmosphere of picture collections, second-hand bookstores, and anthropology museums, Reichek collects photographs taken at the ends of the earth. By carefully editing and altering (cropping, enlarging, hand-coloring, collaging) this borrowed material, Reichek coaxes new readings from old images. In re-presenting early-twentieth-century ethnographic photographs, Reichek turns the tables to reveal the cracks in anthropology's rigid, authoritarian method. "Preserving the antique is a colonialist mentality. All cultures are in flux. We are looking at them, they are looking at us." Free of nostalgia (a term invented in 1688 by Johannes Hofer, an Alsatian medical student; nostalgia, from the Greek roots meaning "return home" and "pain," was regarded as a medical problem until the late nineteenth century), Reichek's work does not sentimentally yearn for the past.

Photography has been described by Stanley Cavell as "a medium for making sense" and Reichek's work is about making sense, taking delight in cultural incongruities while avoiding a traditionally linear view of history. Reichek's photocollages and room-sized installations pointedly break down the notion of a correct and singular viewpoint. Her work is never didactic; her arrangements of photographs set up dialogues, introducing a range of considerations and contradictions. The inset images in her photocollages appear like rips in an otherwise carefully composed surface; like peepholes, the insets offer a surprising glimpse, reminding us that there is never one version to any story. In *I Drank The*

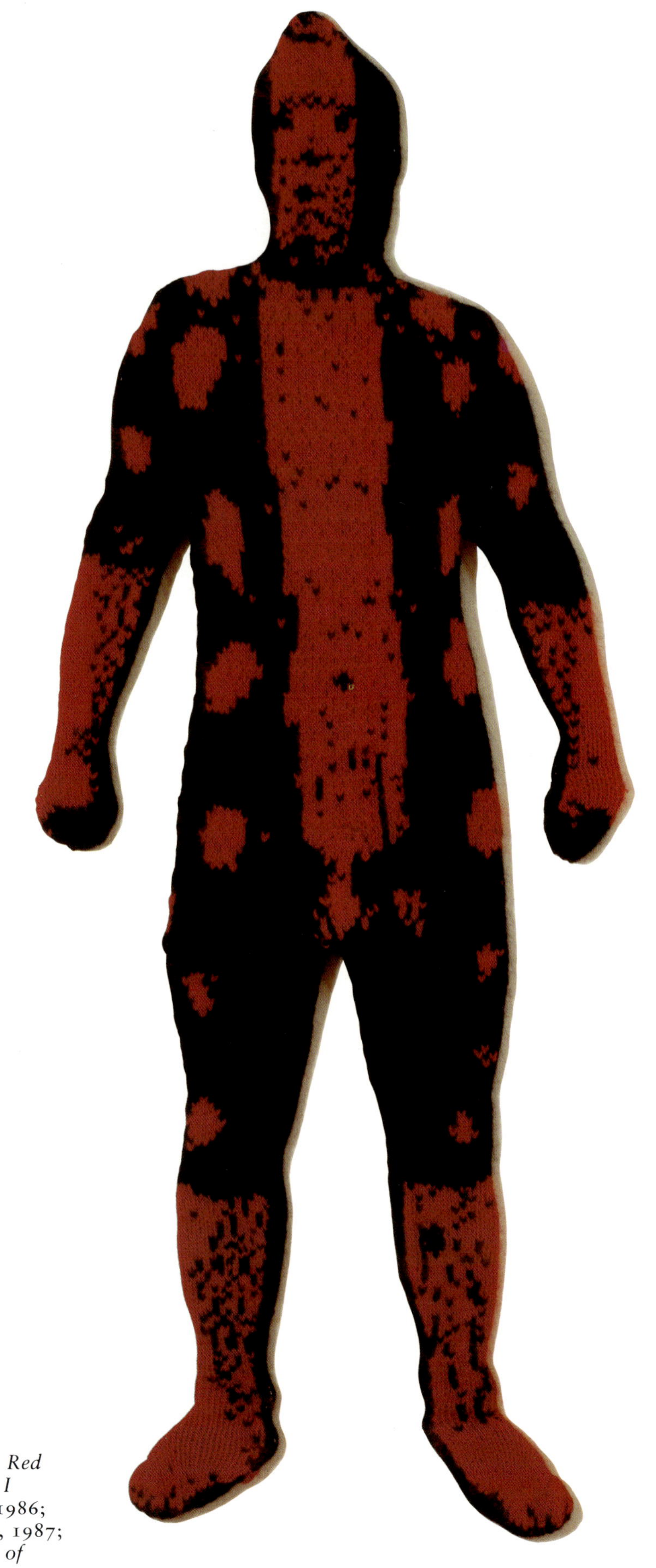

Elaine Reichek, right: *Red Man*, 1987; page 28: *I Drank the Zambesi*, 1986; page 29: *Desert Song*, 1987; pages 30–31: *Burden of Dreams*, 1987.

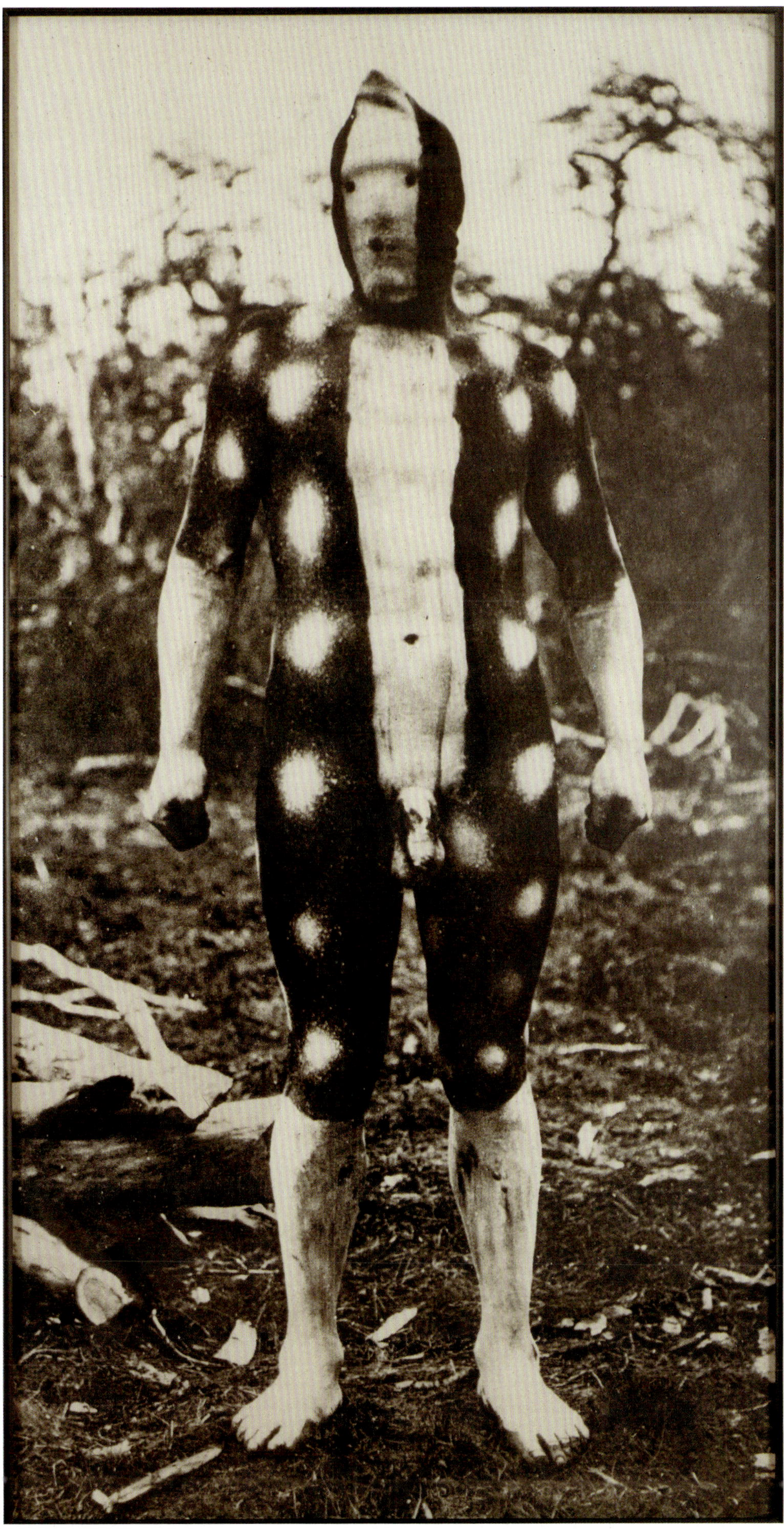

Zambesi, 1986—the mysterious title taken from a travel guide—characters imbibe the exotic. It's the heart of darkness peddled as the flavor of the month as everyone tries to get a taste of the Other: monkeys in dresses, women in animal skins, rain umbrellas as parasols, light bulbs as necklaces. As so often in Reichek's work, the notion of exotic here has no fixed meaning.

Reichek has referred to the hand-coloring of the photocollages as "homogenizing the time." It is a democratic gesture, diminishing any sense of priority among the images and establishing them as equal parts of a whole. In *Ticket to Paradise*, 1988, a painting of Jamaica Bay by the nineteenth-century American landscapist Martin Johnson Heade is hand-colored in pale postcard tints. The sublime landscape envisioned by the Hudson River painter dissolves over time into a tourist's souvenir. Once the wilderness has been tamed, nature is reduced to just another photo opportunity. As in the tradition of English landscape painting, the beauty and importance of the countryside rests in its commercial potential—it is beautiful because you can own it.

In Reichek's room-sized installations, the information surrounds us. The past and present appear in the same moment, creating yet another dimension. In the darkened room of *Desert Song* a pile of broken cameras lies discarded in a corner, a depleted oasis of voyeurism. "The desert is a place of great aestheticism and great luxury. The desire ranges from the spiritual to the carnal," Reichek notes. She has referred to her working method as "free associating"; references abound. In *Desert Song*, the Egyptian pyramids are presented simultaneously as architectural wonders of the world, ten-cent picture postcards, and a monumental movie stage for Elizabeth Taylor's Cleopatra. The central image from *Desert Song* is a classic scene; nomads and camels in the desert, palm trees swaying in the misty distance. The scene is both romantic and fraught with anxiety; all of the figures, men and animals alike, are looking in different directions. "If you look closely, something is happening. A storm is brewing." Reichek has located that ephemeral moment, changes occurring out on the horizon, and framed it. In *Desert Song*, a woman

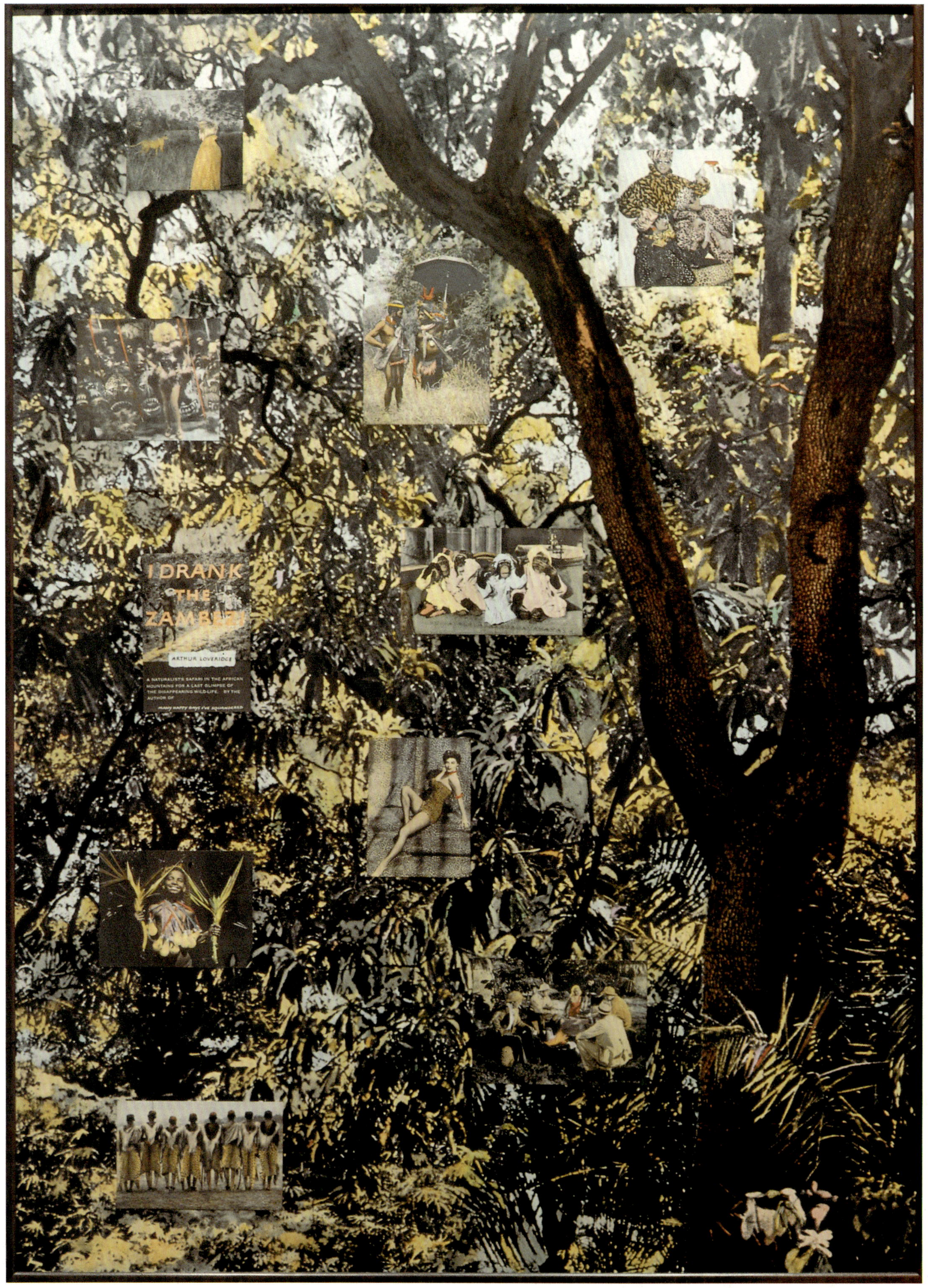
I DRANK THE ZAMBEZI
ARTHUR LOVERIDGE
A NATURALIST'S SAFARI IN THE AFRICAN MOUNTAINS FOR A LAST GLIMPSE OF THE DISAPPEARING WILD-LIFE. BY THE AUTHOR OF
MANY HAPPY DAYS I'VE SQUANDERED

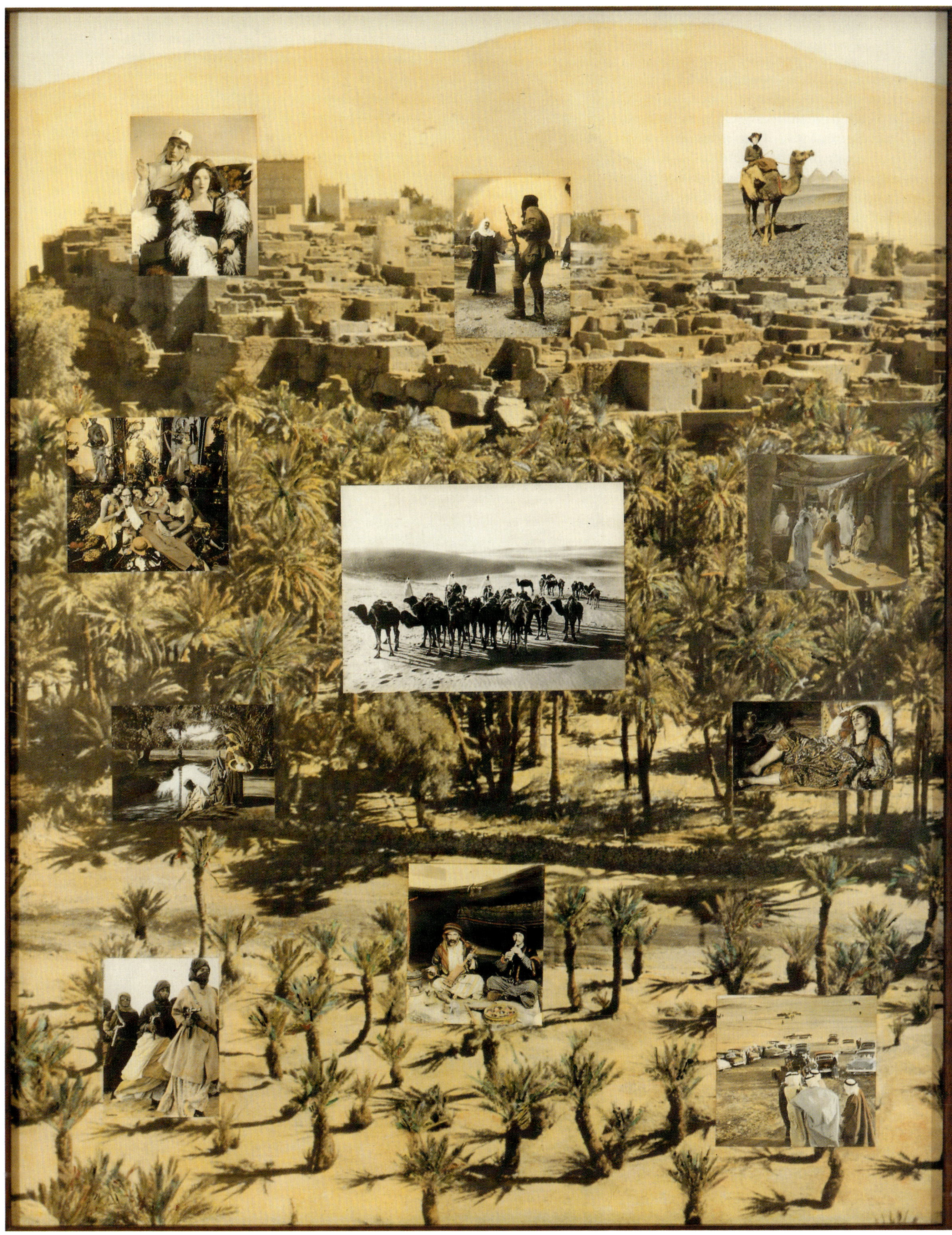

in Victorian safari-wear poses on camelback; the photograph is from the nineteenth century but the woman's face is Reichek's. "I try to include myself in the work. I am implicated. The work is about my own desire and guilt."

Since the late 1970s, Reichek has worked from "photographs into knitting," translating found images into three-dimensional objects. Working from a series of ethnographic studies of the Tierra del Fuegans, taken between 1908 and 1921 by Martin Gusinde, a German Jesuit anthropologist, Reichek has produced a series of knitted men, decoratively patterned after their now extinct, hand-painted human counterparts. Darwin loathed the Tierra del Fuegans, dismissing them as a people "with no form of art, only a crude form of body painting." Within fifty years of contact with Europeans, the tribes of Tierra del Fuego were decimated. The beauty of that lost culture is found, at least through allusions, in Reichek's work. The knitted men appear like shadows, visual puns on the embodiment of spirit. Displayed alongside Gusinde's photographs, they appear to be stepping outside the last remaining document, regarding their own lost history.

In Truman Capote's story "Music for Chameleons," the narrator visits the Caribbean island of Martinique. His conversation with a local aristocrat, an elegant woman "perhaps seventy, silver-haired, soigné," reveals the island's intricate culture and complex history. Nothing is simple, no natural "paradise" is serene. When the narrator takes notice of a black mirror, his hostess explains that in the late nineteenth century artists used black mirrors to "refresh their vision"; this one "belonged to Gauguin. You know, of course, that he lived and painted here before he settled among the Polynesians." The conversation continues. They talk about Carnival and murder; the narrator considers again the black mirror. "All the while the black mirror has been lying in my lap and once more my eyes seek its depths. Strange where our passions carry us, floggingly pursue us, forcing upon us unwanted dreams, unwelcome destinies." Reichek's work has captured the essence of the black mirror, refreshing our vision and unearthing our dreams.

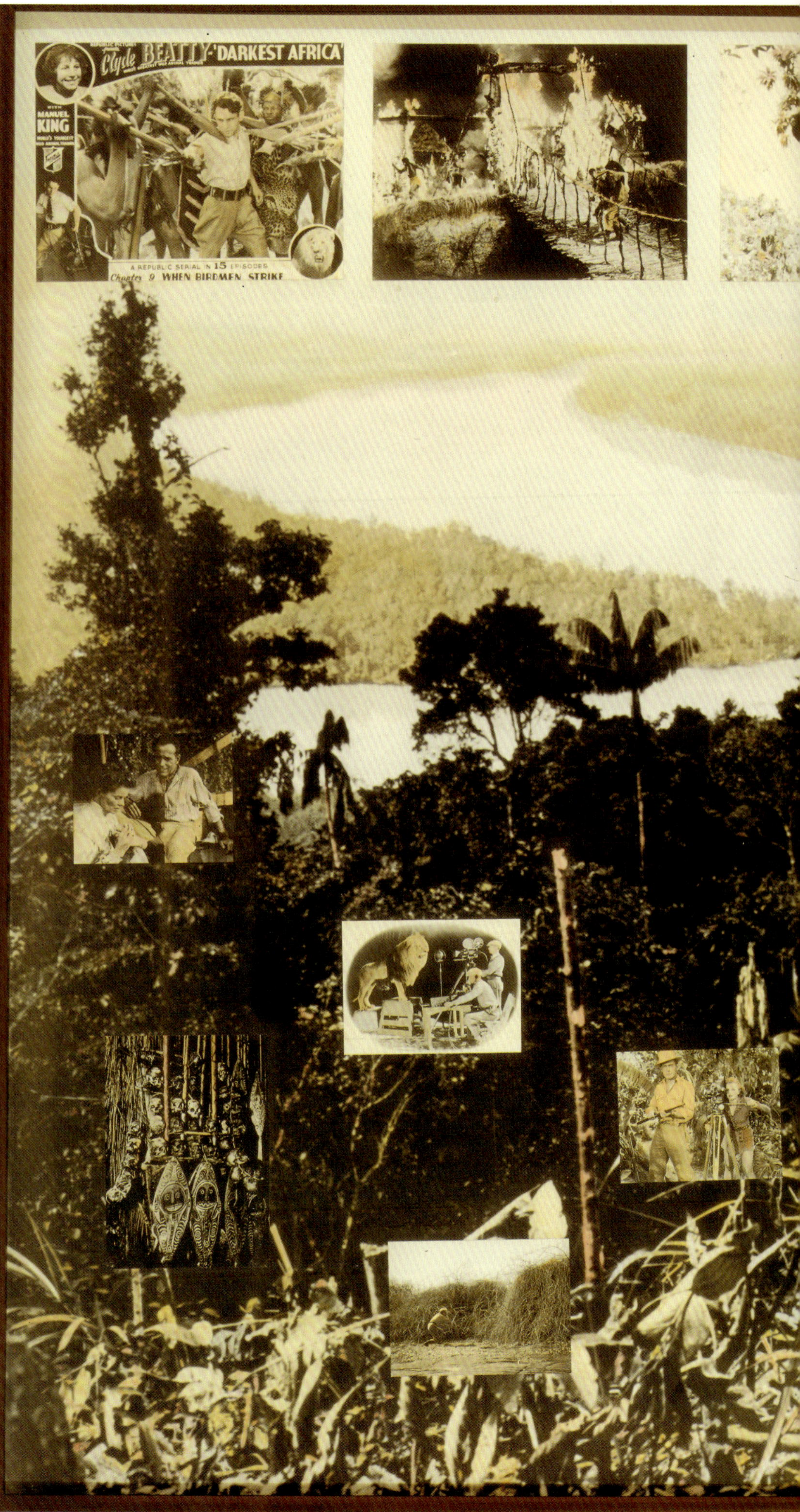

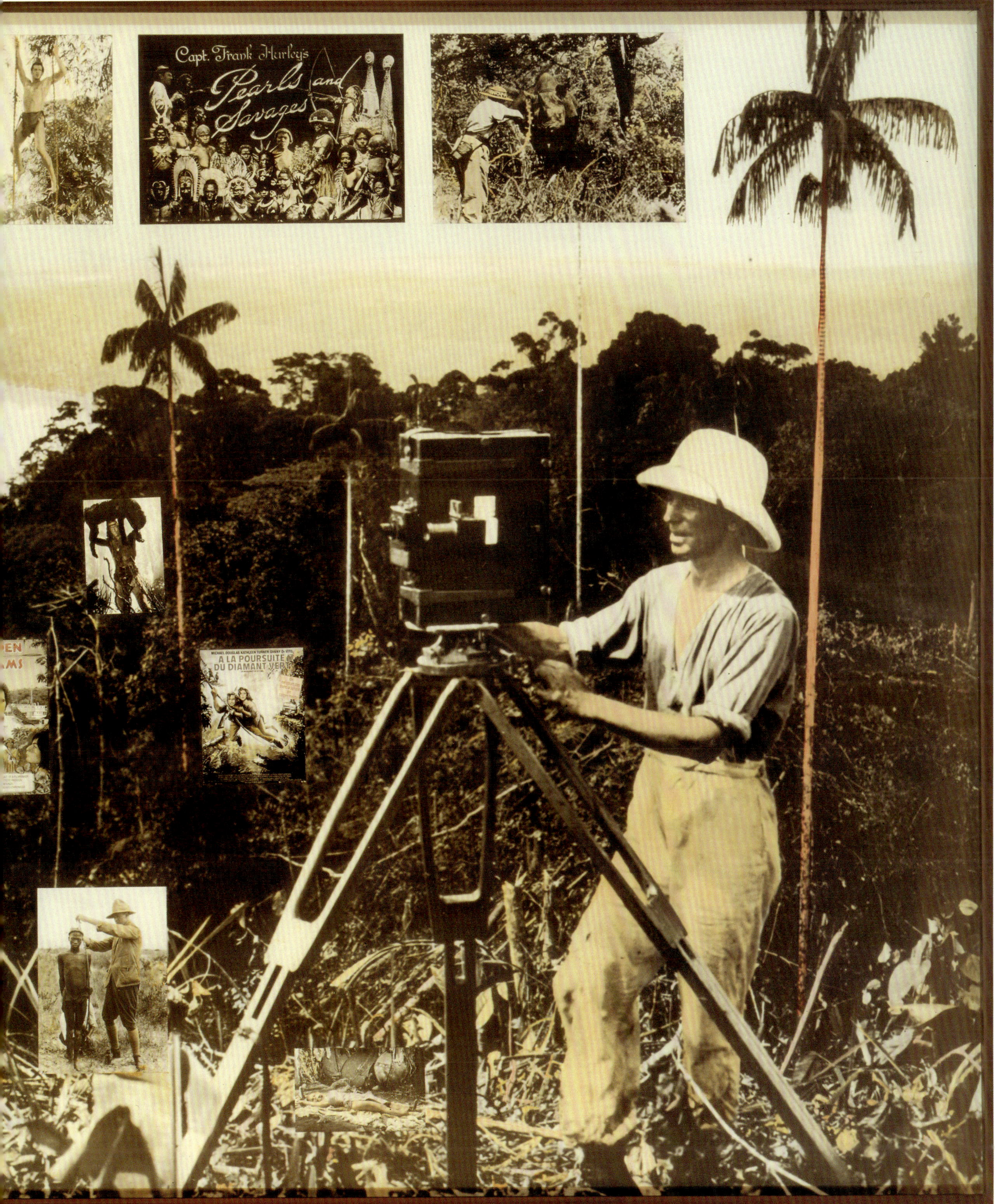
Capt. Frank Hurley's
Pearls and Savages
A LA POURSUITE DU DIAMANT VERT

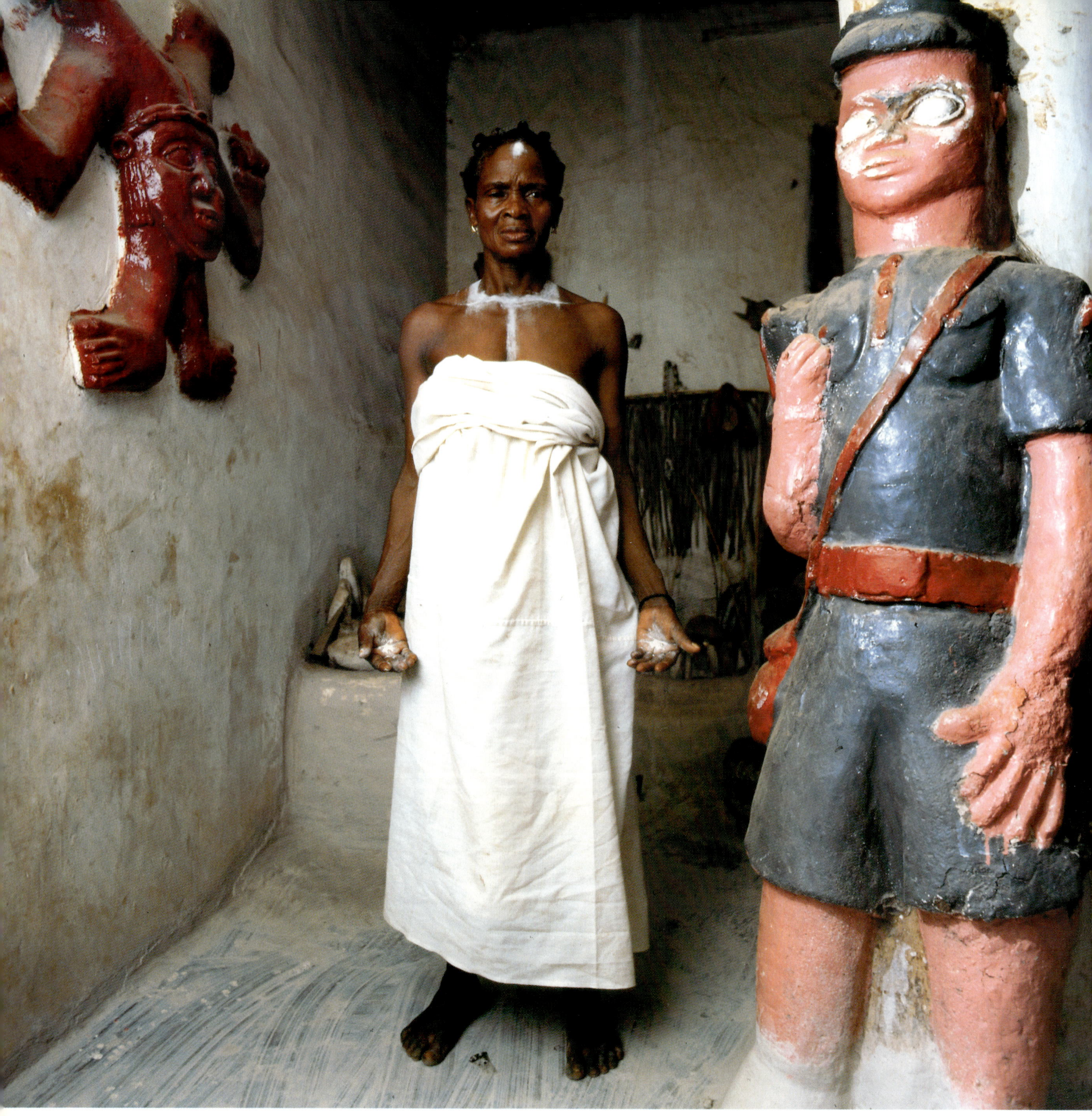

An Olokun priestess in front of her personal shrine. The figure on the wall to the left represents Ofoe, the messenger of death. The unusual arrangement of his limbs is a metaphor for the unpredictable timing of death.

Sobriety and Variation: Notes on Brazilian/Yoruba Sacred Altars

By Robert Farris Thompson

We move in the study of Afro-Brazilian art—whether originating from the Yoruba of western Nigeria or the Bokongo of Bas-Zaire—from naive appreciation to strategy and spiritual discernment. At the turn of the century, to study the candomblés of Brazil was to study "the marginal." No matter how loving the account or how full the documentation, a critical phrase here, a demeaning title there, placed the findings outside the level of civilizations we believed in. The candomblés and their rich art, in other words, were at one time cast in zones of moral indiscernibility.

Now all that has changed. To begin with, Brazil is one of the major nations of the world, a third of a continent, comprising a major portion of a language family more populous than that of French. And within that automatic importance, of size and population, surges the richness of Brazil's black culture, defined in brilliant variations.

The emergence of Yoruba-influenced Benin shrine art and Yoruba-influenced altar art in Brazil, both richly illustrated here, proves (as if proof were needed) that the split of Italic into Spanish and Portuguese has no copyright on the classicizing process. For if to watch a world classical tradition unfold is to witness multiple associative values—permanence, moral center, spiritual continuance—in motion across incredible stretches of time and space, then the sobriquet of Bahia, "the Rome of the Africans," alerts us to this double diaspora, this salutation of things and deeds classically black, within settings classically Iberian. The Mediterranean, after all, remains forever half an African sea.

There is a fortuitous (because that is where Phyllis Galembo has worked) but historically right quality to the triangulation that we witness here of two classical African—Yoruba and Edó—civilizations in comparison with perhaps the most intensely Yoruba-izing city in the New World, Bahia.

We are studying Edó as an extension of Yoruba religious influence in architectural and ritual actions present in Nigeria today. In terms of matched artistic and intellectual intensities, Bahia is to the original Yoruba and Edó as Alexandria was to Athens and Rome. Time will test and deepen this asseveration.

If we focus on the Yoruba-derived religions of Bahia, we find the ancient constants. For example, we discover the [Yoruba] enabling power of the gods, *àshe,* returned in the virtually identical Afro-Brazilian concept, *axê,* embedded in time-resistant stones, uplifted or concealed on altars. We find *axê* exalted in the presentation of cloths and paintings and statuary, surrounding the most important altars, where stones are guarded, where god-objects appear in powerful arrangements.

In Yorubaland and Bahia, the thunder axes of Xangó, the metal fans of Oxum, the mystic iron bow and arrow of Oxossi, are objects of constancy and sobriety. But variation defines the way servitors shape and embellish such objects. And variation defines the styles by which the altars of Black Bahia are completed.

Afro-Bahian altars are not sublanguages of the spirit, cast forever in the shadow of the Roman Catholic Church. They are, in and of themselves, "diamonds of becoming." To borrow the phrasing of Gilles Deleuze and Felix Guattari in their brilliant study, *A Thousand Plateaus:* "[Their] value is to trigger uncontrollable movements and deterritorializations of the mean or the majority." Thus, if we compare the hundreds upon hundreds of vernacular altars among the blacks of Bahia, something remarkable emerges. In reimagining motifs from Rome and Ketu in favor of "differences in dynamic," the servitors in Salvador have elaborated, I think, one of the great altar traditions of the world. These altars have been designed not only to guard stones of permanent residences of the spirit; they were also constructed to honor God's own demand for artistic creativity, as a sign of respect. In short, they were made to set the *orisha* in motion, to leap the ellipsis of the flesh.

The situation is far too rich to entrust to any single school or discipline; a thousand monographs, it does not matter, there will always be nuances beyond.

Thus followers of the *orisha* spoke to Phyllis Galembo, as she prepared these photographs, in the freshness of individual phrasing. Obaluaiye they salute as "king of fevers"; Iemanjá dances with eyes closed, "because if she sees, Exu, the trickster, arrives." The latter comment, in effect, glosses eyes-closed *orisha* dancing in Bahia as amuletic harmony.

Galembo asks fundamental questions, as if we knew nothing, which, considering the infinity of the *orisha,* seems appropriate. Thus she asks, "Who is Oxum?" and is told, Queen of the waters. "Who is Iansa?" Queen of the sword, the fire, the storm, the lightning. And just when we think we know all we need to know about a famous deity, Ogúm, one of her informants can shock us back to humility by adding a luminous

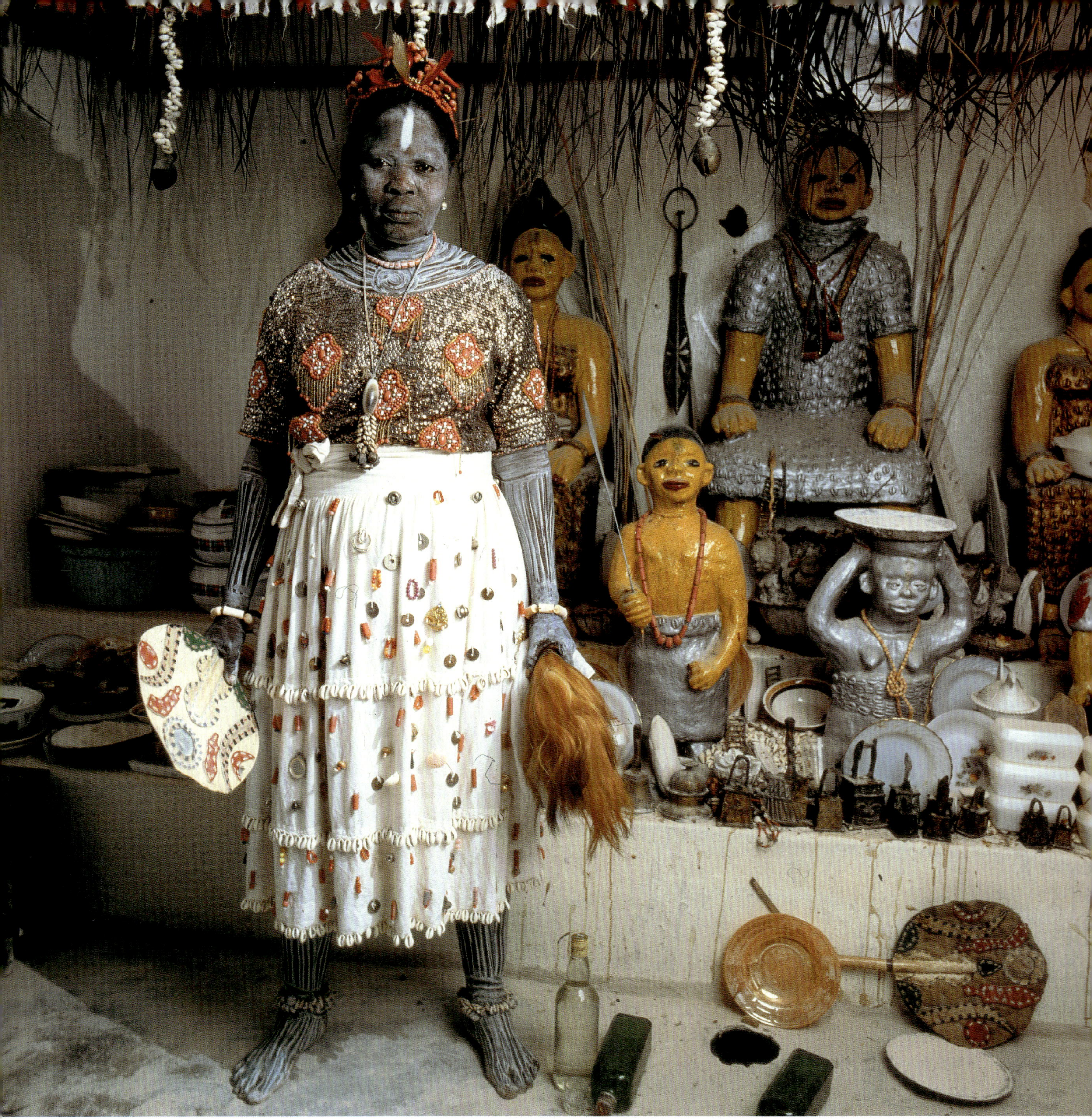

An Olokun priestess in front of her shrine. The image of Olokun in the background is flanked by attendants and guardians modeled of clay and other materials, and painted with commercial pigments. Imported objects signify the importation of wealth, in accordance with the Bini proverb, "Rivers ever remain small that do not stretch their fingers to the sea."

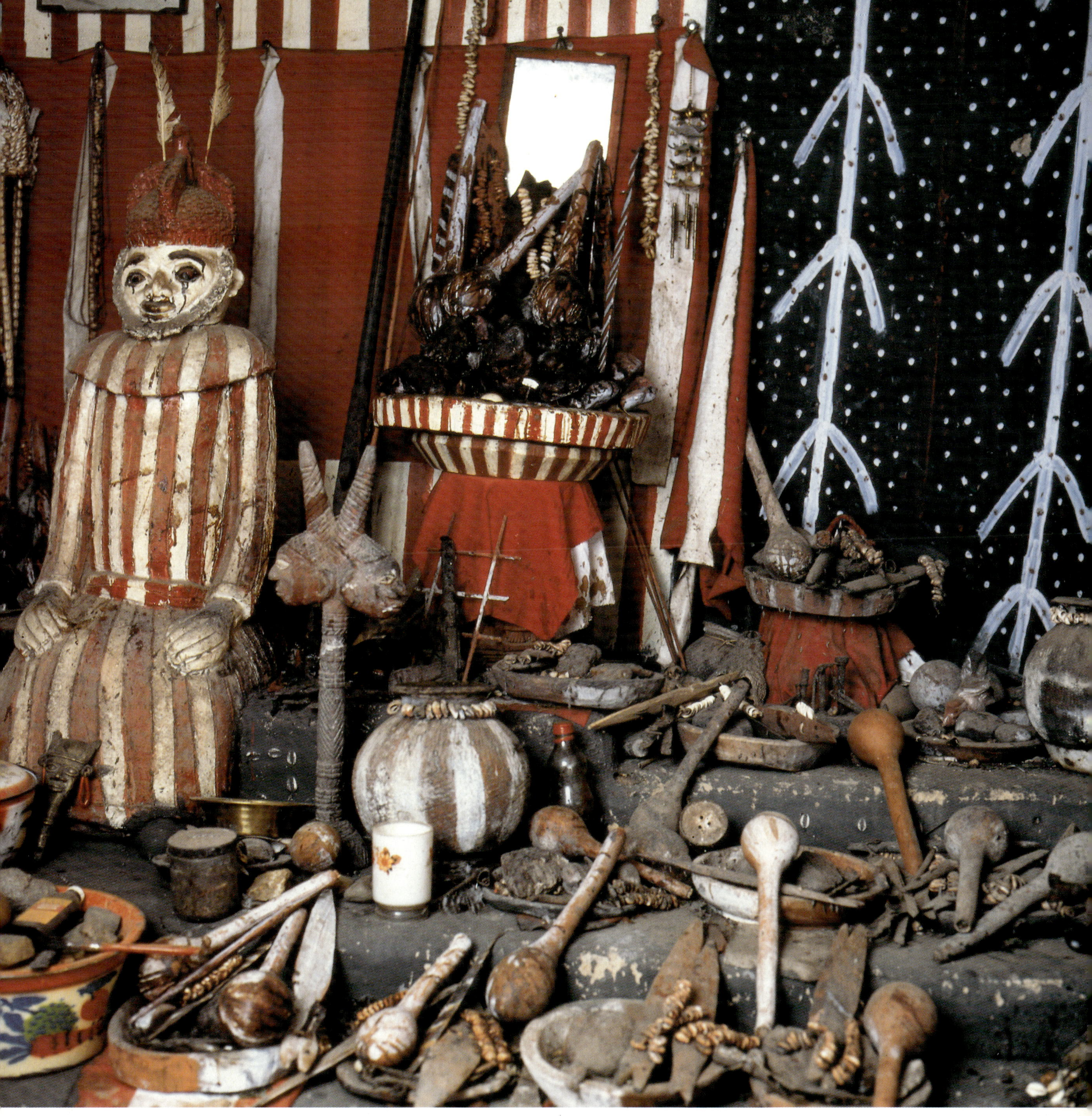

Sángò shrines being developed under the direction of Madame Agbonavbre. Each of the shrines in the foreground belongs to an initiate who is being instructed by this priestess.

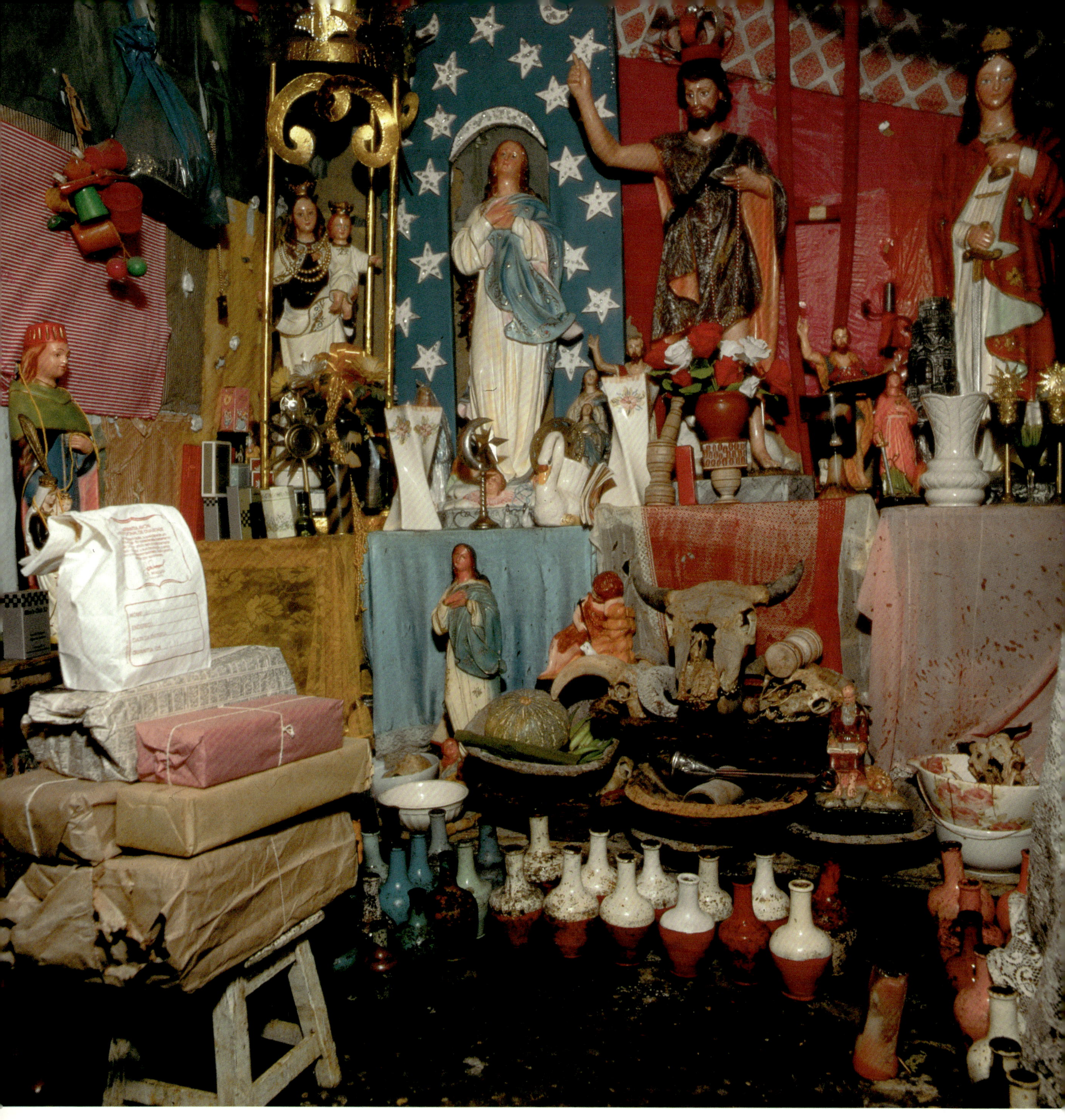

A shrine to Iemenja, with representations of the moon and stars.
A good example of syncretism in candomblé.

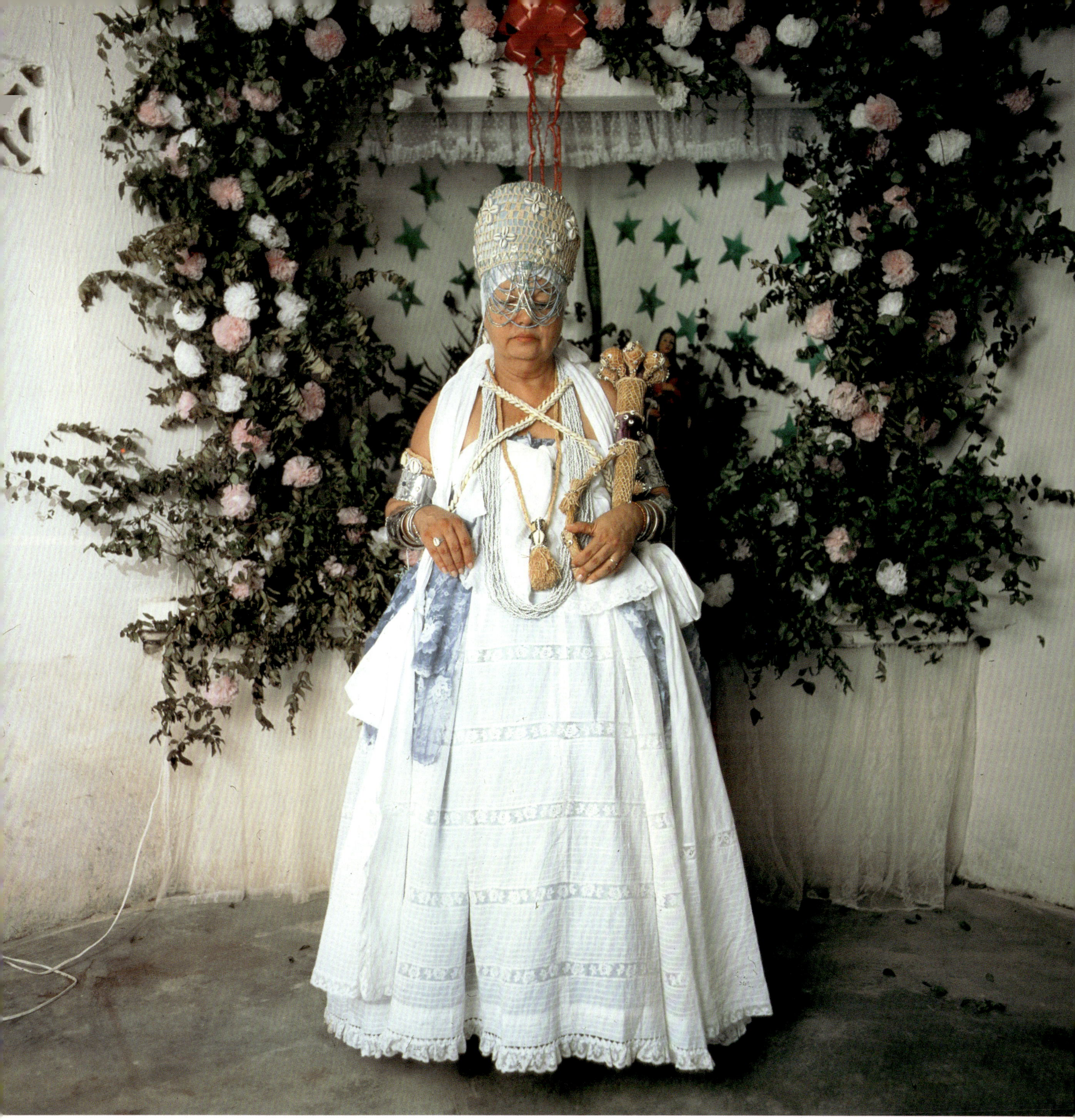

A devotee of Nana, shown holding a staff of palm frond fibers.
This deity represents the courage and accomplishments of women.

fragment of unrecorded understanding. Everyone in Yoruba studies knows that Ogun, in West Africa, is lord of war and iron. But an Afro-Bahian refines this vision: "Ogúm is the god of peace, [for] at his feet there is a lamb, the son of peace." Ogúm, in this interpretation, represents full military preparedness, and this in turn makes waging war, for enemies, not viable.

In focusing on the altars of Bahia we need first to establish the semantic range of the concept of altars in the West. From remote antiquity we discover associations of elevation (from the Latin *altus*, high), scent, and illumination (from the Latin *ardere*, to burn). Compare *Exodus* 38: "the altar of burnt offerings." This suggests a preference for the Western altar—that which elevates, illuminates, burns.

In cultural contrast, consider the terms in which the Yoruba regard the concept of altar: as *ojú òrìshà* (literally, the face of the gods) or *ojúbo* (literally, the face or point of sacrifice). *Ojú*, in classical Yoruba, simultaneously refers to eyes, face, and surface. There is a further nuance to the term *ojú*, namely, gateway, portal, door. Compare the phrases *ojú ona* (literally, "face of the road," or gate) and *ojú ilé*, (literally, "face of the house," or door).

Thus, a Yoruba altar is a face of the gods, a sacred surface, an area where spirits are venerated. As to the altar/surface concept, recall the Yoruba phrase for a railroad train—*oko ojú irin*, literally, "vessel upon the face of iron, or vessel gliding over an iron surface, or vessel on iron's own altar." Conceptual phrasing becomes pure poetry.

Face implies focus. This grants the Yoruba servitor the conviction that he has a point wherein to assuage the gods, as he might offer an honorific beverage to an elder. Altar seen as face means altar seen as place to feed or offer drink. The metaphor breathes life into an abstract raised structure, with a flat top, upon which offerings are placed. Adherents to the *orisha* thus approach this "face," this "surface," this "door," to establish a continuum between this world and the next. This modicum of cultural preparation allows us to examine Phyllis Galembo's photographs of Yoruba-Bahian altars with an increased appreciation.

A few examples may demonstrate the rich vocabulary of meaning these altars embody. One image shows an altar to the Yoruba deity of chance and vicissitude, Exu. The surface of the floor is part of the altar. It is studded with bottles of palm oil and other liquids for the god. Elevated portions of the altar (called *pepele* in Bahia, just as they are in Yorubaland) lift up, to the informed gaze of the initiates, the *iba exu*, earthenware containers in which primordial images of the trickster are built up in clay, blood, shells, and other ritual substances. These presences confront us with the strange sparkle of shell-embedded eyes, with a frozen shell-embedded mouth. The shells in

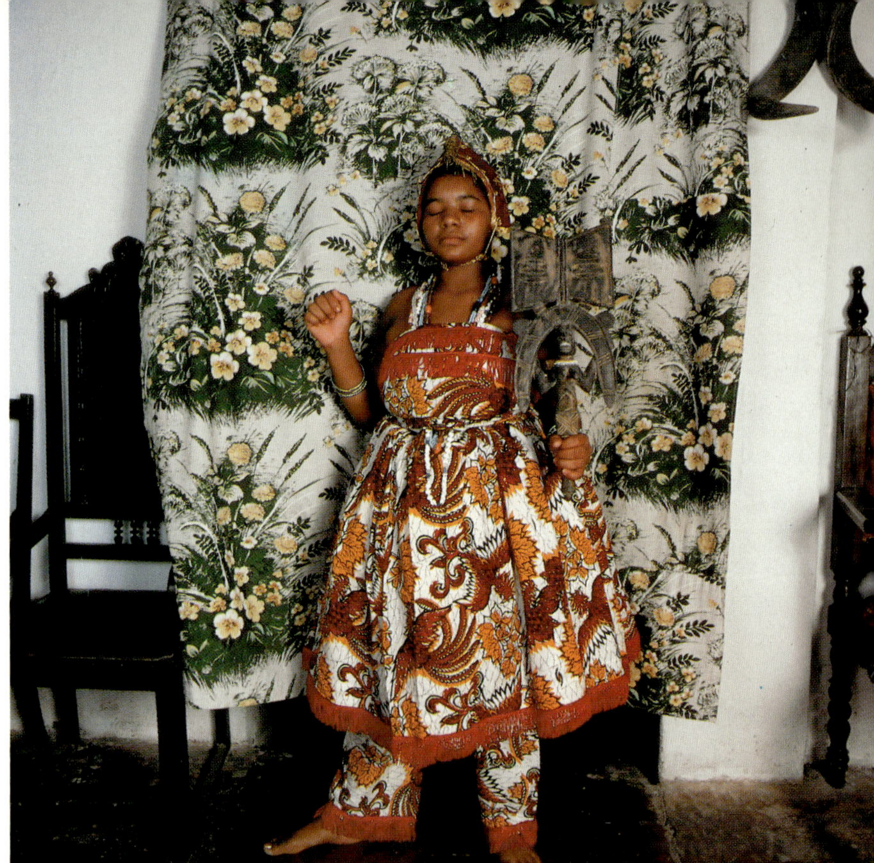

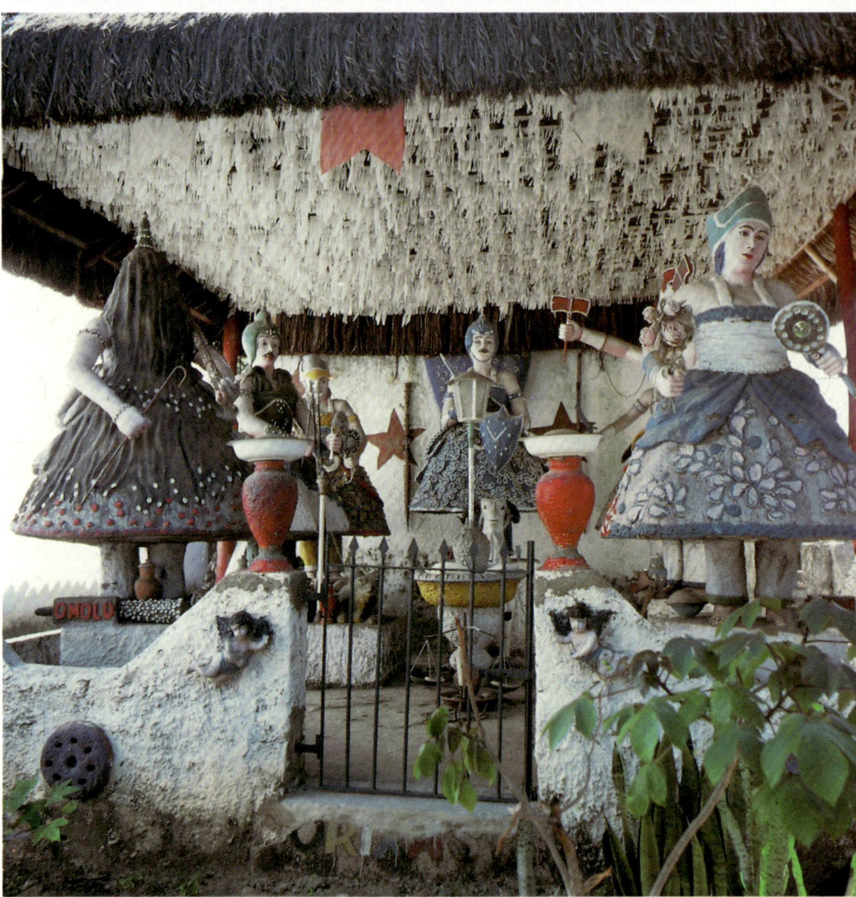

Top: A follower of Shango, the god of thunder, lightning, and fertility, who is commonly syncretized with the Christian Saint Barbara. The devotee shown here carries Shango's common symbol, a double axe, the tool with which he dramatizes moral vengeance and intimidation.

Bottom: This altar-gateway leads to a shrine punctuated by images of Omo-Olu, Iemanja, and other spirits. Omo-Olu appears as a kind of walking broom, bristling with lengths of imported African straw. The blue of Iemanja, with her spangled skirt, promises increase and plenty.

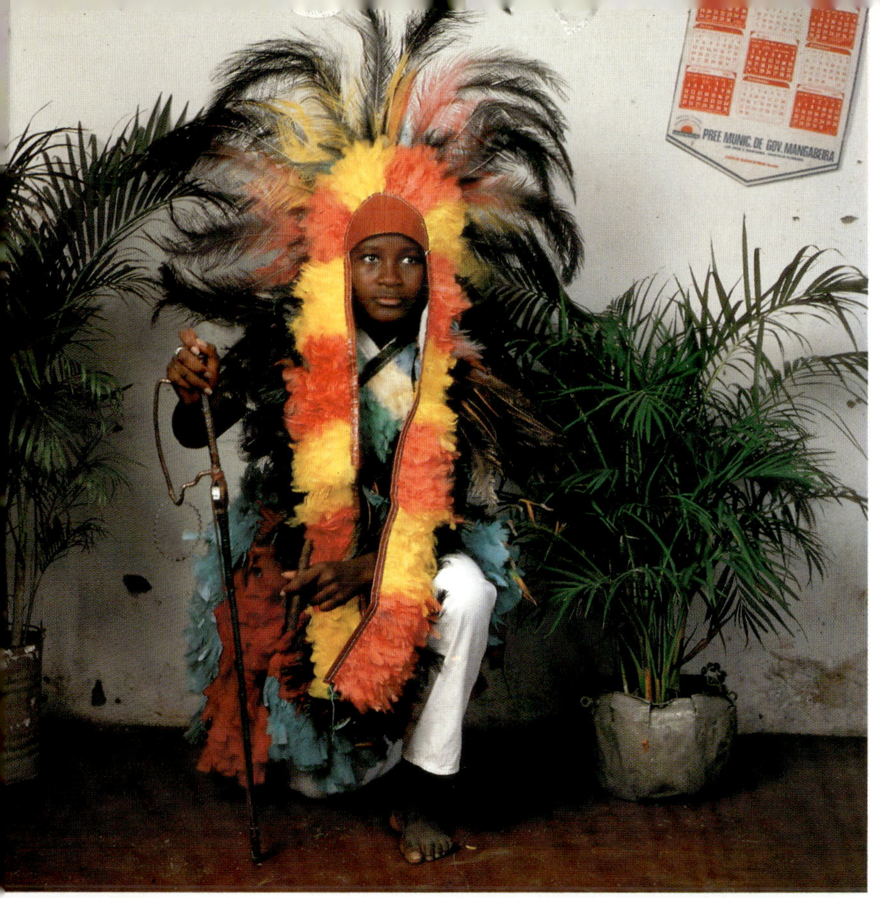

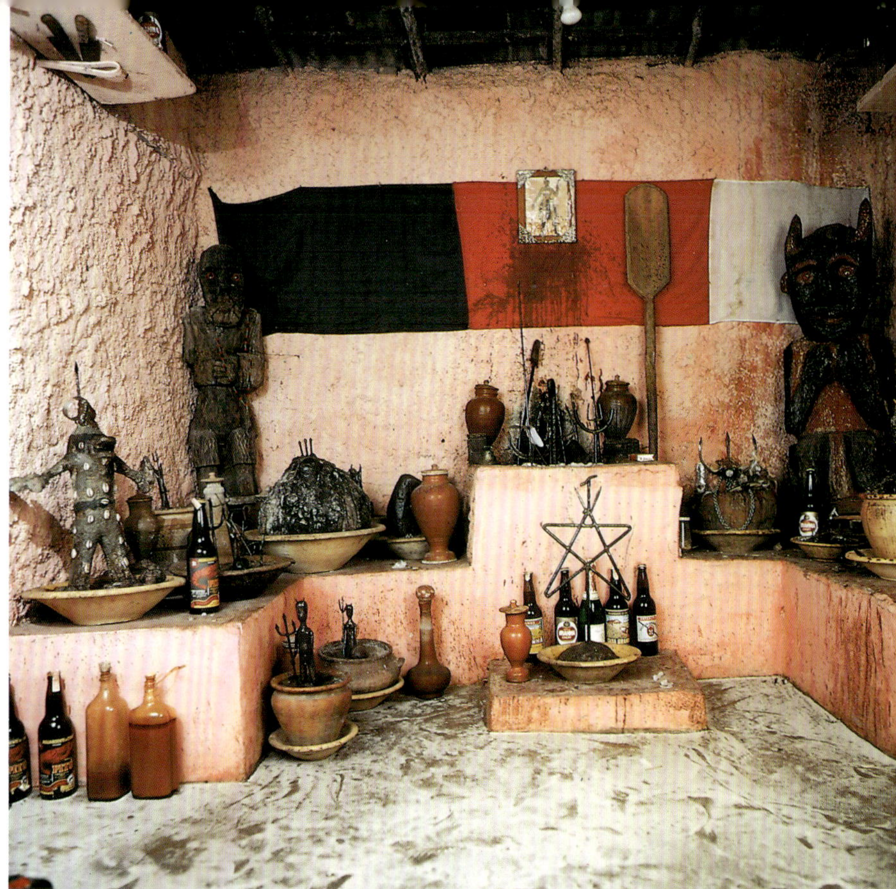

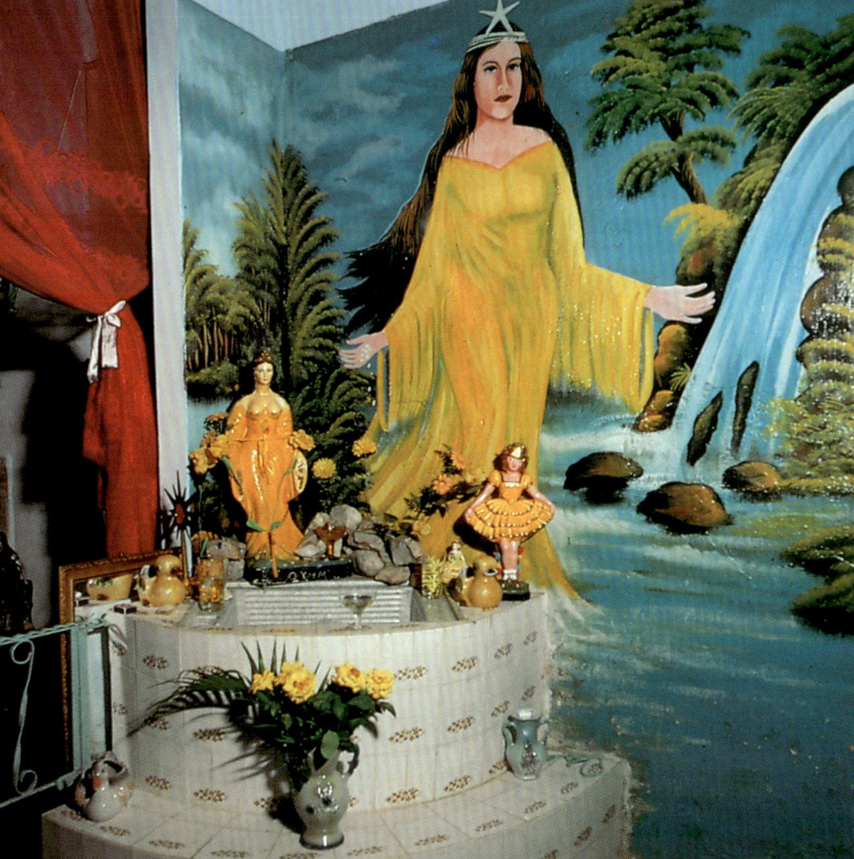

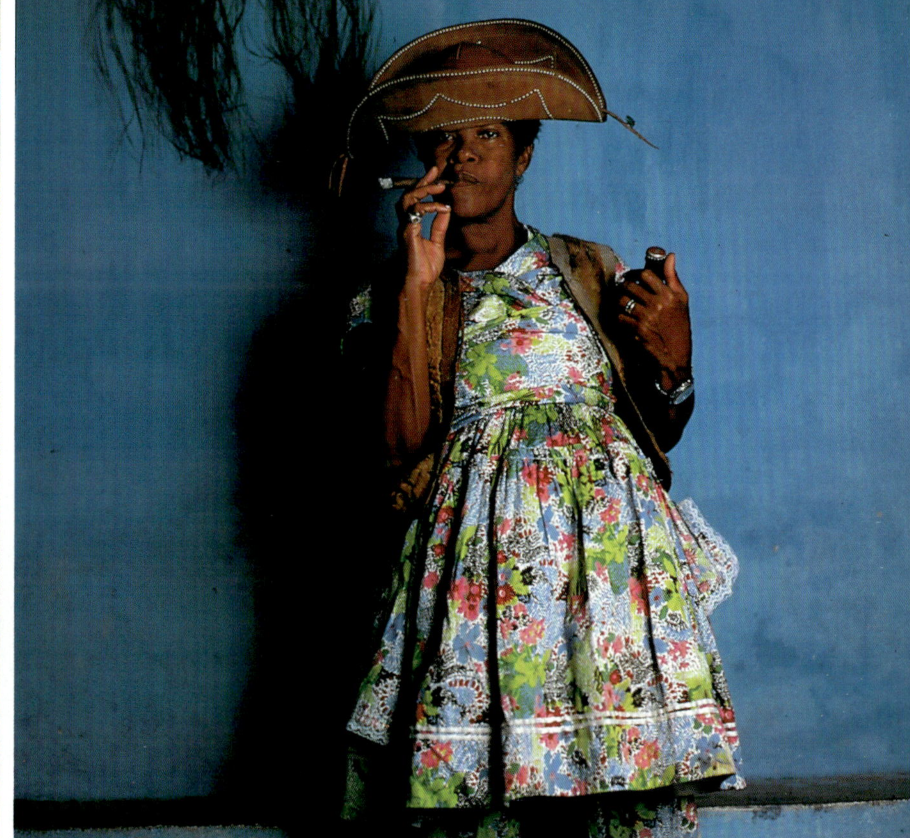

Top: A follower of Caboclo, an Amerindian deity found in candomblé and Umbanda, the fusion faith of Rio.

Bottom: A shrine to Iemanja, the deity of motherhood and the birthplace of life on earth, the ocean. Mother of rivers, her color is blue and her symbols are fish, round fans, crowns, and eathernware vessels filled with seawater.

Top: An altar to Exu, the Yoruba deity of chance and vicissitude. The elevated parts of the altar present *iba exu*, earthenware containers in which primordial images of the trickster are built up in clay, blood, shells, and other ritual substances. The highest portion of the altar elevates *quartinhas*, clay vessels which often enclose cool water, for ritual assuagement of the deity.

Bottom: A follower of Caboclo.

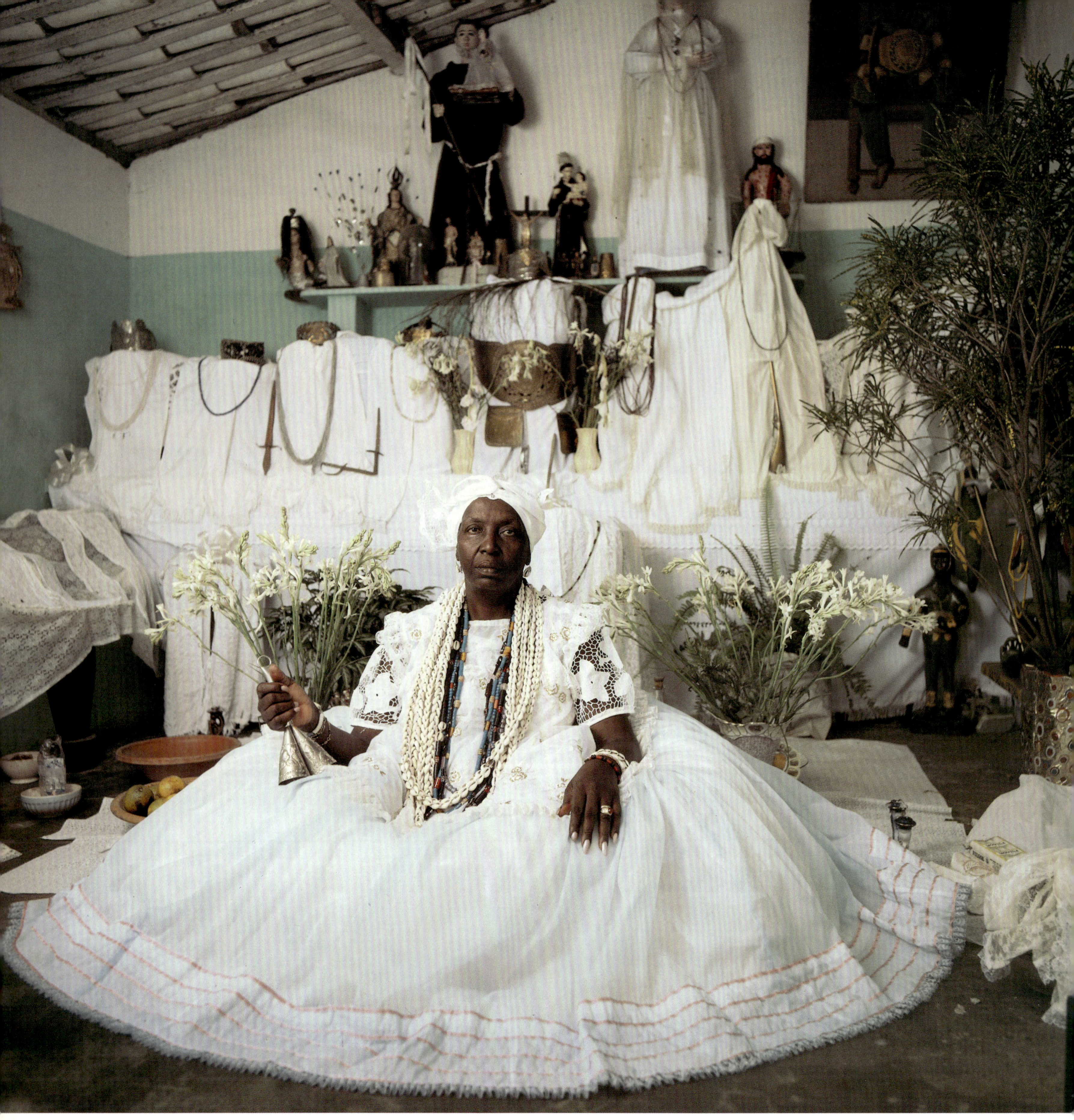

Cloth-embellished altars, recapturing the glamour of heaven, persist in Bahia as a living tradition. The head priestess of this shrine, dressed in luxurious lengths of immaculate cloth, is seated among guarded receptacles of *ashe* wrapped in immaculate white cloths, as well as an intervening array of flowers.

traditional Yoruba rituals are used in divination. This warns us of the trickster's power to observe—and transform—destiny.

The highest portion of the altar elevates *quartinhas,* small clay vessels which often enclose cool water. They are statements of reconciliation, of a return to freshness and composure. The corners of this gateway to Exu are guarded by wooden images, one of which is horned. This associates, through a false analogy (which, unfortunately, has acquired much currency in the popular imagination of Brazil), Exu with Satan. This association works only if we see in this comparison the Satan of the Book of Job. For there the famous adversary came to test—and thus confirm—the patience of a righteous person.

The photograph captures a further element of Exu's confrontational presence. The keeper of this shrine paints the emblems of Exu in his colors, red and black. Witness the triple banner, crimson, black, and white, colors of violence and purity and the night. On the altar is a paddle, referring both to travel and, perhaps, to punishment. Finally, a star, set in a central portion, cosmologizes the setting. But it also smacks of the influence of *Umbanda,* the fusion faith of Rio. It is, I think, an invasion, of one of the myriad star symbols of *Umbanda,* one of the so-called *pontos riscados,* that are to be found within the world of this Rio-originated religion. Purists rarely admit such things. Nevertheless, Rio/Bahian fusions inform the vitality of certain shrines.

In ancient Ife, altars sometimes combined images and attributes of the god of divination, Ifá, with images and attributes of other *orisha.* This made the point that "many *orisha* work together with Ifá," that "Ifá is not alone." Similarly, on another cloth-canopied altar we find Oxossi, lord of hunting (and fishing, too, in Bahia) honored with bow and arrow painted in bold red upon the wall. *Iansan,* correlated with the chromolithographs of Saint Barbara, and *Iemanjá,* once again the mermaid, march together at the top of a tall domestic corner-altar. Finally a servitor stands by, holding the fish and the fan, the water and the wind, powers of *Iemanjá,* within his hands. Such objects safeguard the narrative richness of the *orisha.*

In ancient Yorubaland, white cloths for Obatala were placed on altars as outward manifestations of his inner purity. Cascading cloths announced the power and the prestige of Yemoja upon her altar in Abeokuta. Cloth-embellished altars, recapturing the glamour of heaven in full-dress architectural settings, persist in Bahia as a living tradition.

Galembo has captured something more. Her photograph (page 40) shows not only the guarded receptacles of *àshe,* wrapped in immaculate white cloths, plus an intervening zone of flowers, but a head priestess herself, in luxurious lengths of matching immaculate cloth.

This mother of the spirits is seated where things are grasped in themselves. Ritual textiles and the person coincide with essences of purity and potential.

A final example of the altar-gateway is a shrine punctuated with three-dimensional images of Omo-Olú, Iemanjá, and other spirits. The former appears, essentially, as a walking broom, bristling with lengths of imported African straw, *palha da costa.* The broom's basic structure is defined in straw. Straw sweeps pestilence upon the immoral, and protection upon the righteous. Both premises are signaled in the broomlike image of Omo-Olú, also called Master of the World, Obaluaiye. This note of terror and decorum in the image of Omo-Olú is relieved by Iemanjá's blue promise of increase and plenty, all stemming from the sea. One look at her spangled skirt and we find ourselves in the presence of her plenitude. Whether the red *quartinhas* which flank this portal to the gods limn the dangers which lie in store for the promiscuous, or for other reasons, I cannot say. But the firmament of crepe which decorates the ceiling speaks of ritual ecstasy. Crepe paper ceiling decorations tell us that the hard-working devotees who flock to this shrine do so in a spirit of celebration. If their conscience is clear, they know these powerful figures will surround them with truth and love. Those who built this shrine, who keep it at a pitch of power, receive quiet but overwhelming gifts. For example, night after night, when gods and goddesses make their appearances, they frequently hug the devotees, or, sometimes, place their right hand upon their heads, a gesture which proclaims the peace surpassing human understanding.

In any event, among the Ijesha and Oyo Yoruba, Oshun/Oxum is praised as Olomi Ide, which means, literally, "Mistress of rivers turned into flowing, liquid brass." The image refers to the fact that traditional Yoruba attribute particular strengths, particular powers, to brass (ide). To the Yoruba mind, several *orisha,* but especially Oshun, move with the sacred force of this molten metal. As one traditionalist told me in Ekiti, "Brass—look at it, see something fast, moving, murmuring, like bracelets chiming on the wrists of Oshun, like water racing over sands or stones." Absorb this vision and think of the fast, immediate punishment of the Ogboni Society, the sign of which includes a male and a female figure, rendered in brass, joined by a chain in the same speed-implying metal. Absorb this vision and think of the lightning flash of Shango, reflected in the chain of brass through which he disappeared into the earth, in the darting motions of the brass mask of his own ancestral spirit, Alákoro. And finally think of love-drenched Oxum, who can swim into our lives with the speed of a minnow, with the flash of a golden carp in light-pierced waters, in the liquid hips of a stunning woman, who promises her lover that his loneliness is ended, that he will swim directly within her ecstasy forever.

APERTURE SYMPOSIUM
at Esalen Institute

The World's Reality

In a world both increasingly fragmented and incrementally interdependent, the boundaries of existence are being remade daily. New technologies redefine our relation to the environment, upheavals in social structure and the breakdown of systems of identity threaten cultural norms; new political realities impose long-range conditions for change.

The deliberate naïveté of the chosen title for this gathering, "The World's Reality," reflects a recognition that new strategies for emotional and intellectual survival are necessary. . . .

—from the announcement of the Aperture symposium at Esalen

In the following special section, Aperture is proud to present a series of articles based on ideas and issues that arose during the course of "The World's Reality," a symposium that Aperture organized and which was held with the generous cooperation of the Esalen Institute in February 1988. Beginning on page 44, Nan Richardson, former editor of *Aperture* and a conference participant, describes the challenging presentations and intense debates of the conference itself. On page 50, Megan Biesele describes the situation of Namibia's Bushmen, as they respond to the radically changed economic and political circumstances they find themselves in; in the next feature, beginning on page 58, Elizabeth Weatherford, of New York's Museum of the American Indian, discusses the growing use of media by native peoples to record their own histories.

One of the major disappointments of the Esalen symposium was that Omar Badsha, the South African photographer and editor, had been refused a visa and would be unable to attend. This year, though, Badsha was finally allowed to travel abroad, and during his stay in New York he spoke on the role of photography in the struggle against apartheid. Finally, starting on page 66, we present a selection of video stills from Edin Velez's *Meaning of the Interval,* a meditation on modern Japan—caught, as is every other culture, between past and future; these images, photographed by Ethel Velez, are accompanied by an essay by Karoline Postel-Vinay about the seeming incongruities of contemporary Japan.

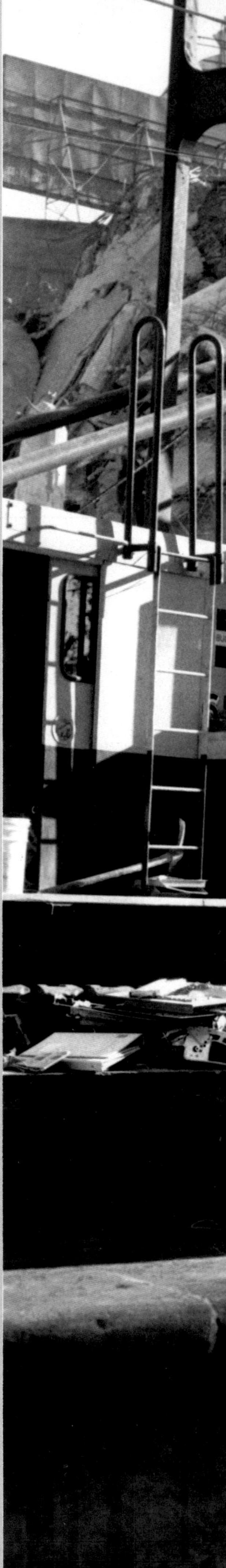

Ricardo Block, from *Terremoto,* 1985

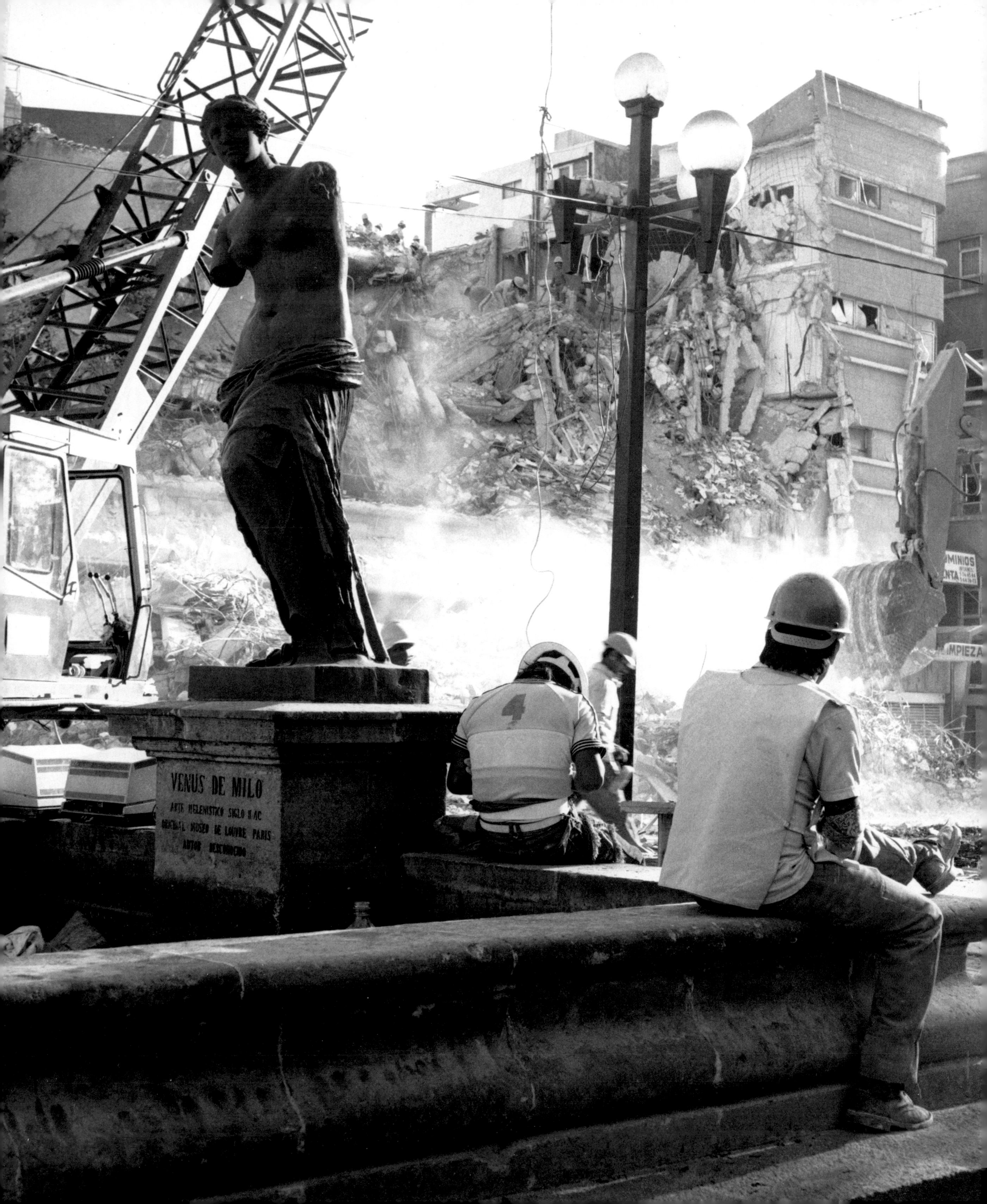
VENUS DE MILO
ARTE HELENISTICO SIGLO II AC
ORIGINAL MUSEO DE LOUVRE PARIS
AUTOR DESCONOCIDO

The Past Becoming Future

By Nan Richardson

If he is honest, [the ethnographer] is faced with a problem—the value he attaches to foreign societies—and which appears to be higher in proportion as the society is more foreign—has no foundation. It is a function of his disdain for, and occasionally hostility toward, the customs prevailing in his native setting. —Claude Lévi-Strauss, *Tristes Tropiques*

Two years ago, Aperture invited a group of twenty photographers, filmmakers, video artists, and anthropologists to meet for a five-day conference, hosted by the Esalen Institute in Big Sur, California.

Esalen was having its twenty-fifth anniversary that year, and seemed less the legendary mecca of 1960s human-potential experimentation than an idyll framed by mountains of eucalyptus and wild sage sloping to flowering meadows, vertiginous cliffs, and an ice-blue sea. Michael Murphy, one of the the original founders, inherited the land for this spa-cum-religious retreat from his grandfather, and that week, as the monarch butterflies began their seasonal migration and covered the ground with color and vibration, we were truly in another-worldly reality. Against this backdrop, the conference took place, questioning whether the artists' "authentic response to the world's contradictions," as poet Patricia Hampl argued, was "to indicate the path between reality and men's souls."

The consensus was that the paths are many and varied. Robert Levy, an anthropologist at the University of Southern California at San Diego, led with a comparison of Tahiti and Nepal, commenting that we were witness to a global imbalance in cultures, within which balance, however precarious, still managed to exist. While Tahiti is a society ruled by common sense, where tradition and modernity coexist, Nepal's city life is largely defined by heredity: in jobs, in the caste structure, in the sacred art used to tell stories that explain the shape of the world. Describing those cultures as "lived" rather than "thought about," Levy raised the issue of the inadequacy inherent in judging work foreign to our culture and experience, and questioned the outdated anthropologists' view of "privileged truth."

Edin Velez began his video *Meta Mayan II* by deciding to forego questions of subjective or objective, and to move from documentary to more personal expression. Born and raised in Puerto Rico, and now living in New York, Velez "was searching in other Latin countries for what I hadn't experienced in mine: identity, a sense of belonging somewhere." In Guatemala he joined a Jesuit project documenting grassroots community organizations working in the shanty towns of Guatemala City. While there he became fascinated with the Mayan perception of time and culture, and started to use video in nearby villages. The film alludes to events in Guatemala in the 1980s, a time when 50,000 Indians were killed by the Army, their villages were burned, and survivors were herded into "model" settlements. In an extraordinary sequence, the camera follows a Mayan woman down a road as she turns, confronts the camera, and walks on. Velez commented that, "While this isn't an active incisive political documentary—I didn't feel I could, or wanted to, do that—there are a lot of things that are not on that tape, that you live on a day-to-day basis. You experience them knowing that you're really not doing much that will change the situation, and that it will go on—and probably get worse. You can leave, but they'll be staying." (A feature on *The Meaning of the Interval*, Velez's reflection on cognition, taped in Japan, is presented on page 66 of this special section.—Ed.)

James Clifford's phrase "ethnographic romanticism" was advanced by Megan Biesele, then teaching at Rice University, in Houston, to describe the prevalent bias in anthropology: the Eden-like pastoral of "death-by-myth" that strips political realities from the picture, so that, as Biesele contended, "you can't see that they're still there, they're hungry, and their land is being taken away." She discussed the ways in which social documentation was moving away from speaking to others, in favor of ways people could speak for themselves. "Translation itself is a political act," she asserted, "and the broad translation of cultures in particular is a very political activity." Biesele pointed further to the enfranchisement in current anthropology of new forms: the ethnographic novel, the autobiography, and the use of a multiplicity of voices in continuing dialogue, which has been slowly replacing the authoritarian voice of the documentarian.

The film Biesele showed, *N!ai, the Story of a !Kung Woman,* by colleagues John Marshall and Claire Ritchie, told in N!ai's own words the story of her life over thirty years, the changes the Bushmen of Namibia's Kalahari Desert have undergone in moving from a past as hunter-gatherers to their current status on a reservation set up by Namibia's South African rulers. (For an update on Biesele's work in Namibia, see her article on page 50.) Beisele spoke of her own deepening involvement in the area, first as a folklorist and then, as the !Kung asked for specific help, as an active advocate, founding the Kalahari Peoples' Fund to support practical and political work. "Finally," she concluded, "it comes down to an art, an art of presentation, as true in photography as in anthropology. The cutting edge is to bear witness to the fact that it's not over yet; people are in the process of creating their own reality, and they ask us to listen."

The entire Esalen community met the following night to screen *First Contact,* a riveting documentary history of the first encounter, in 1930, between twentieth-century Australian whites and the pretechnology "Stone Age" highlanders of Papua New Guinea. Who were these sky-beings, who flew on great birds? Perhaps their own returning dead, who could cap-

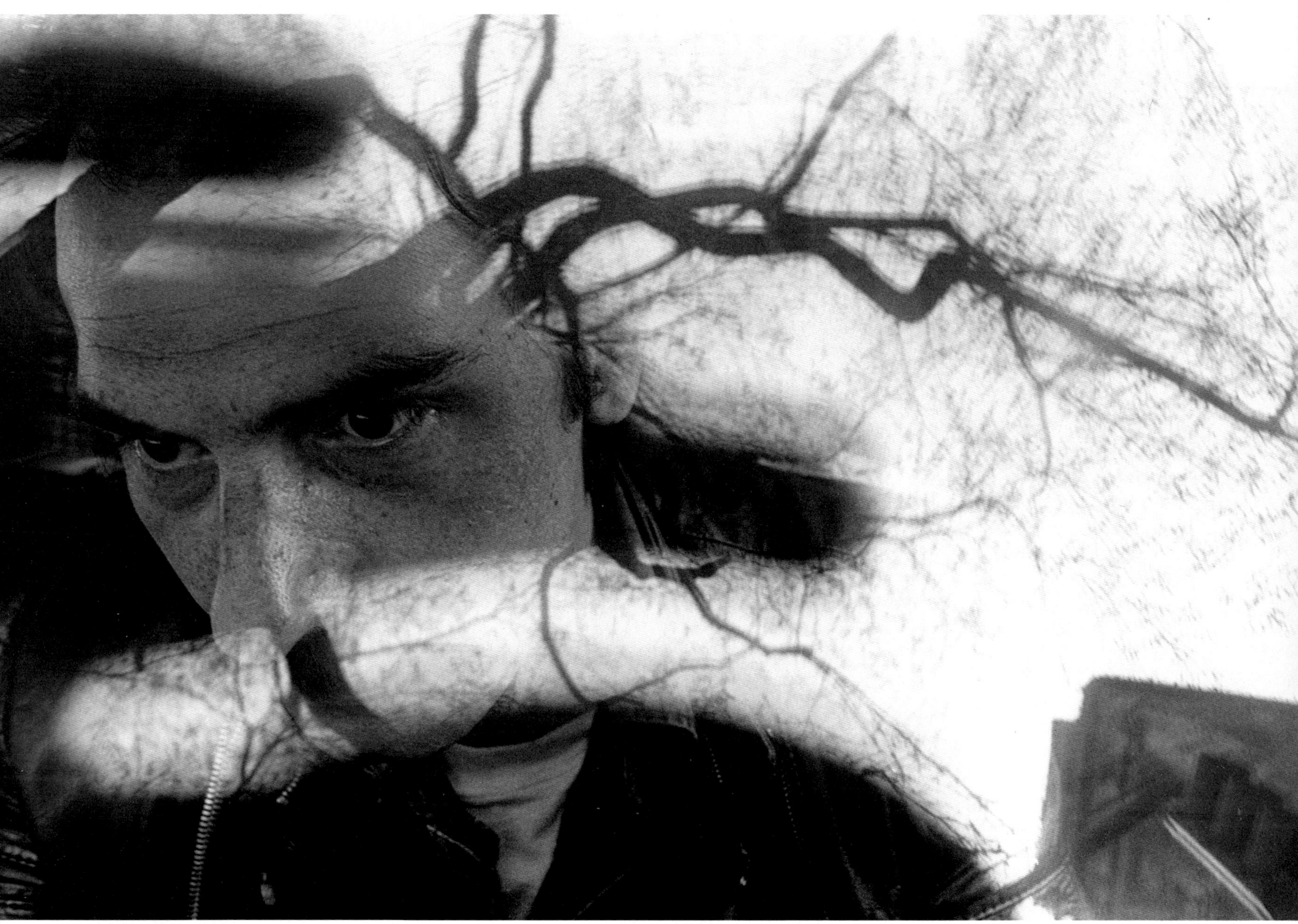

Eugene Richards, from *Below The Line: Living Poor In America*, 1986

ture the moon from the sky and put it in their tents, who searched the rivers with a dish looking for their bones; Michael Leahy, an adventurer in search of gold, made stills and home movies of the first sightings; his films were rediscovered fifty years later by filmmakers Bob Connolly and Robin Anderson, who conducted in-depth interviews with Leahy's colleagues, as well as natives who remembered that shocking, humorous, profound moment when two alien cultures collided. *First Contact* is a story of conquest, a chastening lesson in history, but told in the words of those who experienced that great cultural change, it is chiefly about the power of memory and history.

Peter Raymont, a Canadian filmmaker from Toronto, showed his award-winning film *Magic in the Sky,* the story of Eskimo communities in the grip of change as TV arrived in their villages in the late 1970s, and of their efforts to set up their own broadcasting network in response. Initially sent by the National Film Board to teach filmmaking to the people of Frobisher Bay in the Canadian Arctic, Raymont soon began to feel the need for a film that would raise issues of cultural sovereignty, control of technology, and the overlaps of myth and reality. Raymont quoted John Grierson, father of documentary film, as saying that "Art is a hammer, not a mirror," as he described his next project, on the creation of the Eskimo stereotype, from the first "discovery" by white explorers, through Robert Flaherty's *Nanook of the North.* Gilles Peress summed up the discussion of Raymont's film, saying that it "suggests how much there is to do in documentation between our culture and other cultures. What you describe is the moment of negotiation, the moment of interface."

Alex Harris, of the Center for Documentary Photography at

Duke University, presented a series of photographs he made in New Mexico, some of Harris's neighbor, an elderly Mexican-American named Jacobo, and others of the interiors and objects of the houses of local people, bursting with "color as accidental as we see the world; color as decoration, rooms that changed colors in six months, aged and changed and transformed." Together with Margaret Sartor, he then showed work from *The Cordoned Heart,* a book of photographic essays conceived when the Carnegie Corporation began a major study on poverty in South Africa that involved economists, historians, anthropologists, labor organizers, and doctors. (Omar Badsha, who edited the book, is interviewed on page 62.) "We were very careful making this book," Harris said, addressing the issue of possible reprisals by the South African government. "There is no single photograph in it that is technically illegal, so the book could not be banned on any grounds and is being seen all over South Africa." These photographs show a history of the country that simply was not being seen: demonstrations of a million people that were never reported in the press (before these mass gatherings were banned); union meetings where the officials asked to have the meetings covered, even though the photographs were often confiscated and used by the government in treason trials. The exhibition (which toured on portable panels to community centers and other spaces) has been seen by many people, particularly black South Africans.

Sartor noted that "South Africans feel themselves fighting something so big and pervasive that it is, quite openly, a battle they are waging. The discussion was: how shall we use our cameras? Simply to let a reality that is there tell its own story; or as weapons in the struggle?"

Pablo Ortiz Monasterio, editor and photographer, presented a passionate portrait of his native Mexico City, images Velez characterized as "magical realism": fire-swallowers in the boulevards, teenagers with handguns, children selling plastic robots, and Day of the Dead celebrants. In marked contrast, he also showed an earlier project on a fishing village, where the photographs had a more lyrical character. Ortiz Monasterio spoke of reconciling the inherently colonalist act of taking photographs with the need to return something to the subjects. Ten percent of the books made on the village were given to its inhabitants, he reported; "One old man looked at a copy for several minutes before opening it: he looked at how it was done, what sort of materials were used. This object that had come from the outside represented *them.* Some things they liked, others they didn't, but *because* it came as this object, everything was important. It made them discuss things that they didn't feel were very important, socially or politically, but they *became* important precisely because they were in the book."

Bill Viola, a video artist from Long Beach, California, attended with Kira Perov, presenting his tape *I Do Not Know What It Is I Am Like,* a phantasmagoria of primal images: chicks emerging from eggs, snakes crawling across golden goblets, zebras in a neon night. "I wanted to be able to use duration itself as material in a work," Viola reported, "to fight against the incredible pressure to condense that our culture feels. I wanted to be able to make a shot that is too long, so you get a little uncomfortable, to keep stretching, stretching—like a rubber band—stretching till you let go—POW!—and all the images come flying at you.

"There are cultures that transmit knowledge through physi-

Robert Levy, *Nepal: The Living Goddess, Kumari,* 1975

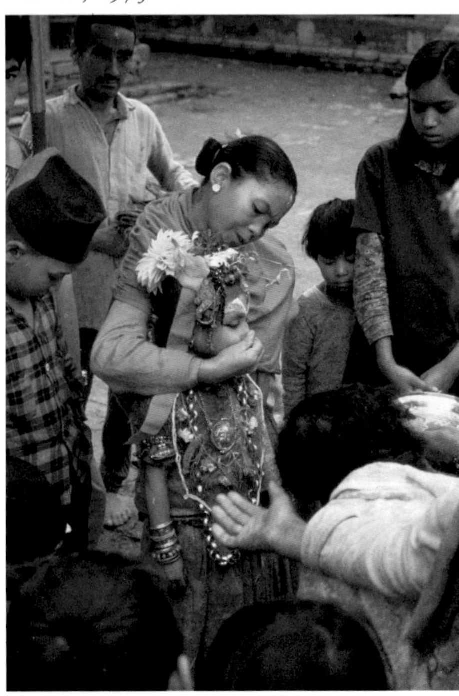

Pablo Ortiz Monasterio, *Ritual prayers to Pascual Abaj, a pre-Hispanic stone in the highlands of Guatemala,* 1989

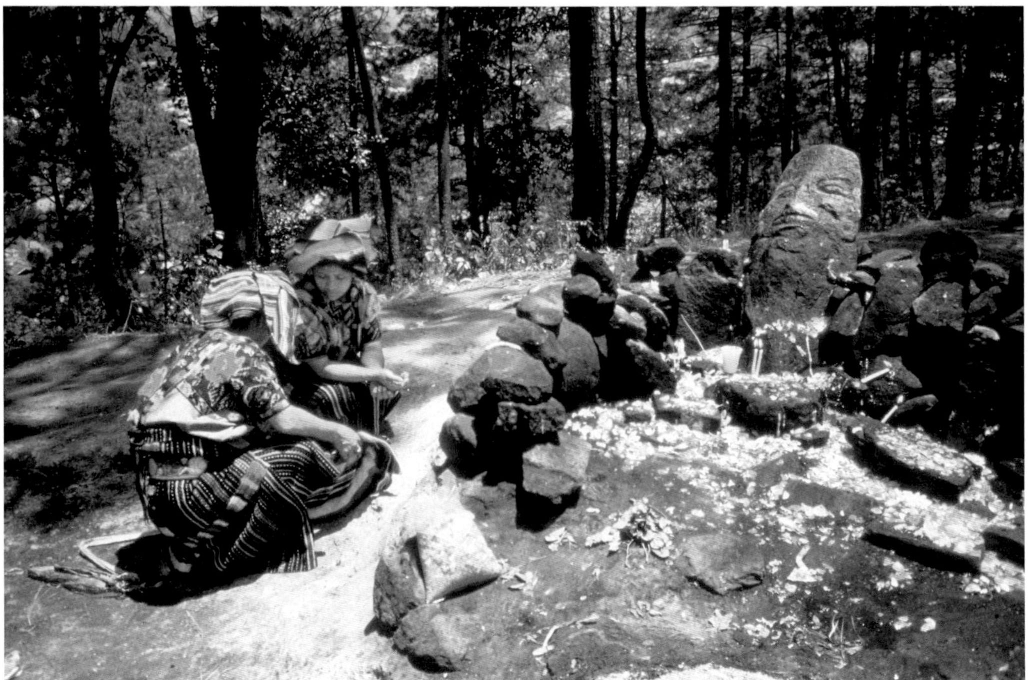

cal experience," Viola concluded, "while in our lives it is abstract, book learning. I want to make those two things equal: a monitor flashing, black and white, light and dark: that's the purest state video can be in."

Proprietary attitudes toward the developing world clashed with accusations of romaticizing tendencies in the presentation of Pedro Meyer, whose book on the Mexican oil industry was commissioned by Pemex, the giant oil conglomerate, for the fiftieth anniversary of the industry's nationalization. "At the time of the nationalization, oil was in the hands of American, British, and Dutch companies, who paid no taxes, who exploited the workers, and over whom Mexico had absolutely no control," Meyer began, projecting layouts of portraits and reminiscences by the workers who participated in the historic event. Meyer went on to photograph Pemex's factories, processing plants, pipelines, and oil fields, but chose not to depict the omnipotent union. "Corruption comes from the power they have to influence Mexico's major employer, the key to the country's economy," he argued. "I cannot photograph the payoff, so I chose to ignore the union entirely—in itself a statement of major proportion." "There are all kinds of ways to intimate corruption," Eugene Richards objected, "the way you hold the camera, with light, by your own emotions. To leave out this crucial element is just a cop-out." A heated discussion followed, ending with Ortiz Monasterio's contention that in any project "you have to think of where the work will be published, who is paying, and the moral and ethical question of whether you should accept it at all. The bureaucrats who spent millions of pesos on this project thought of it as a celebration, and Pedro had freedom—but only to a point. In Mexico we don't have too many opportunities—period. *Any* space is a fantastic opportunity; and even if you can only suggest the problems, it is still better than nothing."

The dilemma of corporate sponsorship was also raised by Eugene Richards, who reported that Consumer Reports, who published his book *Below The Line,* used it "to advertise their social concern. They agreed we could talk with people and discuss what it means to *struggle with* poverty, because people never think about whether they are poor or not." Nevertheless, Consumer Reports subtitled the book *Living Poor in America.* Richards said that he had insisted on using the words of the subjects, rather than the "name" writer the publisher wanted: "Though their perceptions of themselves were absolutely untrue, even in untruth, they were fascinating and important." Comments on his work suggested that he was stretching photography towards film or video, which seemed even truer in his next book, on emergency-room medicine, where, he said "I was trying to get all those voices around me to bend; the heroism and bad humor, the screaming and the noise, the sound of the drum, the monitor, so like the heartbeat, which, when it stops, is the most awesomely frightening time, while the technician plugs his machines, the doctor emotes, the health aide thinks, 'Shit, I have to clean this up,' and the student freezes in fear. You put these voices together, and that is reality. Between

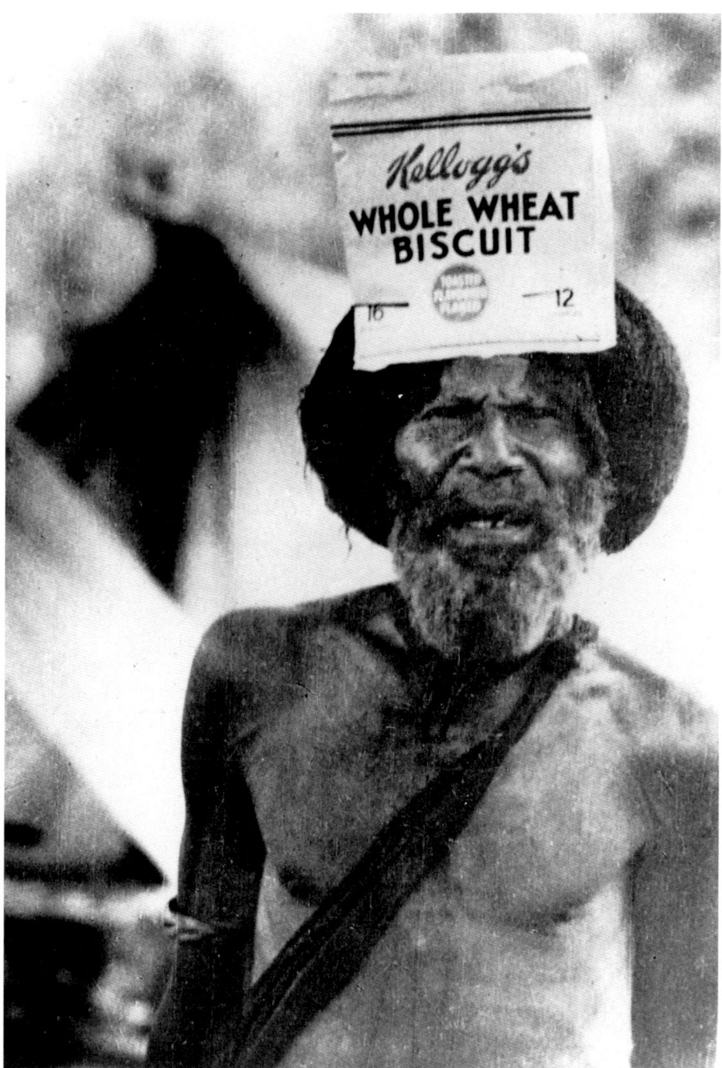

Still from *First Contact,* a film by Bob Connolly and Robin Anderson, 1983

themselves, as they take off the rubber gloves, they call it 'The Knife and Gun Club.' So that's what I titled the book."

"How can we as filmmakers start to approach how people see themselves?" asked Lenny Kamerling in introducing *The White Dawn,* a film he and Sarah Elder produced. "To create not an informational film, not an anthropological film, but an experimental form that captures time, the texture and fabric of life, and that people would be able to look at and say: 'This is what our life is about. This is a fair representation?' " Using terms like "native empowerment," Kamerling described how the community of Bethel in Alaska (where Kamerling has worked for twenty-five years) became an active participant in deciding where the film would be shot, the rules to be followed in filming, what could and could not be looked at. Concentrating on the overwhelming social problem in the north, alcoholism, and Bethel's role as an administrative center for 200 outlying villages, Kamerling explained that although Bethel, like other towns in Alaska, voted to ban the sale of alcohol, they allow its importation "so that the forty-percent white popula-

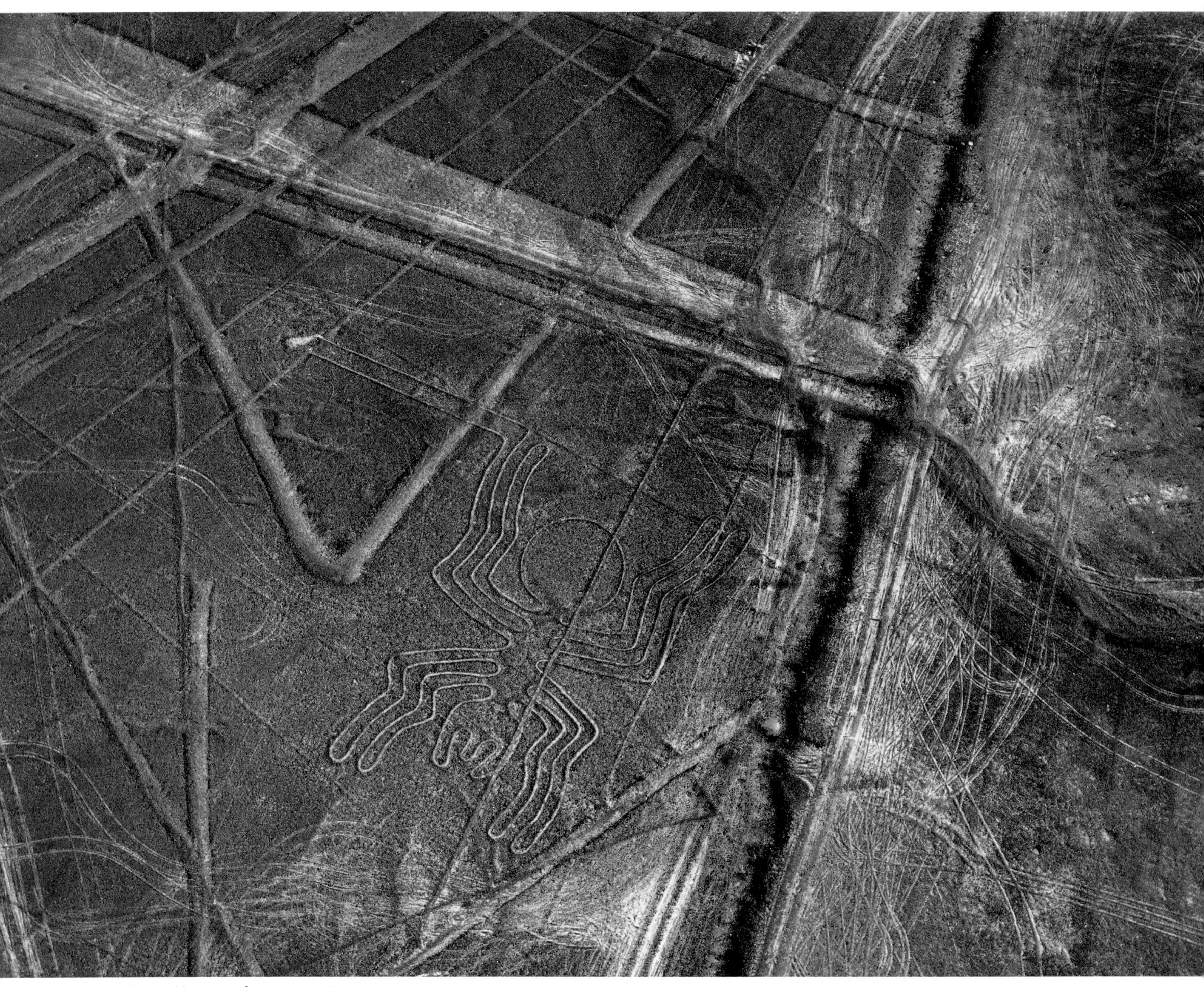

Marilyn Bridges, *Spider, Nazca, Peru,* 1987

tion doesn't have to go without theirs." "It's created a ripe environment for bootleggers," he added. "People there are very sophisticated about media," Kamerling explained, "and instead of the stereotypes in films like *The Savage Innocence,* where Anthony Quinn played Hollywood's idea of an Eskimo, Inuits now want the visual record of their culture to be revised to incorporate their reality, their self-image." As Biesele concluded, "The natives never thought 'taking an image' was stealing their souls, but just exposure on someone else's terms, and the lost comforts of top-down interpretation, as Lenny has shown, are gone forever."

"I guess in a way we all photograph who we are," began Marilyn Bridges, dating her interest in photographing the spiritual centers of the world from her teenage involvement in Indian ceremonials and ritual dancing. Bridges has followed her aerial images of sacred landscapes of the Incan, Mayan, and American Indian cultures with a new series of markings modern man has made. "Man is the earth, and the way we treat the earth is the way we treat ourselves," Bridges commented. "I'm doing this work now to remind people that the earth is sacred. The anthropologists of the future will look back at us and wonder—but it would be hard to make a pastoral out of our society."

Several other films were screened at the conference, though their authors were not able to attend. Chick Strand's *Anselmo and the Women,* about a wife, a husband, and his mistress, presented a social dilemma through the voices of the three characters, and different kinds of psychological reality in a Mexican village. Later, Frederick Wiseman's extraordinary documentary on a Southern school for the blind, *Blind,* was screened, long into the night. Wiseman's deadly accuracy and deliberate use of "real time" is a test of attention span, but the aggregate picture of the life of these children was a poignant and powerful one.

A short video interview with Robert Coles, the leading child psychiatrist in America and a legendary teacher at Harvard University, speaks of learning from others, and emphasizes a motivation born in passion. Coles relates his fateful encounter with six-year-old Ruby Bridges, a black child who broke the segregation barriers in New Orleans schools in the sixties, and how the impact of her courage led to his twenty-five years of study among children of all nationalities and classes, culminating in the Pulitzer-prize-winning book series, *Children of Crisis.* Coles's depth of concern, personal charisma and lucid intelligence came through clearly in the film.

Lastly, Trin T. Minh-ha's film *Naked Spaces* created a strong reaction, among the participants, with Biesele querying the broad generalizations that form the interstices of dialogue—for example, "Religion is the absence of conflict." Biesele objected further that the film was "picked piecemeal out of Dogon mythology—which the Dogon themselves, a highly tricky people with complex metaphysics, have articulated and put together. Why mix it with surface Western and maybe Asian/Vietnamese impressions?" While the film started out as a real critique of anthropological categories, its argument didn't sustain itself. But the epigrammatic statements created a ritual rhythm of presence and absence, un-Western, unfamiliar, providing an intense and fitting ending for the conference.

Gurdjieff tells a story about a group of people gathered together in the desert sand, who cross the vast expanse on stilts so that their heads are above the storm, never seeing, never touching the ground. The Esalen conference was like some Gurdjieffan journey, an encounter where things were left rather than said, where all the travelers were touched, not by the trajectory, but by the tangential. We came together to consider the ethics involved in using visual media (by its nature intrusive, and perhaps, colonialist), and to examine the intentions, origins, and consequences of the signs and meanings we ascribe to our own experience or the experience of others. If during our five-day encounter we never arrived, perhaps it is because the journey continues still.

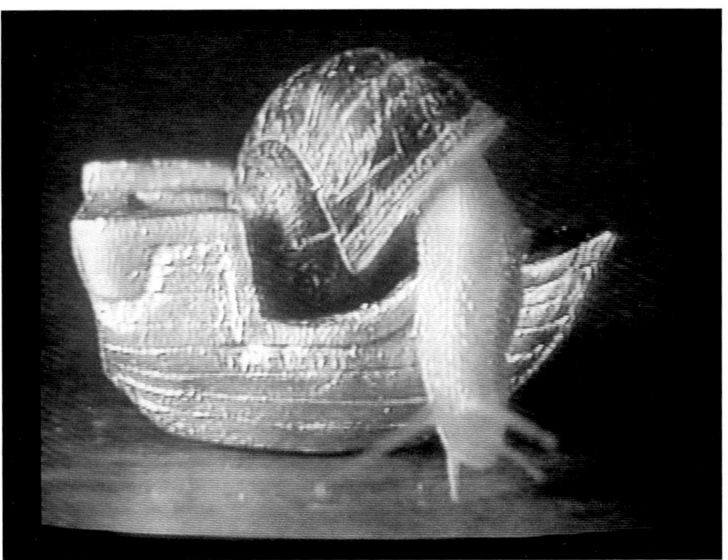

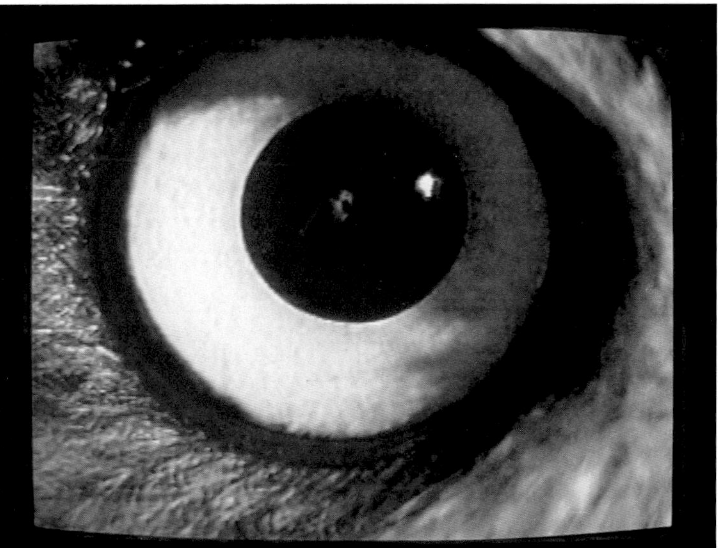

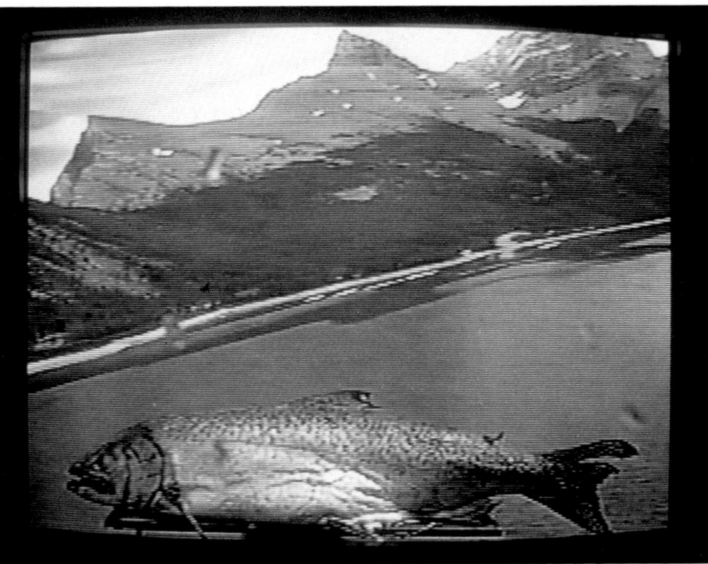

Video stills from Bill Viola, *I Do Not Know What It Is I Am Like,* 1986. Photos by Kira Perov.

Reclaiming a Cultural Legacy: The Ju/'hoansi of Namibia

By Megan Biesele

There are two kinds of bioscope [movies]. One kind shows us as people like other people, who have things to do and plans to make. This kind helps us. The other kind shows us as if we were animals, and plays right into the hands of people who want to take our land.

—Tsamkxao ≠Oma, /Aotcha, Namibia

The Ju/'hoan Bushmen of Namibia are in transition, not in the old sense of traveling from one water source to another, but in the current exigency of changing their lifestyle in order to survive. They have lost the vast expanse of the Kalahari Desert that enabled them to live, as had the generations before them, from hunting and gathering alone. They have been reduced to the depths of poverty and degradation in rural slums. Now they are struggling to adapt their ancient ways to modern necessity, and to hold onto their remaining land.

Namibians are preparing for profound changes, as seventy-five years of South African colonial domination comes to an end and independence under majority rule begins. The new government's policies on rural development and ethnic minorities will affect the Ju/'hoansi greatly, but in ways as yet unknown. What the Ju/'hoansi do know, however, is that their survival depends upon the ability to raise themselves to subsistence level, like other Namibians, by supplementing their hunting and gathering with gardens, cattle, handicrafts, education, and employment.

Several thousand Ju/'hoansi still hunted large animals with poison arrows and gathered wild food in Namibia until the late 1950s. They lived in mobile bands of about forty, each group centered on a *n!ore*—"the place to which you belong" or "the place which gives you food and water"—where their ancestors had lived for as many as 40,000 years.

In the past forty years, however, life has changed drastically for the Ju/'hoansi. They lost seventy percent of their traditional area, called Nyae Nyae, in 1970 when the South African administration carved the country up among ethnic groups, reserving much of it for the white minority. Nearly all Ju/'hoan bands migrated to the Bushmanland administrative center, Tjum!kui, where they were given a school, a clinic, a church, a jail, and a few jobs. But Ju/'hoansi called Tjum!kui "the place of death" for its overcrowding, alcohol-related violence, desperate poverty, and social disorganization. Their feelings for their *n!ores* remained deep. "Your father's father's *n!ore* is a place you do not leave," says Tsamkxao ≠Oma, a forty-five-year-old Bushman who heads the Nyae Nyae Farmers Cooperative.

Some seven hundred Ju/'hoansi in twenty extended family groups have reestablished their communities at their ancient places in a program parallel to the "outstation" movement in Aboriginal Australia. Socially these communities are like the nomadic camps of previous days, but economically they are

Bottom, left: John Marshall filming, c. 1952; Bottom, right: Lorna Marshall interviewing a Ju/'hoan informant, c. 1952: Opposite page: stills from *N!ai, the Story of a !Kung Woman*, a film depicting thirty years of N!ai's life, by John Marshall, 1979

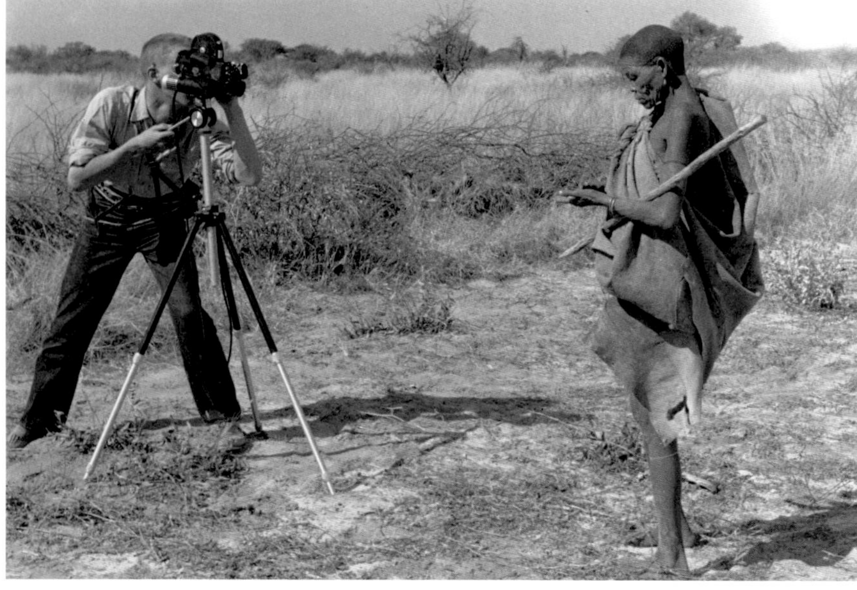

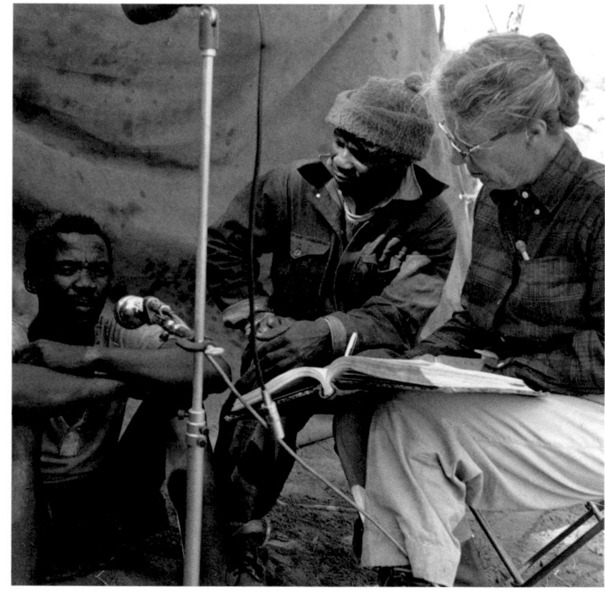

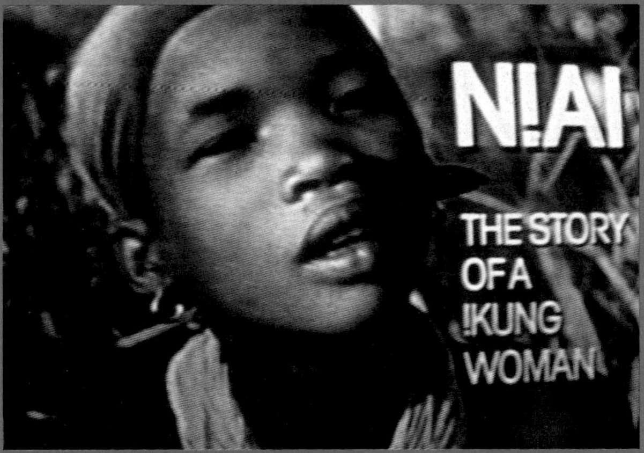

N!AI

THE STORY OF A !KUNG WOMAN

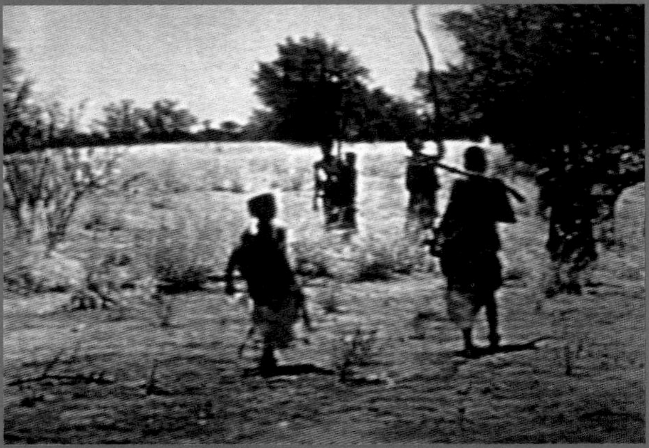

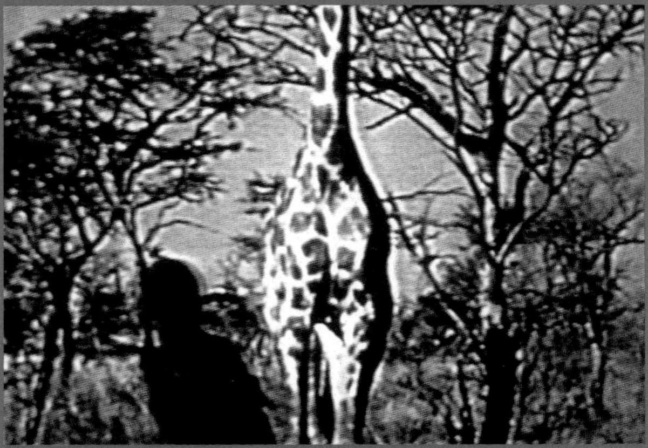

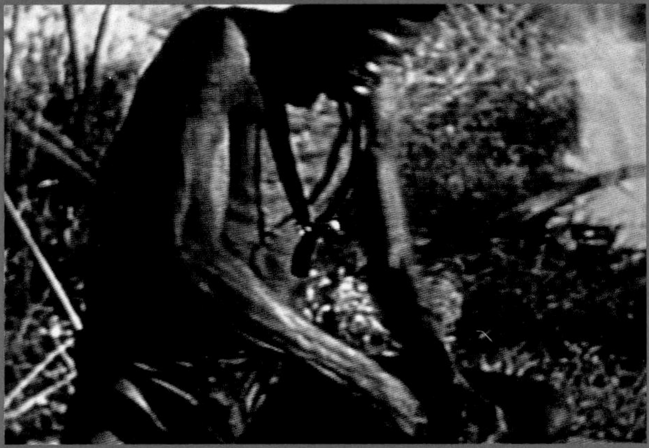

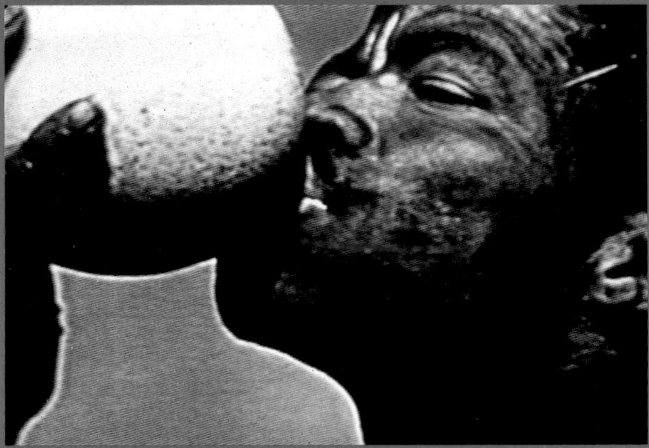

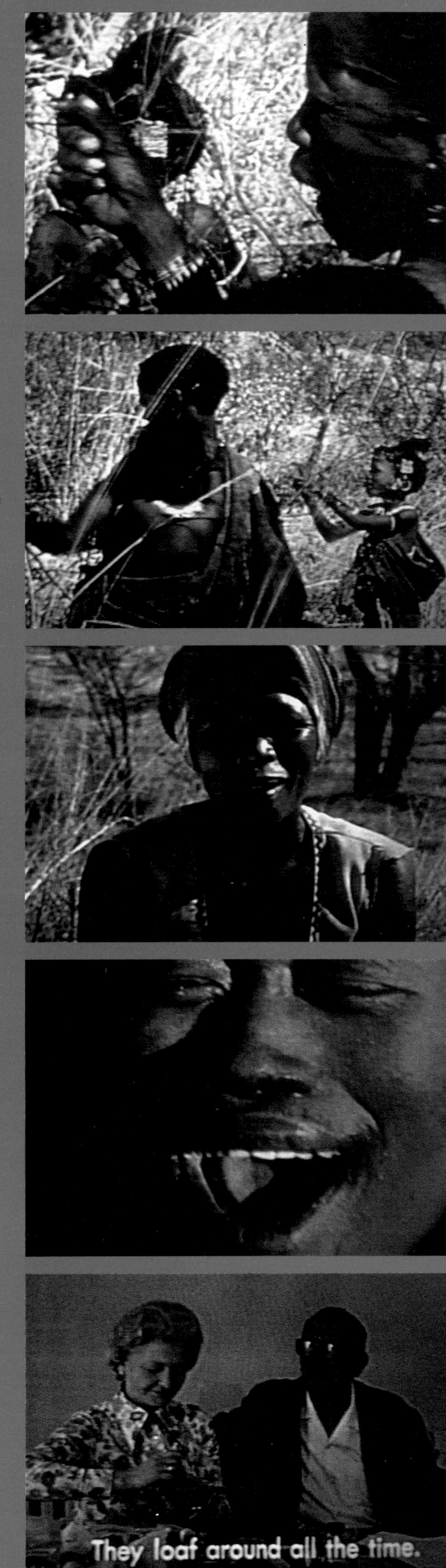

building a stable mixed economy of hunting/gathering, small-scale cattle raising, gardens, and handicrafts.

Ju/'hoan farmers struggle against lions that kill their cattle, elephants that trample gardens and pull out water pumps, and unhelpful or hostile officials who believe them incapable of development. They also struggle within themselves to adapt the cultural rules and values of their foraging life to an agricultural one. But most are adamant about not returning to the rural slum of Tjum!kui. "We must lift ourselves up or die!" people say to each other now. A new spirit of possibility is palpable in the cheerful, though struggling, communities.

Ju/'hoan efforts to raise themselves to subsistence level coincide with massive political changes as this country of 1.3 million people nears its long-awaited independence from South Africa. The old German colony of South West Africa, which South Africa has ruled since conquering it in 1915 during World War I, is Africa's last colony. Renamed Namibia after the Namib Desert, it has recently (November 1989) completed United Nations-supervised elections for a constitution-writing assembly, has adopted a constitution (January 1990), and will gain sovereignty once the new government is in place, probably in April of this year.

The new government will inherit the legacy of apartheid, which deepened the economic and cultural divisions among the country's eleven ethnic groups. Most Namibians, including Bushmen, live well below the poverty line even for the Third World. They depend heavily on a kin-based economy—one brother keeps cattle while another hunts; a cousin works in the city and brings goods home when he can. And they rely on rights to land and resources they don't have to pay for.

Under South African rule, seventy percent of the Namibian population has been squeezed onto thirty percent of the land. The rest has been reserved for diamond mining, white-owned commercial farms, and tourism. The land set aside for Bushmen was reduced in 1978 from 45,000 square kilometers to 6,000 square kilometers, an area sufficient to support only 162 people by hunting and gathering alone. Without more intensive food production, Ju/'hoansi are doomed to remain wards of some government, dependent and vulnerable. All but 3,500 of Namibia's 33,000 Bushmen live outside Bushmanland, working as laborers for white and black farmers or living on the edges of rural communities, dependent on the few family members with work.

The half-dozen groups of Namibians labeled as Bushmen were never united politically. They speak several languages, some mutually unintelligible, and live in widely separated areas of this vast desert country. They had no traditional chiefs or headmen and, thus, no regional government, as other ethnic groups had under South African rule.

Historically the Bushmen were exterminated as vermin; today there are still many people who regard them as lazy, unteachable, and constitutionally unable to plan for the future. They have remained at the bottom of every social ladder, a minority misunderstood by white and black alike.

But celebration of old ties to the land and to their culture is strong among Ju/'hoansi today. At a recent all-night dance under a clear black sky pricked with stars, men drummed and women went into healing trances and cured each other by traditional laying-on of hands. Di//xao ≠Oma, Tsamkxao's sister, her two-year-old bouncing in a sling on her back, suddenly left off singing and flung her hands toward the sky. A spectacular and inexplicable pencil of light was poised like a shot arrow among the stars, and it hung overhead for many seconds. "Yes!" she cried exultantly. "We're dancing and our old, old people see us!"

The real voices of the Kalahari, Di//xao's and others, have rarely been heard outside their own communities. However, as some of the world's last hunter/gatherers, Ju/'hoansi have become a focus of scholarly and human interest. Their lifestyle provides clues to the ancient world from which our civilizations sprang. The "Ju/wa" or !Kung Bushmen are familiar to Americans through films such as *The Gods Must Be Crazy* (parts I and II) and through Elizabeth Marshall Thomas's book *The Harmless People*. They became popular—but remained isolated.

The American filmmaker John Marshall and his associate Claire Ritchie are now working on a depiction of the Ju/'hoansi that shows a very different side of their lives. After eight years of practical development work with the Ju/'hoan communities, Marshall and Ritchie have recently returned to their work as filmmakers to continue the process of documenting Bushman lives begun by Marshall's family during the 1950s, and are assembling a film trilogy on the history of the Ju/'hoansi's struggle for self-determination.

The history of Marshall's forty years of film made with the Ju/'hoansi reads like a primer on the changes which have taken place in both human-rights awareness and in anthropology during the same period. Marshall's films have moved from the "illustrative" to the "dramatic" (à la Robert Flaherty) and thence to cinéma vérité sequences, eventually culminating in a new style of committed, dialogic, and collaborative film endeavor. Increasingly, Ju/'hoansi themselves are aware of the importance of the process of depiction in presenting their situation to other people. As Tsamkxao ≠Oma said to a newspaperman recently, "I went to a conference in Cape Town last year and found that many people had never even heard of my people. If they do, that may be a way to help end discrimination. Those days we refuse that our children have to hear words like 'Bobiaan' [baboon] and 'Kaffir'."

News of coming Namibian independence startled Ju/'hoansi into political involvement. Through community discussions, this egalitarian people has begun to think of selecting its own representatives and of seeking legal recognition for its ancient system of land use. Members of the Nyae Nyae Farmers Cooperative, a Ju/'hoan community self-help organization, went "on the road," traveling the sometimes impassable tracks of their contiguous *n!ores* to bring the news to far-flung communities, not one of which boasts a radio.

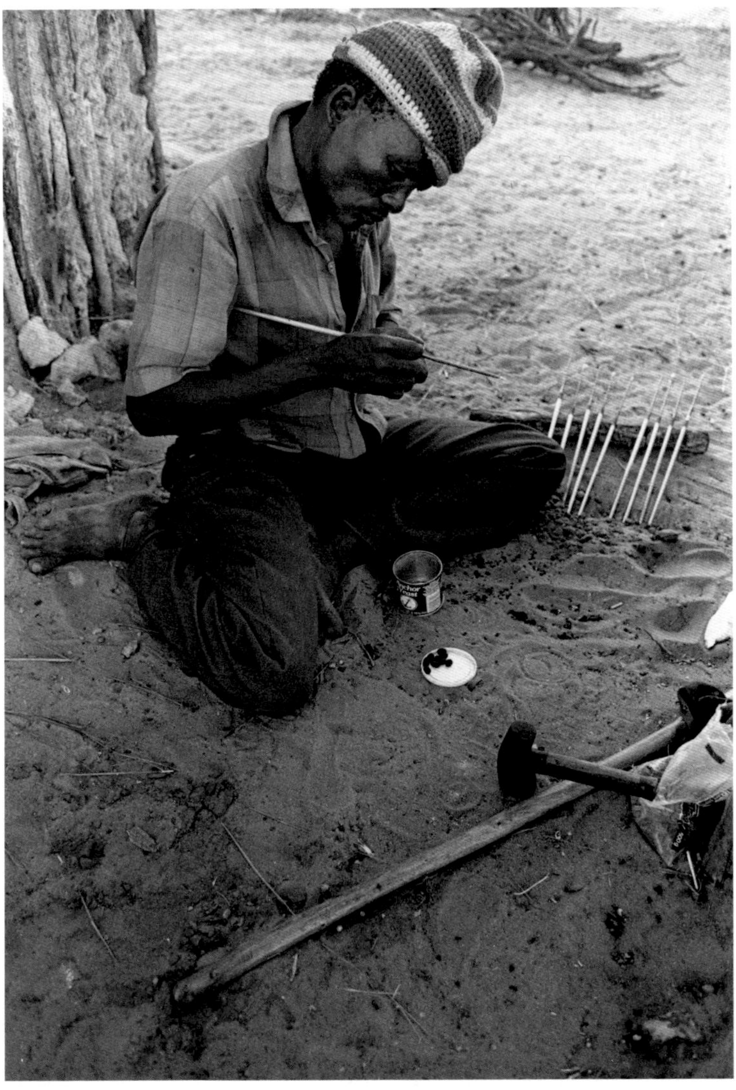

Paul Weinberg, *Poisoning arrows, //Auru*, 1988

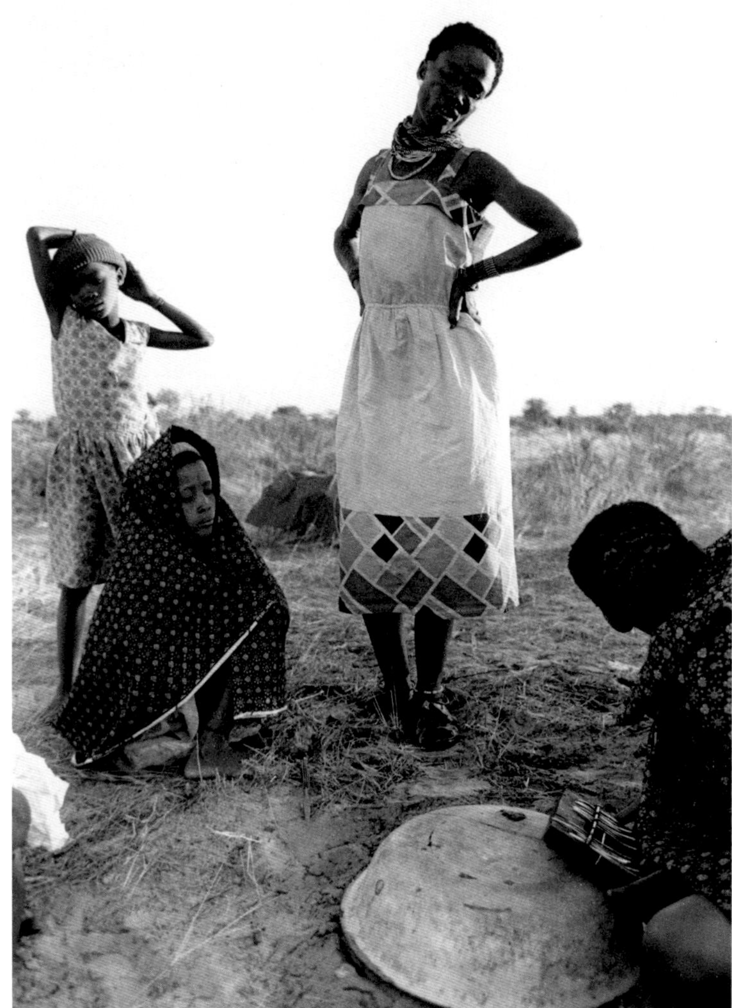

Paul Weinberg, *Playing the dongu, //Auru*, 1989

One clear, hot morning, cooperative chairman Tsamkxao ≠Oma set off early with four companions to drive through heavy sand to communities in the far north. He was wearing a new suit purchased to match the formality of the occasion. When a kudu ran across the track he braked, flung off the coat and his shoes, grabbed his bow and quiver of poison arrows, and went off where the antelope had disappeared. In a few minutes he was back at the truck, replacing unused arrows in the quiver. The arrow in the kudu would do its work slowly and Tsamkxao would return later to track the dying animal. He put his coat back on and resumed the business day.

At the community of N//oaq!'osi, the meeting was held in the shade near a circle of small huts made of sticks and fresh grass. Tsamkxao and the people with him talked about political meetings in Windhoek, the capital, 750 kilometers away.

The talks about elections and other democratic concepts were held outdoors, mostly, with a tree or a shelter of sticks and leaves for shade, or under a pole framework with wild melons sliced and drying overhead. People sat on old blankets or on the silver-grey sand. One day, when the wind was blowing violently and conversation was impossible outdoors, the travelers were forced into tiny mud houses, where entire communities sat on top of each other to hear the news.

At Djxokho, people were delighted to receive the news about the coming independence. "This almost sounds like real help," one man said. A young man named G/aqo asked to speak. Dressed in a South African Defense Force cap and boots, he spoke Fanagalo, the lingua franca he learned in the South African gold mines. With his wider experience and his language skills, he explained to his relatives the laws under which Ju/'hoansi lost so much control over their lives. He added that the Djxokho community had recently complained to the commission that tourists had been fouling their drinking water. A woman named Tsheg//ae added, "I went to talk to these two whites. And I saw that they had stopped their car and entered the reservoir and were swimming. And I said, 'Yo, why have

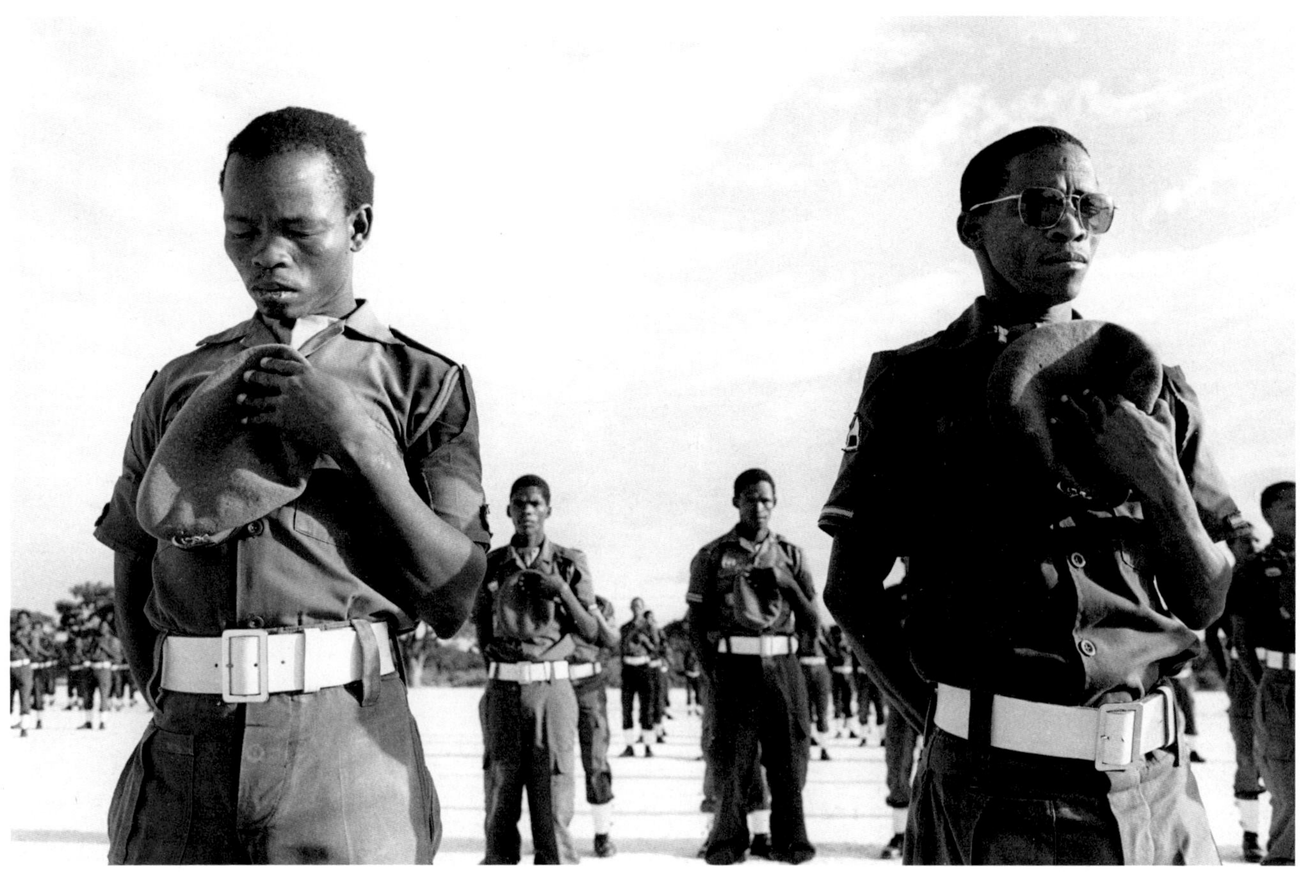

Paul Weinberg, *Prayer Parade, Mangetti Base*, 1989

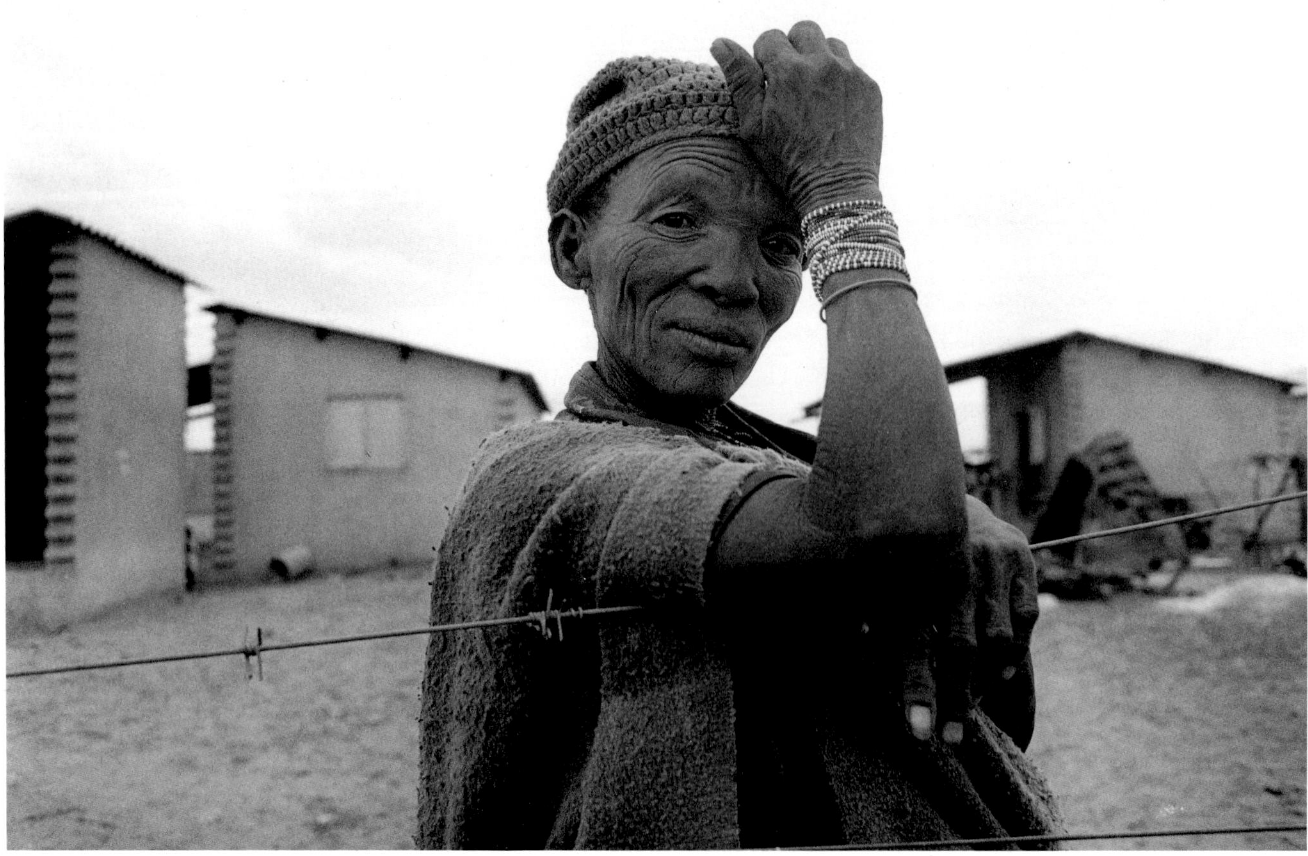

Paul Weinberg, *Location, Tjum!kui*, 1984

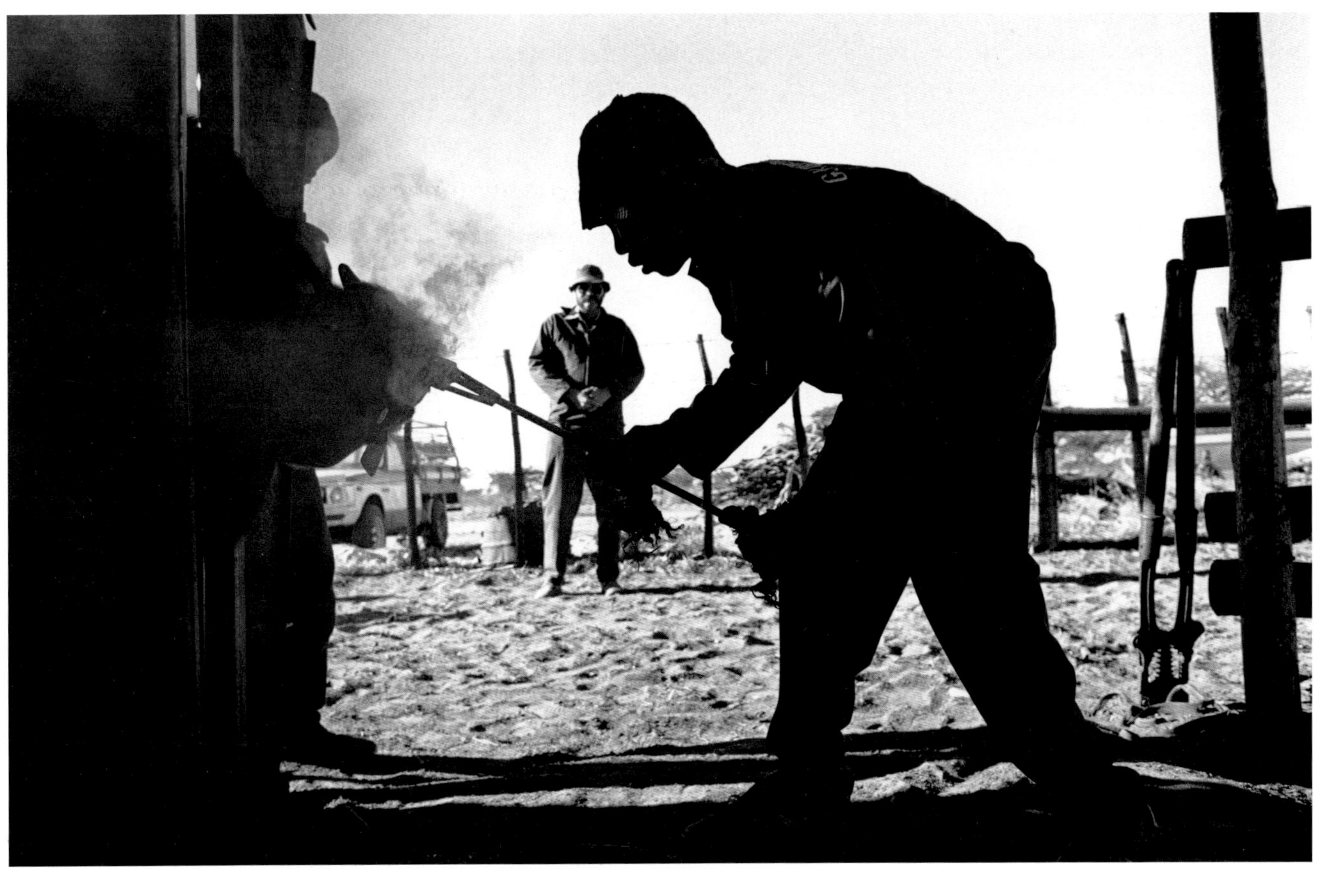

Paul Weinberg, *Branding and dehorning, Gobabis farming district*, 1989

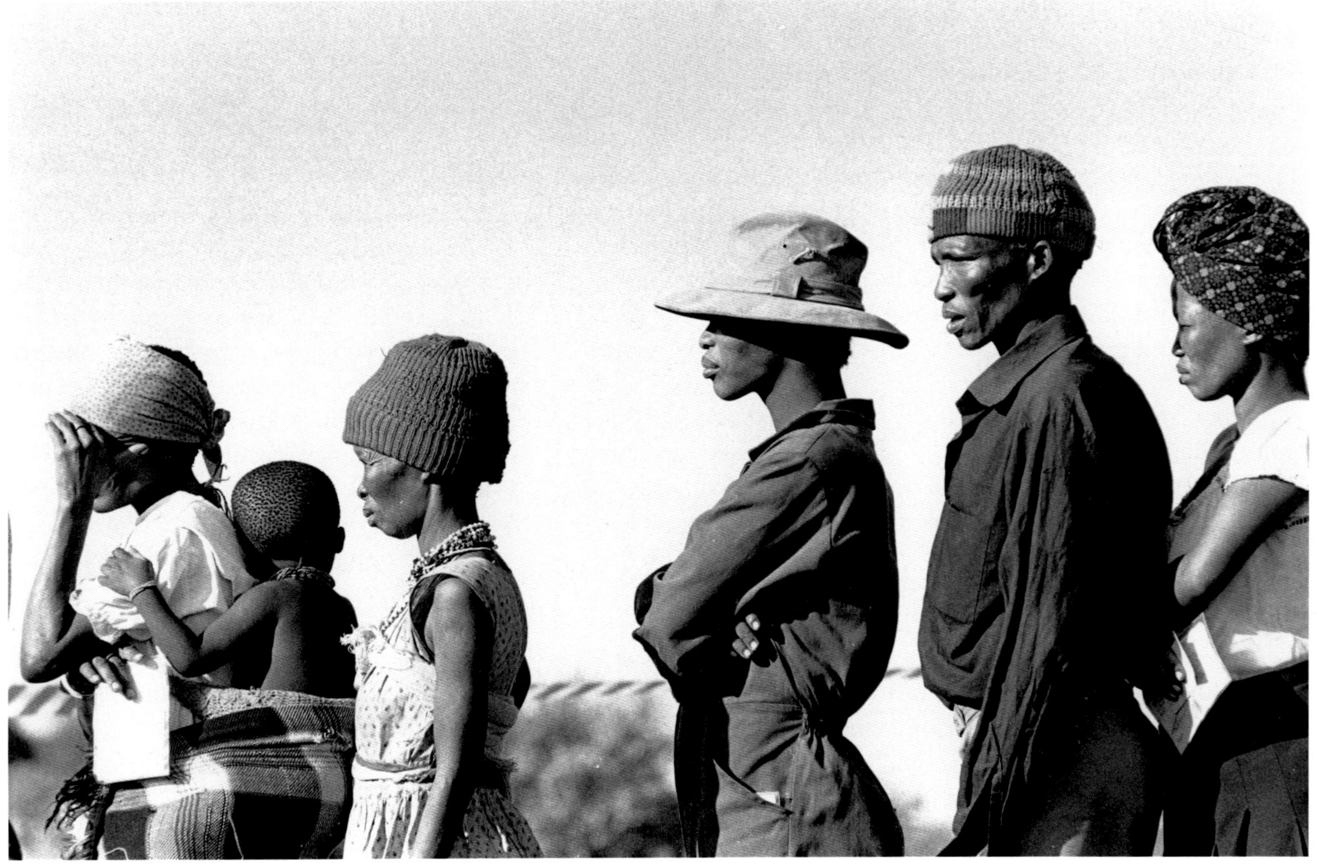

Paul Weinberg, *U.N. elections, //Auru*, 1989

you jumped into our drinking water and put your dirt into it?' And these school-kids got their car number; we had no pencil but they wrote it down with a cinder."

After a while the team packed up to continue the trip. At two other communities that day, the information was passed on and discussed. Having a forum in which to air their grievances seemed to lighten people's hearts, and the trip took on a festive atmosphere.

Ju/'hoansi call themselves "the owners of argument" and "the people who talk too much." For them it's important that issues be discussed and debated by all. None of the language of democracy seems new among them; rather it is age-old. These are the people who gravely said to anthropologist Richard Lee over a decade ago, "We have no headmen; each one of us is a headman over himself." The concept of "one person, one vote" fits right in with their ideology, and, among these sexually egalitarian people, one doesn't have to add, "and a woman's vote is just like a man's."

Since 1986 the Ju/hoan communities have worked to make the Nyae Nyae Farmers Cooperative a democratic organization responsible for many decisions about their development: the establishment of new communities; the location of boreholes; the distribution of cattle to start small herds; and the use of money from overseas organizations. The cooperative has also begun to take on more general political functions, acting, in the absence of a traditional chief, as a communications channel to the administration on issues such as tourism and the local school. It also brings in information that the communities need to hear.

Assumptions not only of uninformed neighbors but of the West's whole science of looking at such people—anthropology—are involved in the question of their future. Anthropology is only now wrestling itself out of the pervasive nineteenth-century romanticism which has characterized Western views of indigenous peoples. One mode of representative romanticism, called "ethnographic pastoral" by postmodern cultural critic James Clifford, has been the style of choice for much verbal describing and picturing of hunting-gathering peoples such as the Bushmen.

Pastoral imagery often shows the lion lying down with the lamb; what results from such a vision when people are portrayed, though, is the suppression both of lively individuals and of the oppressive political realities which confront them. People can despair and quietly die while mythic media paint them as happy savages. Outsiders can perceive them as "children of the earth" with no real need of legal title to land. Myths can relentlessly cast persons living today into a "present becoming past," so that they quite literally disappear before our eyes. Meanwhile, people like the Bushmen are actually engaged in a complex, creative "past becoming future" which is central to their acquisition of personal and political power.

Audiovisual and written media, under the stimulus of what may be called a "revolution of reflexivity" in the social sciences, are becoming increasingly sensitive to issues of representation itself—to devices used to frame and slant depictions; to unacknowledged agendas behind representation; to sexist, racist, ethnic, and class stereotyping; to the suppression of individuality in the search for the "typical"; and to the pernicious romanticism of "timeless" portrayals of the other. Reflexivity, the idea that any grasp of other cultural realities is colored and shaped by our own background assumptions, has had a profound effect on anthropology and documentary media.

Because media have been particularly quick to romanticize these people, the situation of the contemporary Ju/'hoansi and other Bushmen of Namibia has been referred to by John Marshall as "Death by Myth." Their recent history exemplifies the practical problems raised for a developing people by seductive, outmoded representations in both anthropological and popular media. Lately things have begun to change; presentations of these people have begun to move from simplistic, fairytale depictions to multivoiced, complex, often contradictory but always active self-presentations. There is in postmodern social documentation a thorough challenge to naive positivism, and progress toward the reenshrinement of narration as a more natural mode of description than the controlling, expository modes of science. In this new view, the "other" is seen as a person who is continually making sense of himself for himself, and increasingly the observer is included in both the event and its record: in other words, there is progress toward creating common cause in all representations, which are themselves seen as social and political facts.

When someone says, "You Bushmen have no government," we'll say that our old, old people long ago had a government, and it was an ember from the fire where we last lived which we used to light the fire at the new place where we were going.

These words of Di//xao ≠Oma, a regional chairwoman of the Nyae Nyae Farmers Cooperative, show that anthropology's assumptions must necessarily be altered by the experience of really listening, perhaps for the first time, to the words of anthropology's "informants." And listening in the context of shared development activities is doubly productive of real hearing. Anthropology stands to profit greatly from the learning available to it through development projects like the Ju/wa Bushman Development Foundation.

For one thing, experiencing the energy of a people's confrontation with each other in the process of transforming their society provides irreplaceable chances to learn the multiple sides to each question. Ju/'hoansi struggle with many external things, like lions, elephants, and hostile officialdom. But their main struggle is with themselves, as they feint and parry with old ideas, adapting the cultural rules and values that underwrote the old foraging way of life to their chosen, very different one of agriculture.

Marshall and Ritchie's forthcoming film trilogy will show,

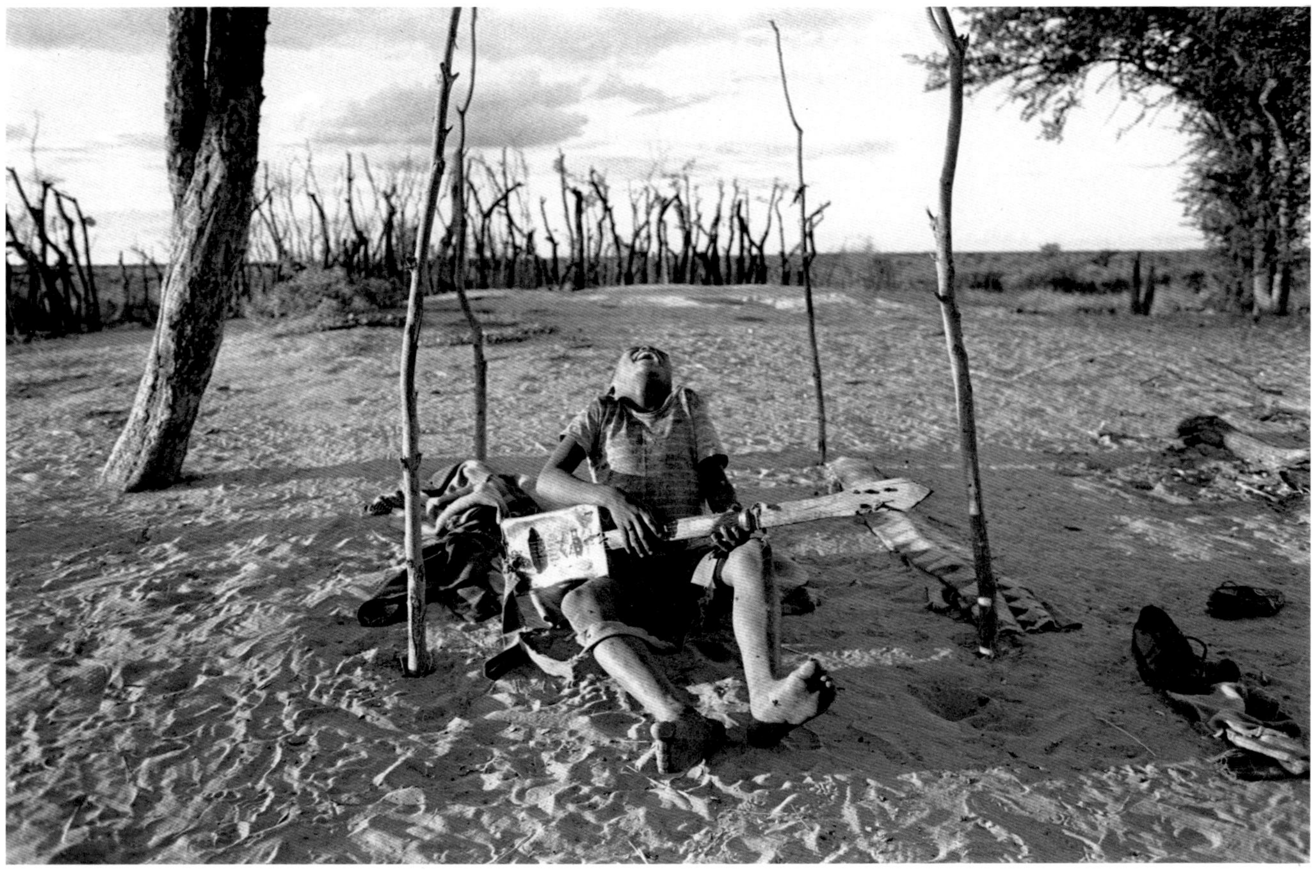

Paul Weinberg, *N//haru-'han*, 1988

as still photographs underscore, how the Bushmen people are creatively engaged with their problematic present life. Neither medium, however, would have been able to portray these realities without the sense of mutual trust produced by the Ju/wa Bushman Development Foundation's decade of advocacy and intervention.

Founded in 1981 by Marshall and Ritchie, the JBDF is a nonprofit organization based at Windhoek, Namibia, which is dedicated to supporting the self-development of Ju/'hoan and other Bushman peoples of Namibia. A sister organization for neighboring Botswana Bushmen, the Kalahari Peoples Fund, was started in 1973 by members of the Harvard Kalahari Research Group. Both organizations have pursued programs of self-help support to Bushman communities which are specifically designed to use the best available anthropological knowledge in service of the people.

The JBDF provides aid in a variety of forms to communities in the Nyae Nyae area. First, it offers support in developing the physical infrastructure needed to develop the mixed local economy (small stock-keeping and dryland gardening, in addition to hunting and gathering), with the Ju/'hoansi supplying the labor needed to install it. This infrastructure includes boreholes and hand- or wind-pumps, to which roads are built by community labor; fencing wire for kraals and cattle crushes, whose poles are cut by community labor; small lots of cattle, all of the work of which depends on community organizing and labor; and vehicles which make possible the convening of Farmers Cooperative meetings from all twenty of the established communities at a central point.

Up to the time of the first free election in Namibia, the JBDF's activities mainly involved community and economic development, and the fostering of communicational skills. Recently it has begun a program of related educational and training projects to enable the Ju/'hoansi to control their own self-sufficient, mixed economy. Much of the work has involved talking and listening as Ju/'hoansi work through the puzzling new problems which face them.

As an anthropologist taking part in this project, I find it a great privilege to participate in a mutual endeavor that involves making sense of a rapidly changing world. We are all, after all, caught in the same dilemma of constructing meaning and order out of fragments of the myths we've held about ourselves. Culture never rests, whether it is technological or "traditional." It develops, and people develop themselves, just as the culture of imaging people itself develops, in the darkroom of the mind as well as in the light of shared work. As one Bushman woman, !Kun/obe N!a'an, expressed it, "If you have work to do you have to do it. If you're behind you have to catch up. It's not a Ju/'hoan thing, it's a human thing."

Native Visions: The Growth of Indigenous Media

By Elizabeth Weatherford

When they were first exposed to film and photography, many tribal peoples could not see the purpose of these media. Introduced by outsiders, the camera seemed one more item, in a long history of contact with Euro-Americans, intended to take from indigenous communities but not give in return. The camera's presence among them did not automatically inspire them with the desire to use it, and in any case native people were rarely offered access to the more specialized tools employed by whites.

But in the past twenty years indigenous peoples in many parts of the world have turned to using film and video for a variety of reasons. By the 1970s the urgency of Native Americans' demands for cultural and political recognition encouraged them to participate in media and increasingly to become producers themselves. In most cases, their focus has initially been on helping to enhance the survival of their own communities. Their works rethink history from native viewpoints, and offer their national cultures the opportunity to recognize their own cultural plurality. Euro-American society remains powerfully nostalgic for a pre-twentieth-century image of Indian and Inuit life. Therefore indigenous media addresses itself to the ignorance of the dominant culture about the realities of contemporary native life.

Indigenous media has developed in a rich variety of ways in the Americas, while analogous projects have been pursued in other countries, such as Australia and New Zealand, over the past twenty years. Ethnographic films were developed to document how indigenous societies live, at first for academic use and increasingly for a general audience. In the 1960s, though, several anthropological projects in indigenous communities began to explore ways to use film to better translate native cultures to Euro-American viewers.

In 1968, in the Netsilik Project, directed by anthropologists Asen Balikci and Guy Mary-Rousséliere and filmmaker Quentin Brown, Inuit living in the central Canadian Arctic were filmed for over a year as they recreated the traditional subsistence and cultural activities they had experienced as children. In 1966, in a workshop in a Navajo community, long before cinema or television were customarily seen on the reservation,

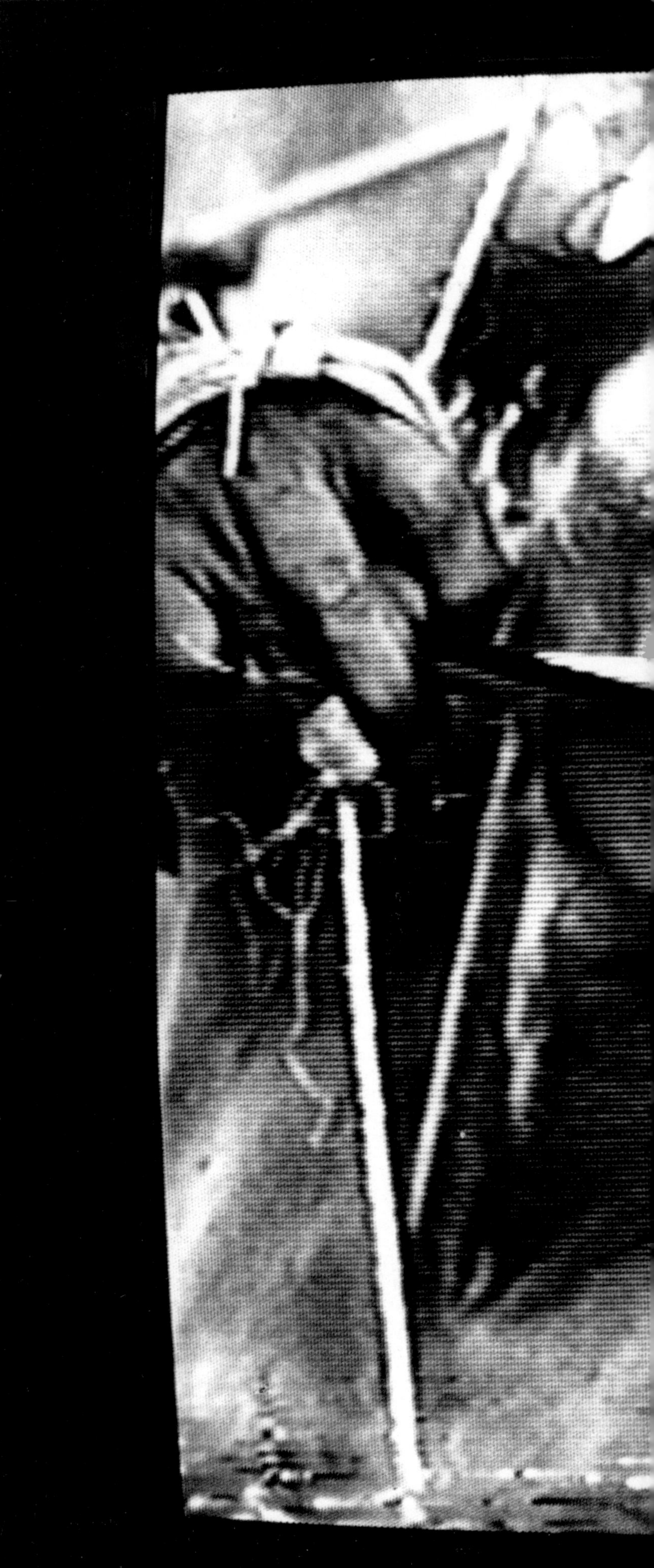

Still from *Video in the Villages* project, Vincent Carelli, executive producer, 1988. A leader of Brazil's Gaviao tribe, which has begun to use video extensively.

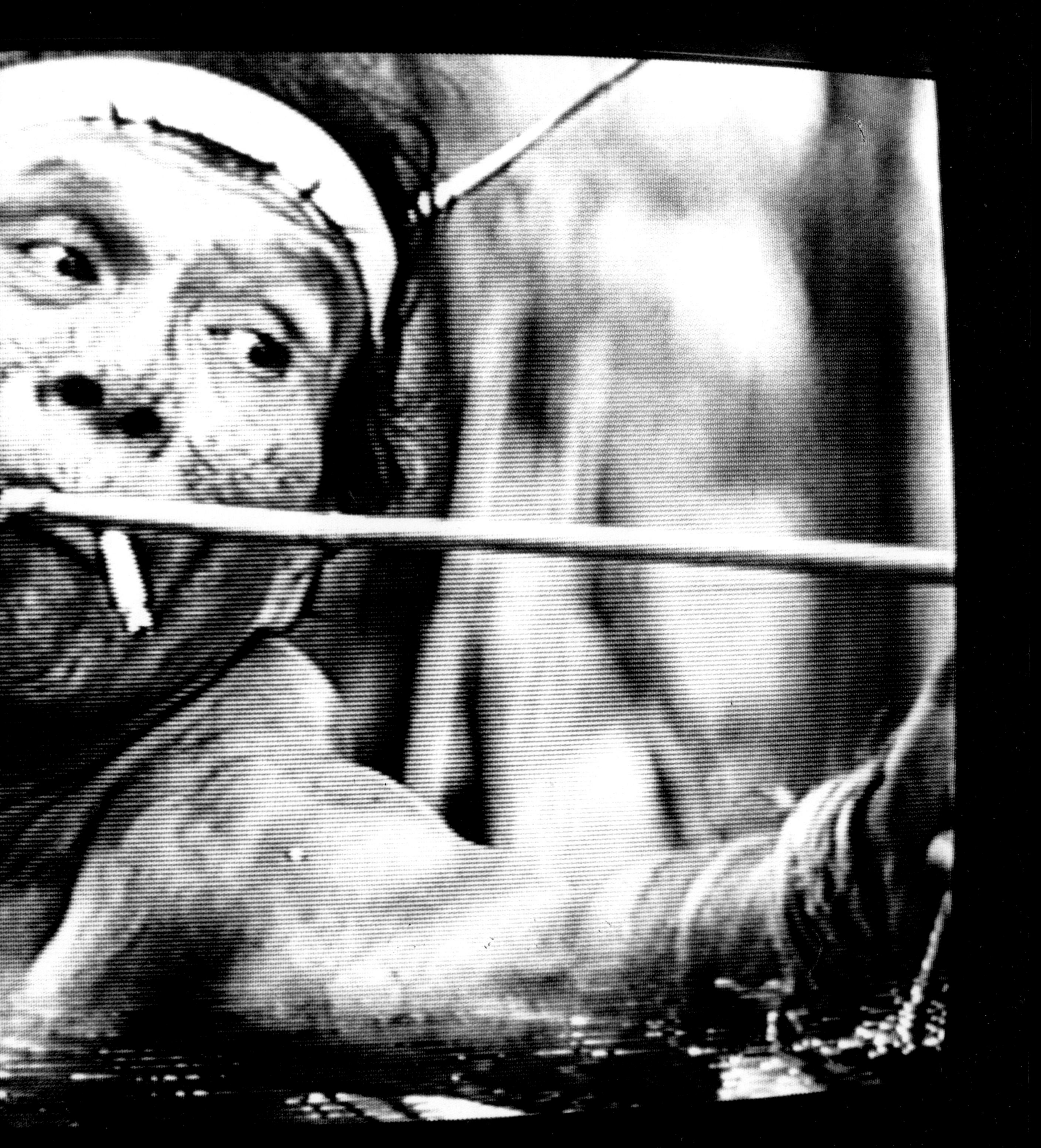

communications expert Sol Worth and anthropologist John Adair introduced film production to see how Indians might express themselves with a film language particular to their own culture. These projects were instigated by scholars, but they contained within them a commitment to involve native self-expression as a component of ethnographic film.

Beginning in the late 1960s, native participation in media production was intensified in several ways. In Canada, the National Film Board's Challenge for Change Project offered film training to various cultural groups, including Native Canadians, in order to broaden the national understanding of Canada's people. In the United States, a documentary series produced by Native Americans, funded jointly for school curricula and for public television, focused on contemporary Indian communities in distinct regions—for example, southern New England (*People of the First Light*, 1979) and Idaho (*The Real People*, 1976). Ideas about empowering indigenous people through film (and by the late 1970s, video) gained wider acceptance.

Because of their experiences with the white world through the years, many native communities are concerned that they receive little benefit from projects conducted in their communities. In response, some film- and videomakers have undertaken to coproduce their documentaries with the native participants. Community members decide who, and often what, will be filmed. Filmmaking expertise is contributed by the nonnative producers. Often they arrange for the community to benefit in other ways from the filming experience, through sharing any profits made by distribution of the productions, or by providing technical training for crew members from the community.

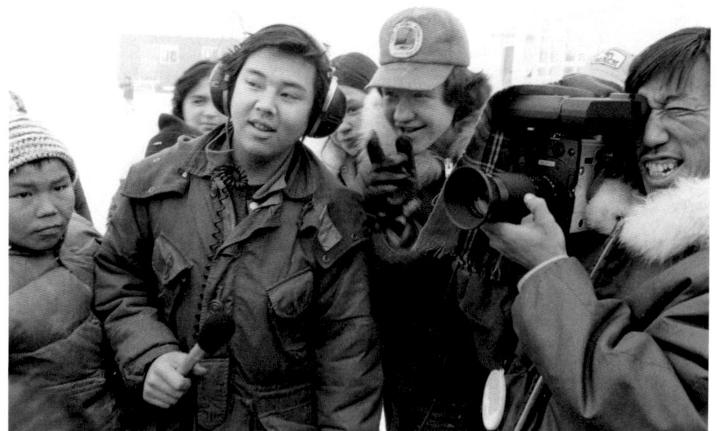

Peter Raymont, still from *Magic in the Sky,* 1981. Mike Angalik and John Allutjut on location in Eskimo Point, Northwest Territories, Canada.

The Alaska Native Heritage Film Project, begun in the 1970s by filmmakers Leonard Kamerling and Sarah Elder, has captured a record of the skills and interests of Yup'ik and Inupiat Eskimo, and show old and new ways of life existing side by side. Native perspectives dominate these films, which are not narrated and in which people talk with humor and insight about their lives. The intimacy undoubtedly stems from the coproduction arrangement, and from the filmmakers' long familiarity with the villagers.

In Brazil, two coproduction projects to document and train Indian videomakers have been ongoing for the past five years. Villagers recognize the significance of these projects, not only as a means of strengthening their cultures, but also as a way for their leaders to address outsiders, both Indian and non-Indian. Because they use video, these projects have also introduced a more accessible technology than film, and as a result some of the tribes have begun to use the cameras and tape recorders themselves.

The Video in the Villages Project, directed by videomaker Vincent Carelli, has filmed more than ten Indian groups at their request, including the Bororo and Guarani. More than 200 hours of video, including records of important ceremonies and events, have been produced. The project has also created video libraries for the tribes, and provides production assistance and editing instruction to tribal members. The Mekaron Opoi Djoi Project has actively worked with Kayapos to provide video training, leaving production equipment in the villages for the Indians' use. Stimulated by recent threats to their continued existence, some Kayapo now videotape the practice of valued traditions, as well as events which are seen as white Brazilian encroachments.

In the 1980s, with the launching of the first Canadian communications satellite, technology for broadcast became available in the Arctic and other remote regions. When native leaders considered the implications of the introduction of television, they actively pressured the Canadian Broadcasting Corporation to launch a native production and broadcast project. Its success led to the formation in 1980 of the Inuit Broadcasting Corporation (IBC), which has seven vastly dispersed production centers and which broadcasts across the Arctic for one hour per week. In addition to IBC, five other native communications societies located across Canada now produce television programs. All stress community control, the presentation of topics of native interest, and keeping aboriginal language and culture alive. A national organization has been formed to lobby for funding for these and other communications groups working in radio and newspapers.

Undoubtedly successful, Canada's native communications societies are still vulnerable. Where legislation and federal and provincial appropriations have institutionalized them, as in the Northern Territories, the future is promising. However, the risk of communications societies being considered merely experimental projects is great. The original IBC project in the Arctic, for example, was sharply cut back within six months of its start. In other regions, with financing dependent on changing public appropriations, the stability of jobs, and therefore the ability to attract a new generation of community members to become producers, can be unpredictable. Once established, the organizations now face the problem of developing a native media with perspectives different from those of the government which sponsors them.

In the United States there are as yet no systematic national or regional programs for developing native communications. The Native American Public Broadcasting Consortium has been limited to working within the public television system, which itself receives low priority in a country with highly successful commercial television. Indigenous media production, therefore, results from individual and local initatives. Only a few tribal communities have been able to commit resources to the salaries and equipment necessary to maintain video production offices and to underwrite projects. One successful community video department, headed by videomaker Gary Robinson, has been run for over ten years by the Creek Nation of Indians. Tapes about its history, rituals, and artists are screened in the tribe's community centers across seven Oklahoma counties, and outside the Nation as well.

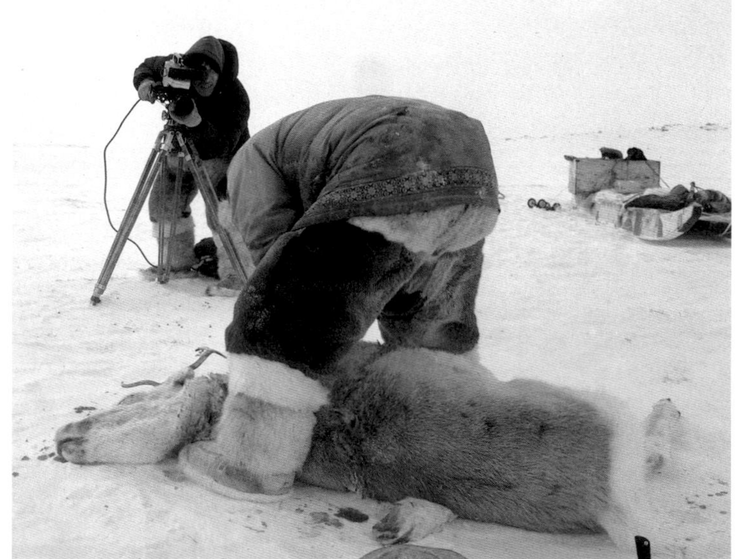
Peter Raymont, still from *Magic in the Sky,* 1981.

Since 1979 the Ute Indian Tribe Audiovisual, on the Uinta and Ouray Ute Reservation in Utah, has documented such traditional activities as drying deer meat, and has also produced animations of traditional tales, and programs on health care and Ute-language instruction. Other Indian communities now commission works from the Ute production unit. Headed by Larry Cesspooch, the production department works to make Ute values more accessible to young Indians who have grown up saturated with Euro-American culture.

Since the 1960s, independent media production has rapidly developed as a strong force in the United States, becoming a means for expressing and circulating critical opinions, alternative aesthetics, and multicultural views. For some Native American media makers the support system has provided them the basis for making highly individual productions.

The work of Hopi videomaker Victor Masayesva, Jr., is marked by its original style. Well-received in the media arts world, it has been awarded prizes at festivals and has been screened on cultural television in the United States and Europe. In *Itam Hakim, Hopiit,* 1984, he provides lyrical images to parallel the telling by an elder of Hopi history from mythic times to the future as predicted by Hopi prophecy. *Ritual Clowns,* 1988, uses computer animation and a variety of other techniques to suggest the roles of tricksters in white and Indian cultures.

Living in Igloolik in the central Canadian Arctic, Inuit producer Zach Kunuk has worked for IBC; his first independent work, *Qaggiq,* 1989, is an enactment by community members of a story about marriage set in former times. Filmed inside igloos, the work reflects a unique sense of space, and the story concludes in Inuit fashion, without the Western emphasis on dramatic conclusions.

Like half the Indians in the United States, Minneapolis-based filmmaker Chris Spotted Eagle has lived predominantly in cities. His films concern themselves with contemporary Native American life and issues of religious freedom and the recognition of Indian rights by the rest of the society. *Our Sacred Land,* 1984, focuses on the Black Hills of South Dakota, illegally taken by the federal government in the nineteenth century, and the Lakota leaders who refuse to yield in their campaign to regain the lands.

What will result from these undertakings in indigenous media is not yet apparent. In addition, support systems for production are often fragile, and the media industries continue to ignore indigenous issues. On the other hand, the foundations have been laid for more native participation in film- and videomaking, and a group of experienced media makers now exists which is committed to seeing it continue.

In a particularly hopeful development, recent legislation in the United States provides public television support for multicultural media productions. In Canada, national offices for the Aboriginal Communications Societies are expanding. And in Brazil, Kayapo videomakers have documented their leaders' successful appeal to the international community to prevent the construction of an immense hydroelectric dam which would have flooded their lands.

Making a New Culture: An Interview with Omar Badsha

By Charles Hagen

In 1988 Omar Badsha was invited to attend Aperture's conference on "The World's Reality" at Esalen, but the South African government denied him a visa to leave the country—as it had for the previous twenty-five years. A photographer, teacher, and editor, Badsha is director of the Documentary Photography Project at the University of Cape Town, and has long championed the use of documentary photography as a tool in the struggle against apartheid. A cofounder of the photographers' cooperative Afrapix, he was involved in editing two recent collections of photographs on the situation in South Africa—*The Cordoned Heart* (W. W. Norton, 1987), and *Beyond the Barricades* (Aperture, 1989). This January Badsha was finally granted a visa, for his first trip ever out of South Africa. We interviewed him during his stay in New York.

Omar Badsha: For me, the significant shift in the arts in South Africa over the past decade can be explained partly by the emergence of the nonracial philosophy of the African National Congress. It is interesting to note that the era of the black consciousness movement in South Africa, the 1970s, was silent photographically. The black consciousness movement produced poets and writers, but no photographers of note.

The '80s was the decade of the image. It was the decade of black and white writers, artists and photographers, working together in one movement. This movement has produced a radical change in the relationship between the artist and the struggle for liberation. The artists found themselves actively creating their own audience—a radical, mainly working-class audience. Whereas in the '70s the black consciousness movement largely attracted the youth and the middle-class intellectuals.

Charles Hagen: What caused the shift from the black consciousness movement to the Congress movement?

OB: Well, because the black consciousness movement was chiefly concerned with the psychological libertion of the black, it was unable to respond politically to events during the Soweto uprisings in 1976. You cannot respond to racial oppression and state repression without developing a political program that takes into account the political interests of the working class and the poor. The youth wanted more than philosophy; they wanted to take up arms. After the Soweto uprising, students joined the underground in droves. Thousands went out of the country for training, and joined the African National Congress.

So in the '80s you had a new culture beginning to emerge, built on nonracialism. This is militant culture, expressed through the mass, grass-roots movement; it has been articulated through photographs, through posters, graffiti, song, dance. But overall, it was the era of the photograph. An important development for photography was the formation of the photographic collectives, such as Afrapix. The idea behind Afrapix was to serve the new movement. Afrapix was formed by people like Lesley Lawson, Mxolis Mayo, Loyed Spencer, Paul Weinberg, myself, Wendy Schweggmen, and Peter Mackensi. . . . One of our major concerns was to become involved in training young photographers, especially black photographers.

CH: An idea that keeps coming up in our conversations is that of forming a new culture. Even the title *Beyond the Barricades*. . . .

OB: Yes, we are at that stage of the struggle where we know that victory is around the corner, and so we have to think about a postapartheid society. We have to go beyond the mental barricades that we have constructed over so many decades of struggle. We have to begin to go beyond the racial barricades. How we are going to do this is at the heart of the debate in our movement and our society.

CH: Is it premature to be talking about "beyond the barricades" when the situation today seems so terrible, with the state of emergency and the ongoing killings?

OB: No, no, we are full of hope. We also know that we are strong and have the initiative to bring about change. We are no longer just thinking about the formation of a nation, we are creating one now. Our movement is in many ways an embodiment of this. Blacks and whites belong to it, and it has been the vehicle through which all the most progressive ideas about what a new nation should be have been articulated. The major concern of the liberation movement is to bridge the gulf between black and white. But at the same time we are very conscious of the fact that our society has a very rich cultural diversity, which needs to be encouraged and preserved. As photographers we are very aware the the process of learning about each other and looking at each other in a new way can be facilitated by the photograph.

CH: You talked earlier about Afrapix's role in informing South Africans about what was happening. How did you do that?

OB: Well, first, we documented things no one else would cover, the beginnings of the movement. Pictures were used by the movement to popularize the message. As the photographers began to become more integrated into the movement, we were called on to document a whole range of issues—for example, forced removals, rent struggles, labor conditions. You must remember that in a highly repressive society the people are afraid of the photograph, because the photograph can be used to identify you. So it is important to remember that in the early

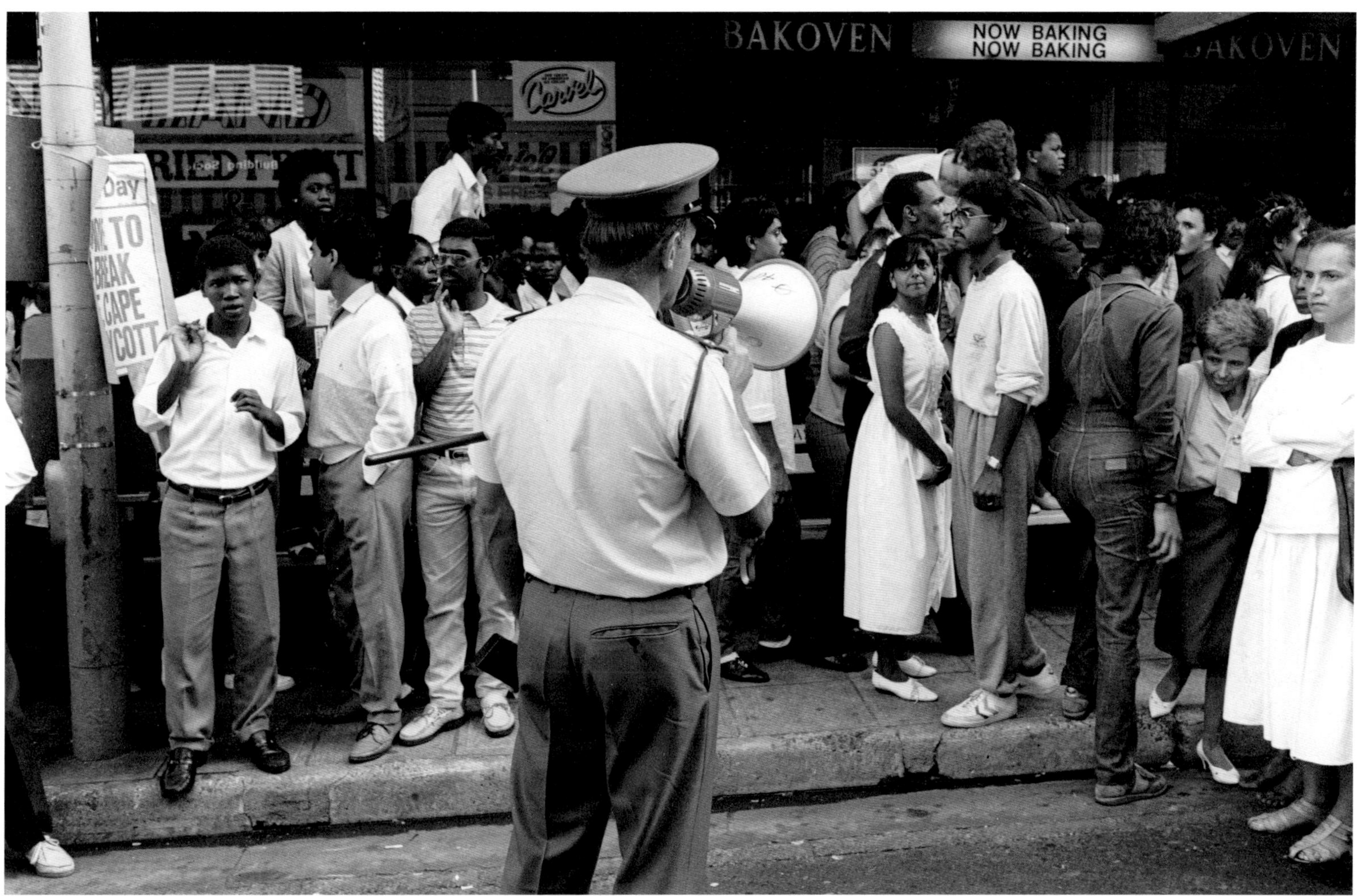

Omar Badsha, from the "People with Megaphones" series, 1985–89

part of the '80s, unless you were part of the movement, people would be very suspicious of you. But as the movement grew larger it became more confident. People were not afraid to have their picture taken. In fact, to be photographed in a meeting or a demonstration became an act of defiance.

Thirdly, in Afrapix, we were involved in hard news, to document and disseminate. Fourthly, we began working on traveling exhibitions and publications—books, calendars, cards. And finally, we were concerned with running workshops. All of these activities we saw as important to the development of documentary photography. We were convinced that as photographers we had a role to play in the process of change, and that a militant documentary photographic tradition was the most appropriate vehicle.

CH: What are some of the books and exhibitions you have done?

OB: Well, in 1979 I did a book on children called *Letter to Farzanah,* which was promptly banned because of the text. The book was done to commemorate the International Year of the Child. In 1985 I did a book on a squatter community in Inanda in Natal. I was involved in the struggle to stop people from being removed, and the book was done to draw attention to the issue of forced removals. The book is titled *Imijondolo,* which means shacks. Then there was the book *South Africa: The Cordoned Heart.* This book and exhibition was done as part of an independent inquiry into poverty in South Africa. In 1984, as part of the campaign against the government puppet tri-cameral parliamentary elections, I did a book on the history of the Natal Indian Congress, titled *Ninety Fighting Years.* Finally, together with Paul Weinberg, Gideon Mendel, and Andre Odenaal, we did the book *Beyond the Barricades.*

CH: Did you have trouble publishing these books, other than the normal financial ones that everyone has? Did the state try to shut you down?

OB: Yes. Any activity that is in any way anti the regime can get you into trouble. *Letter to Farzanah* was banned. With *Beyond the Barricades* we were concerned that the book could land us in trouble because of the state of emergency, so as you can see we are not listed as the editors of the book. We had to look for a legal loophole. The chances of the book being

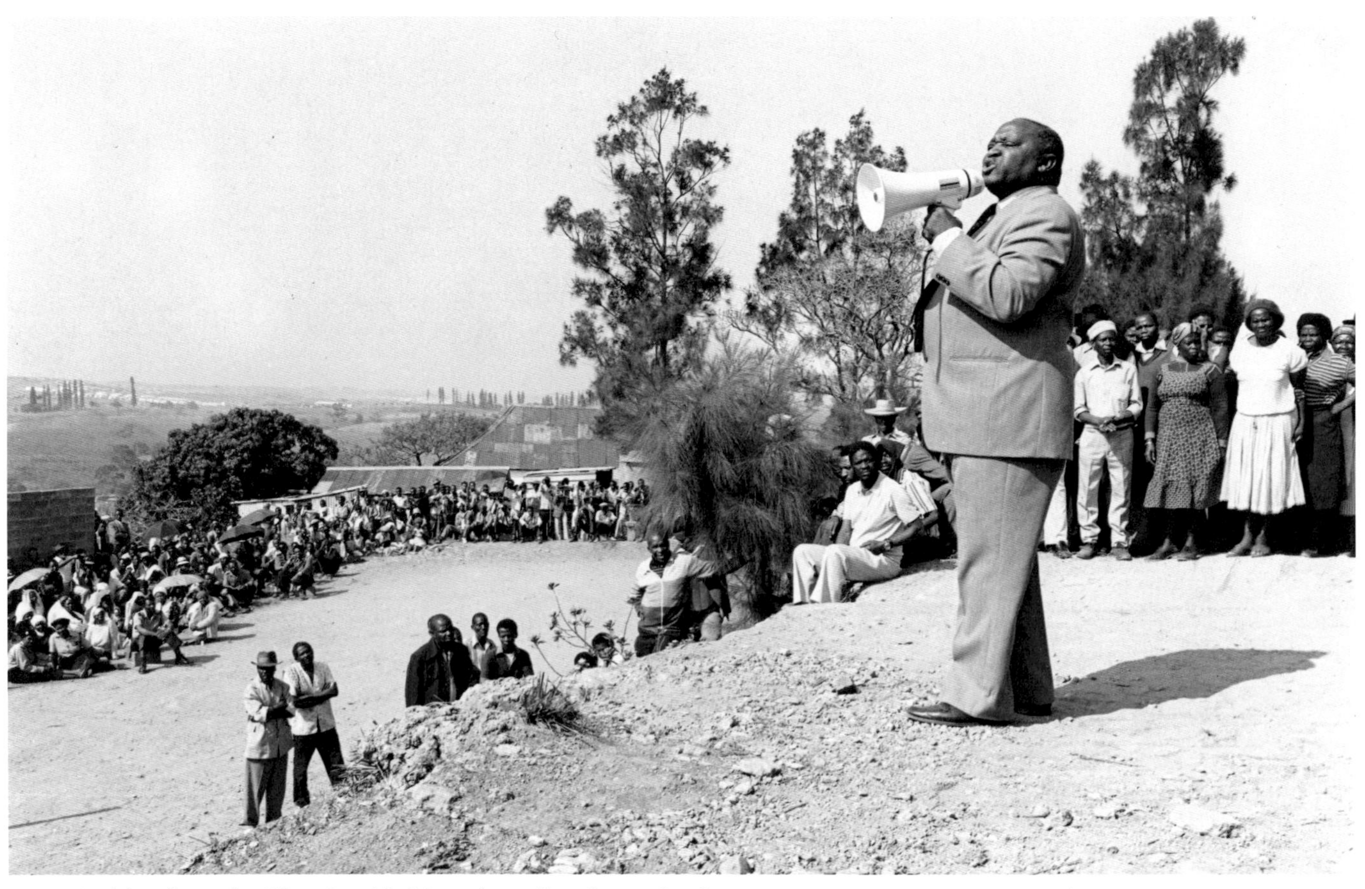

Omar Badsha, from the "People with Megaphones" series, 1985–89

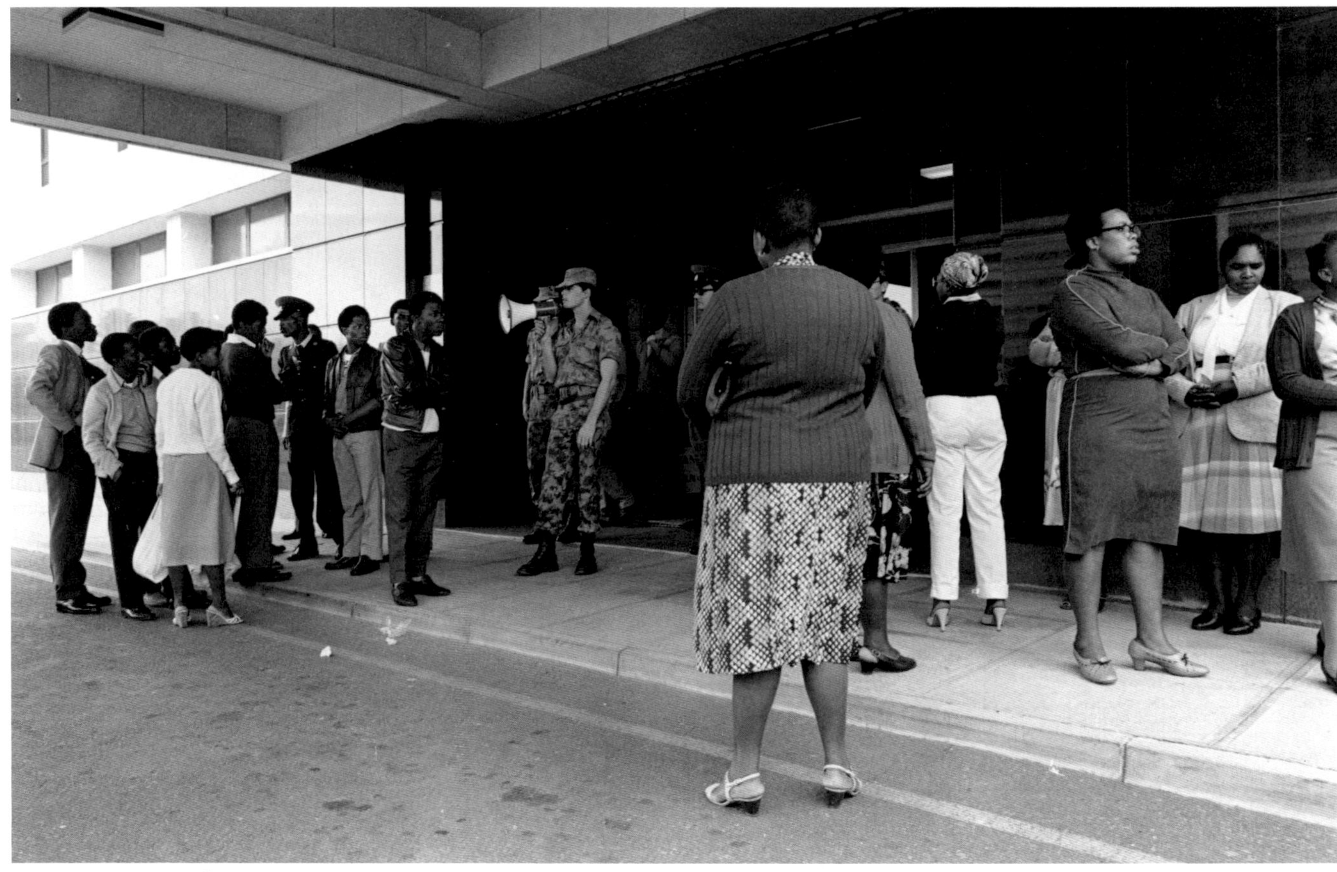

Omar Badsha, from the "People with Megaphones" series, 1985–89

banned in South Africa are very high. Because of the state censorship you tend to also censor yourself.
CH: How are your books sold? Through bookstores?
OB: In some cases through stores; in other cases, like the book on the Congress, through organizations and mass meetings. Because of the mass movement we have begun to develop an alternative audience and distribution network. The photograph book is not the primary form of distributing your photographs. We have the alternative press, but most important of all we have the traveling exhibitions. These exhibitions have become the most important vehicle for our work and ideas. Many of these exhibitions were also done collectively. The collective exhibition has become a feature of the South African photographic movement. Afrapix photographers play a major part in putting together these exhibitions. Today, Afrapix has become largely an agency, but the project I run at the University of Cape Town continues to do what Afrapix started.

Today the project at the university runs workshops. Some of these workshops are directed at helping the youth and young workers, to document these areas as a part of what we call the people's history movement. People's history projects have assumed a political dimension. Since the banning of the ANC and other organizations, the state has tried to suppress the history of the people's resistance. They succeeded to some extent. In the '80s, though, the youth wanted to know about the ANC, about Nelson Mandela. So we began to dig up old photographs. People began to write about the experience of their parents and communities. So pictures began to play an important role in the rediscovery of history. Photographs became an important political tool. The photograph of Mandela became an icon, a symbol of resistance. The photographic image began to emerge on T-shirts, posters, banners, graffiti. The '80s can be said to belong to the photograph.
CH: What kind of places are your exhibitions shown in?
OB: Everywhere—small meetings, halls, schools, conferences, workshops.
CH: Does the state interfere at all?
OB: Sometimes. One thing the state has clamped down on is when photographers are working in so-called unrest situations. They were concerned with their international image.
CH: Because a bad international image would affect the country's economic situation?
OB: Yes.
CH: How effective have economic sanctions been?
OB: Very effective.
CH: Has international consciousness of the situation in South Africa changed much since the press ban?
OB: For a while South Africa was not on your screens. But you must remember that we have the support of the entire world, and as photographers we have directed our work to those support committees around the world, the trade unions, the churches. It might not be on the TV screen or in the mainstream papers, but the South African situation is alive in your country. Everyone in the world has heard of Mandela and Soweto and the ANC. South Africa is the most publicized and most supported struggle in the history of the world. And the visual image has played an important role in that.
CH: What is happening now? What is going to be the effect of the release of Mandela and the other ANC leaders?
OB: Well, we hope that F. W. de Klerk, the President, is really serious and will sit down and negotiate. But the government isn't going to negotiate unless there is a lot of pressure for them to negotiate. In fact, we feel that the talk of negotiations is only a way for them to win some political breathing space, internationally. Even with some political reform, apartheid and the social conditions it has created will remain. As a documentary photographer one has to go beyond the surface. That's what I am concerned with, and talking to other photographers about. What does it mean, to be a committed photographer at this stage in the struggle? How do we see ourselves intervening, making a statement? Because as far as I am concerned nothing has changed, and we have to show that. We also have to constantly take a critical look at the movement. This is one of the most important challenges facing us as artists. We should avoid the errors of other revolutions—"my movement right or wrong."
CH: What are you working on yourself?
OB: Well, one thing I want to do is publish this book on the area I grew up in. I also want to spend time in a little village that I know, in Transkei. Very overcrowded, very poor, but an area that is undergoing rapid social and political changes. In Cape Town I'm working with a number of photographers in working class communities on the people's history projects, and I'm hoping also to take pictures with them in the community.
CH: It's interesting how vital a role documentary photography plays in South Africa.
OB: I think it has played a vital role in all political movements in the twentieth century. Look at Germany and Europe in the '20s and '30s. It was the same in America, with the Farm Security Administration and Photo League. Documentary photography seems to have emerged at a time when society was undergoing a great deal of stress and change, and artists and writers and photographers had to reflect that in some way. Photography has played an important role in influencing people's perception of their society. When society is undergoing massive upheavals, then everyone's issue is your issue. I don't think South Africa is different from any other society undergoing similar transformations.
CH: Well, you seem very hopeful about the situation.
OB: You have to have hope. You know that everything is on your side, you have right on your side. We know that we have to build a new society, a new culture without which we will have no peace or progress. You cannot achieve this without hard work and commitment. As an artist in our society a lot of responsibility lies on your shoulders.

Of Wood and Stone

By Karoline Postal-Vinay

Video stills from Edin Velez's *Meaning of the Interval*

Photography by Ethel Velez

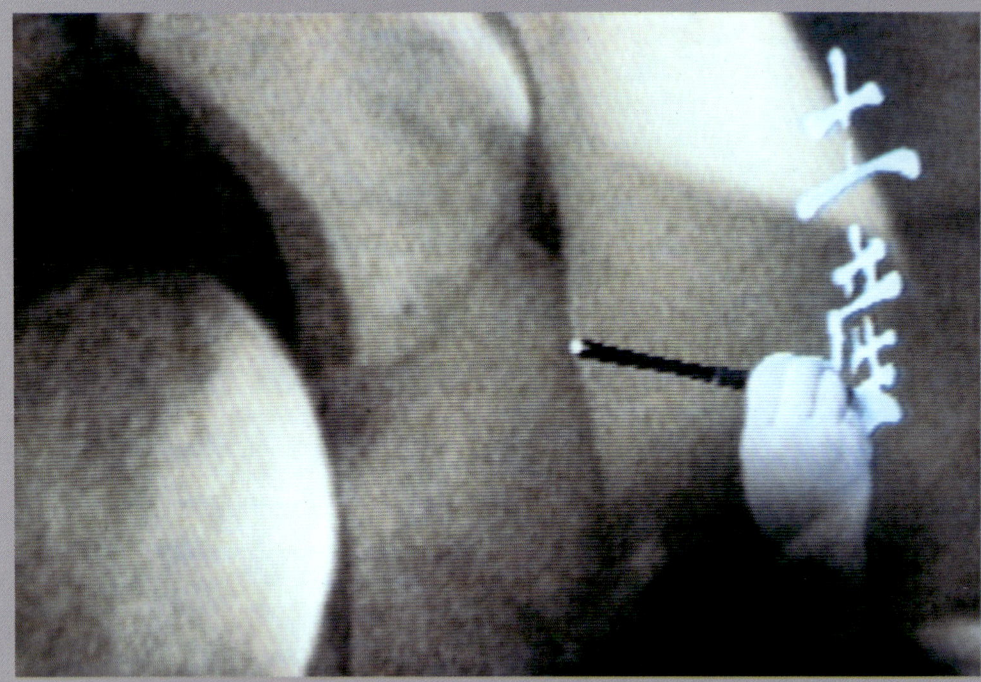

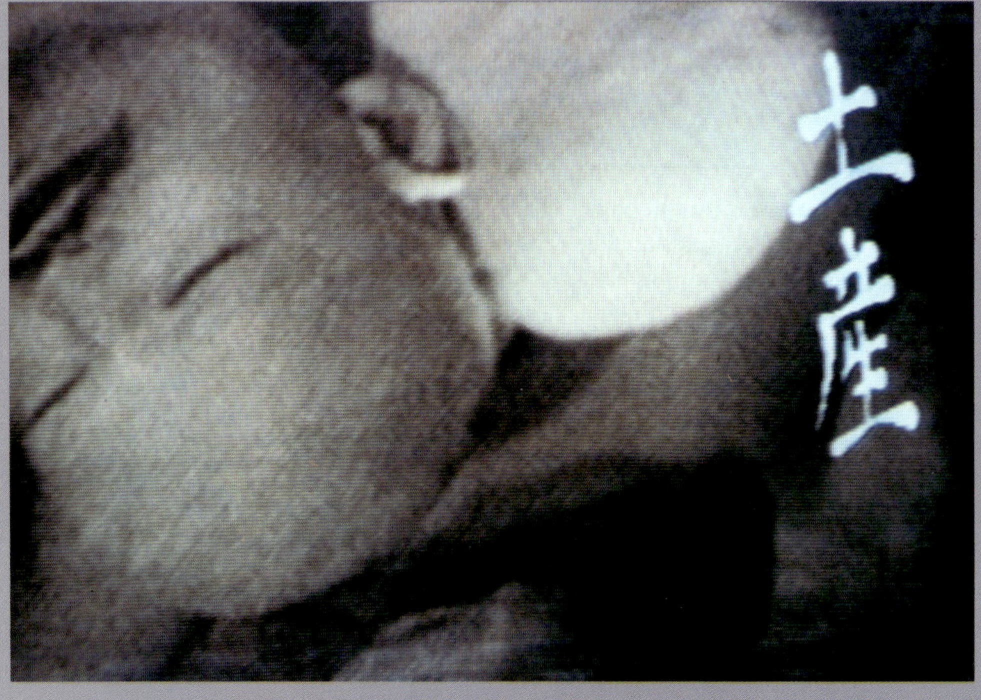

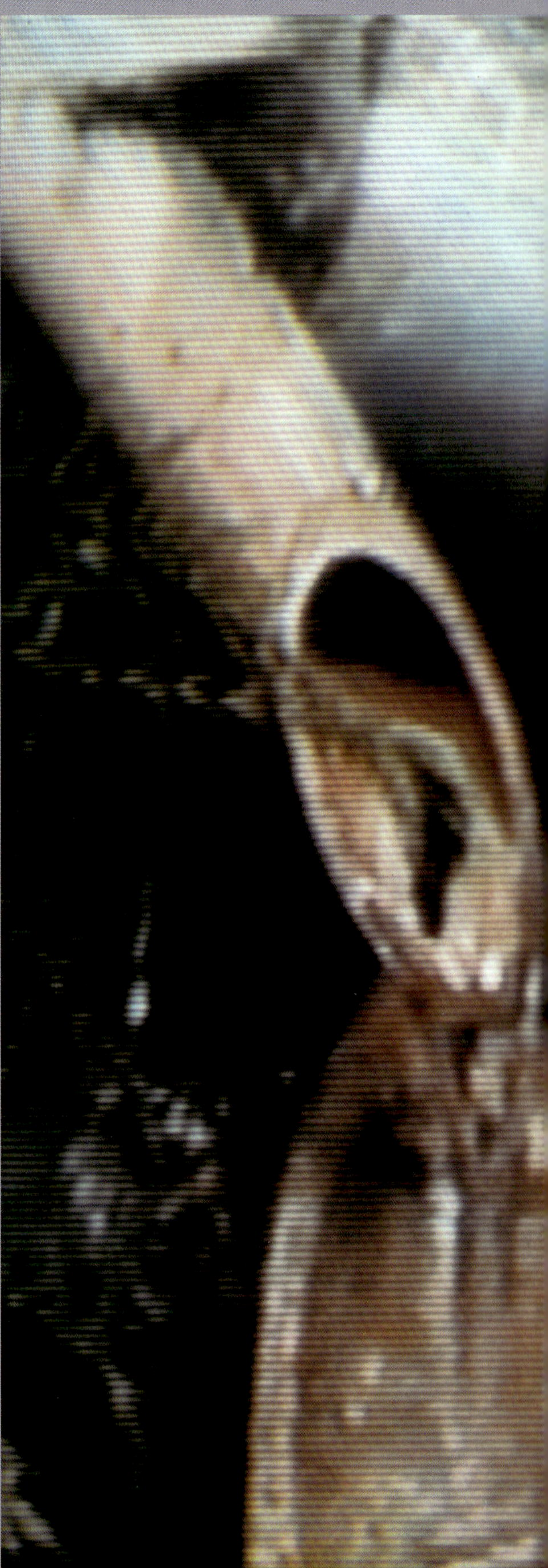

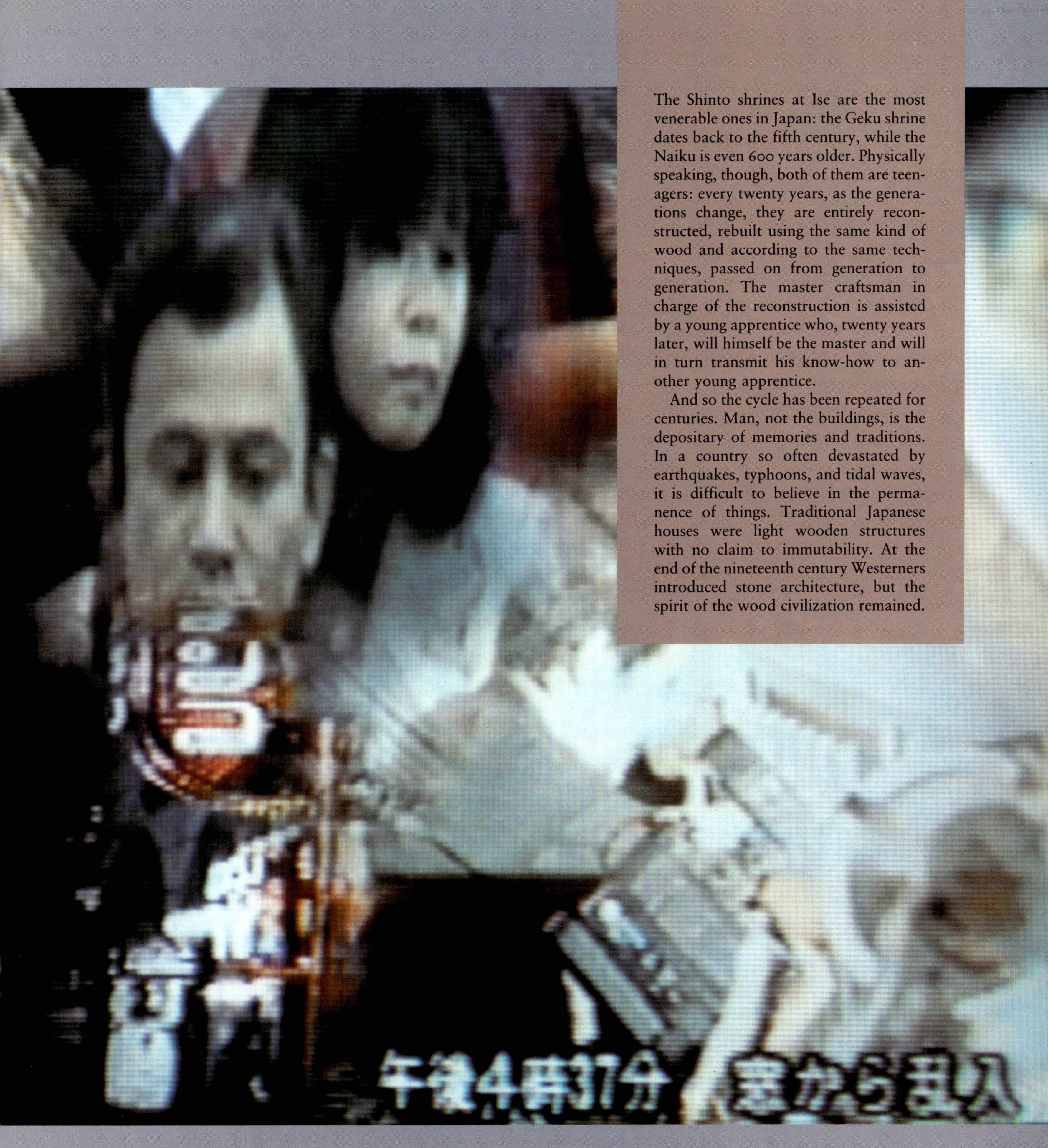

The Shinto shrines at Ise are the most venerable ones in Japan: the Geku shrine dates back to the fifth century, while the Naiku is even 600 years older. Physically speaking, though, both of them are teenagers: every twenty years, as the generations change, they are entirely reconstructed, rebuilt using the same kind of wood and according to the same techniques, passed on from generation to generation. The master craftsman in charge of the reconstruction is assisted by a young apprentice who, twenty years later, will himself be the master and will in turn transmit his know-how to another young apprentice.

And so the cycle has been repeated for centuries. Man, not the buildings, is the depositary of memories and traditions. In a country so often devastated by earthquakes, typhoons, and tidal waves, it is difficult to believe in the permanence of things. Traditional Japanese houses were light wooden structures with no claim to immutability. At the end of the nineteenth century Westerners introduced stone architecture, but the spirit of the wood civilization remained.

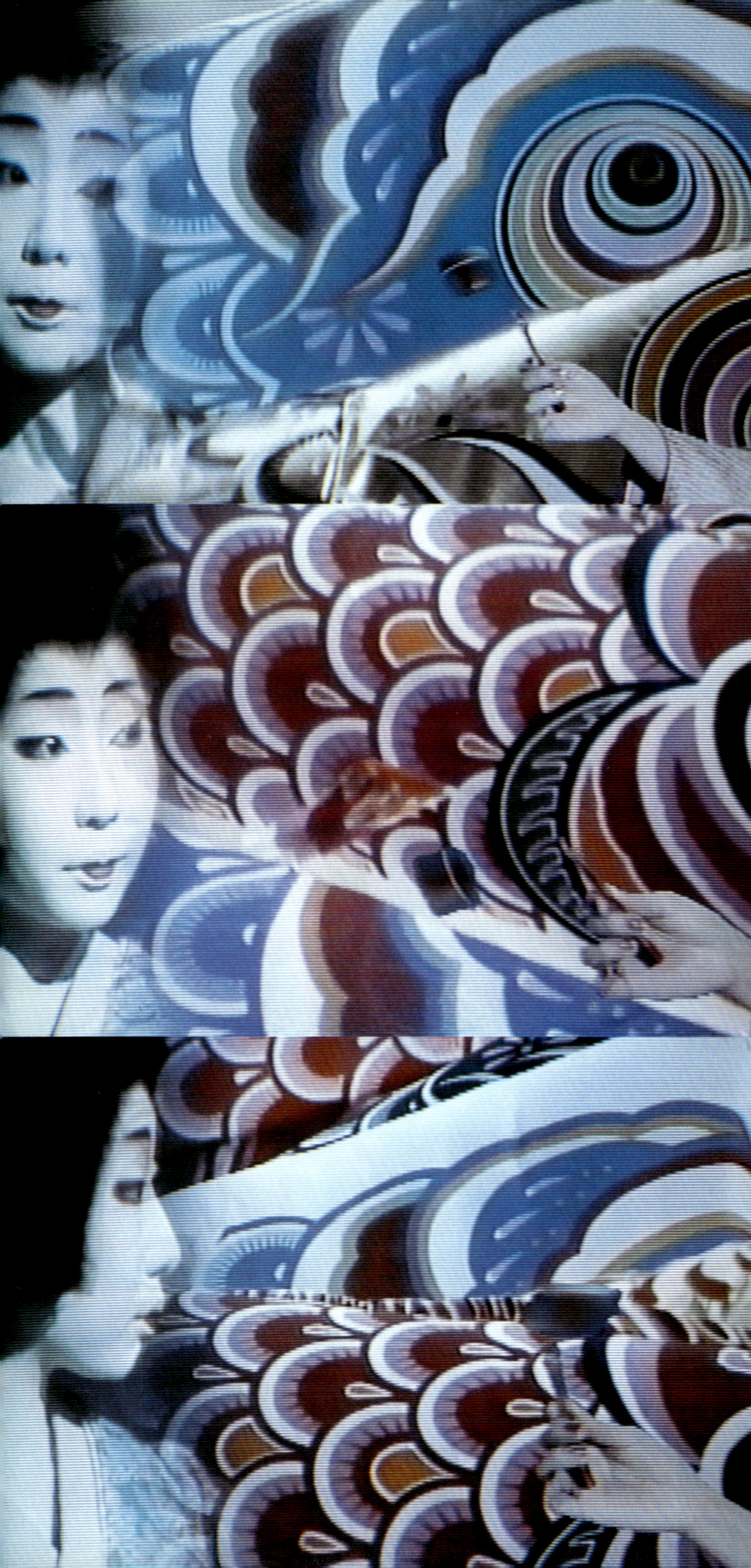

The Japanese frame of mind is one in which old ways can readily coexist with new ones: in which a trendy Nissan sedan can be parked in the enclosure of a thirteenth-century Zen temple, because both of them are significant to today's Japanese people. Our Western stone civilization does not find it as easy to accept the confrontation between Ancient and Modern—or at least the representations of them. We do not mind reading Shakespeare on an airplane; but for many, accepting the presence of I. M. Pei's pyramid in the courtyard of the Louvre was a difficult challenge.

Eventually we are usually able to overcome the feeling of awkwardness provoked by the juxtaposition of old and new. Pei's pyramid is now part of the Louvre—which itself is an architectural mingling of elements ranging from the Middle Ages to the nineteenth century. Yet the bright kimono-clad geisha and the high-tech bullet train of modern-day Japan seem to us contradictory—if not conflicting—images. This is not only a confrontation between old and new, but also one between East and West. Because Japanese modernity was inspired by that of the West, the newest part of Japan looks somewhat familiar to our Western eyes. The traditional aspect of it, though, is surely exotic. Of course the "new" Japan appears to be more thoroughly westernized than it really is: a Japanese homemade hamburger does not taste like an American one.

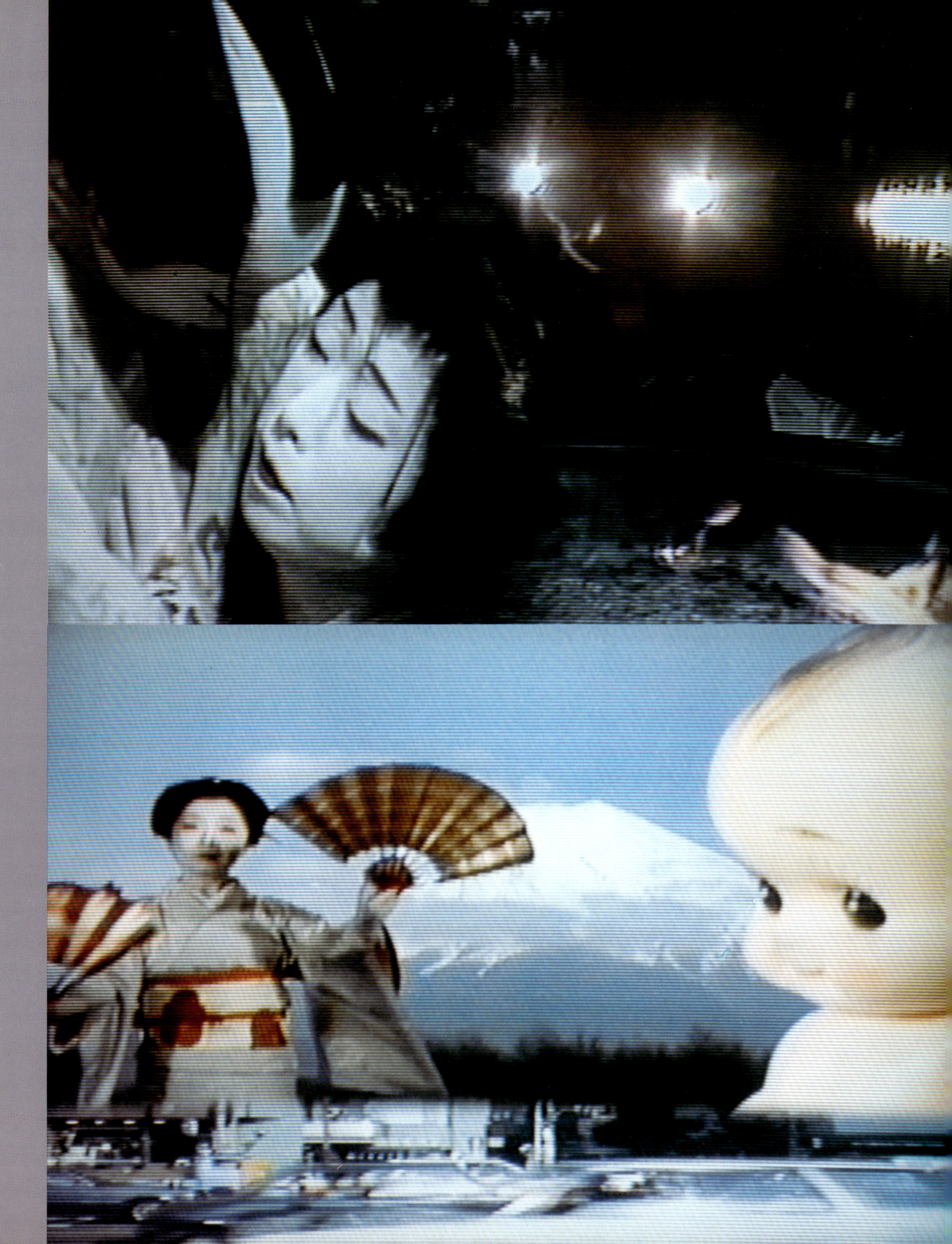

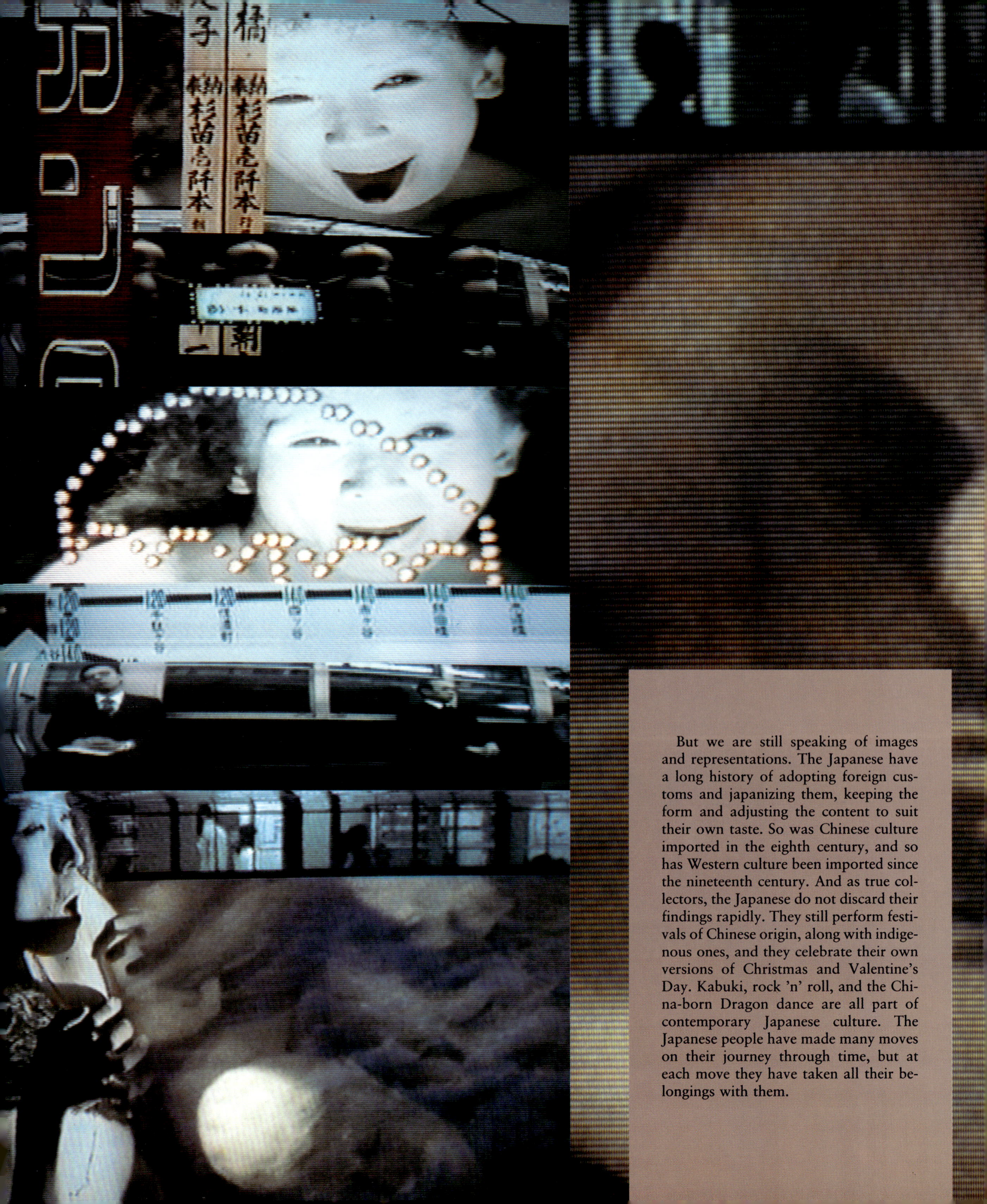

But we are still speaking of images and representations. The Japanese have a long history of adopting foreign customs and japanizing them, keeping the form and adjusting the content to suit their own taste. So was Chinese culture imported in the eighth century, and so has Western culture been imported since the nineteenth century. And as true collectors, the Japanese do not discard their findings rapidly. They still perform festivals of Chinese origin, along with indigenous ones, and they celebrate their own versions of Christmas and Valentine's Day. Kabuki, rock 'n' roll, and the China-born Dragon dance are all part of contemporary Japanese culture. The Japanese people have made many moves on their journey through time, but at each move they have taken all their belongings with them.

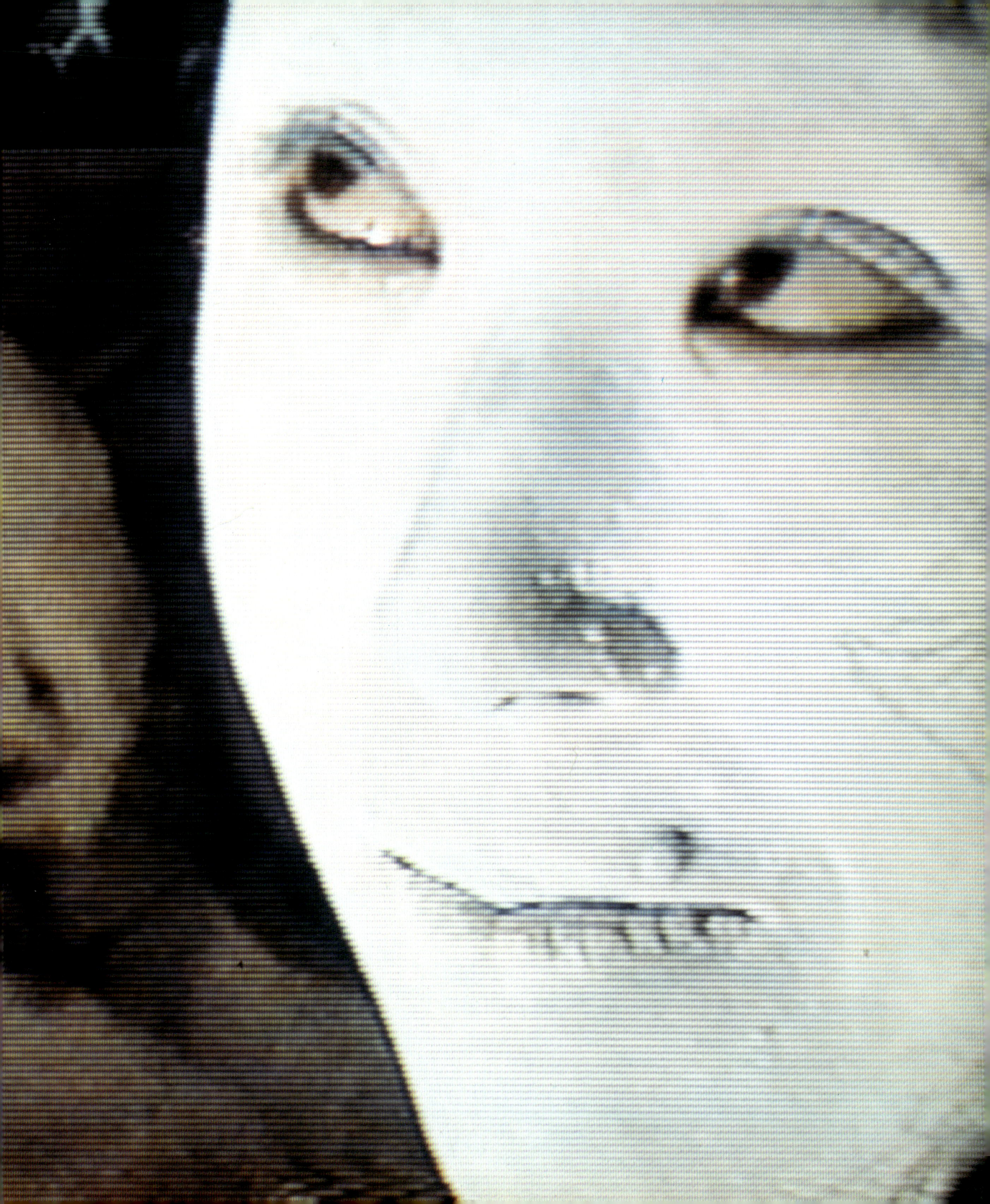

People and Ideas

Videomakers and Basketmakers
By Leslie Marmon Silko

Petroglyphs on rock-outcrops along the San Jose River suggest that the Paleo-Indian ancestors of the Pueblos had already begun to make images of spiritual significance on the sandstone eighteen thousand years ago. Pueblo Kivas have stylized abstract designs painted on the walls and Kiva altarpieces. The Pueblo people had long understood that certain man-made visual images were sacred, and were necessary to Pueblo ceremonial life.

The Pueblo people did not fear or hate cameras or the photographic image so much as they objected to the intrusive vulgarity of the white men who gazed through the lens. My grandfather, Henry C. Marmon, attended Indian school in Riverside, California, which might explain his fascination with and purchase of a snapshot camera in the 1920s. As a child in the 1950s I remember the delight of bringing out the old Hopi basket with Grasshopperman design because Grandma Lillie kept all of Grandpa Hank's snapshots and all the other family snapshots in the tall Hopi basket.

My sisters and cousins and I were too young to recognize the old-time people in the photographs, although often we recognized mesas and hills, certain houses. And so it was necessary that any viewing of the old snapshots in the Hopi basket be accompanied by a running commentary by my father and Grandma Lillie, although they sometimes had to ask Grandpa Hank to help identify the really old Laguna people long dead and gone. The identification of the faces and the places in the photographs never failed to precipitate wonderful stories about the "old days," which in turn brought out other, older stories which stretched far beyond the confines of the snapshots in the grasshopper basket.

Victor Masayesva, Jr., video still from *Ritual Clowns*, 1988

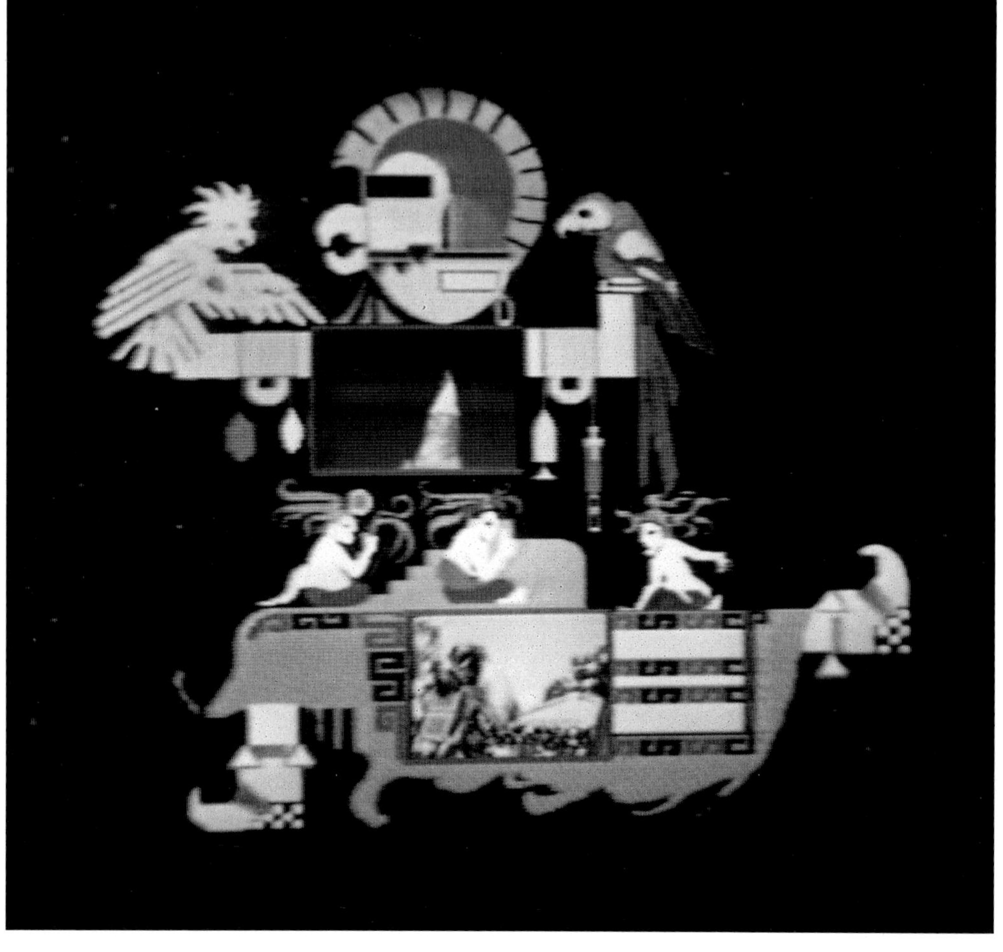

Our family was of mixed Laguna and white ancestry, but as a child I saw that many of the homes of the most traditional and conservative Laguna people included a great many photographs of family members.

At first, white men and their cameras were not barred from the sacred Katsina dances and Kiva rites. But soon the Hopis and other Pueblo people learned from experience that most white photographers attending sacred dances were cheap voyeurs who had no reverence for the spiritual. Worse, Pueblo leaders feared the photographs would be used to prosecute the Cusiques and other Kiva members, because the U.S. government had outlawed the practice of the Pueblo religion in favor of Christianity exclusively.

Pueblo people may not believe the camera steals the soul of the subject, but certainly the Pueblo people are quite aware of the intimate nature of the photographic image. Because Pueblo people appreciate so deeply the power and significances of the photographic image, they refuse to allow strangers with cameras the outrages to privacy which had been forced upon Pueblo people in the past.

But the calculations failed. Eventually

Victor Masayesva, Jr., video still from *Itam Hakim, Hopiit*, 1984

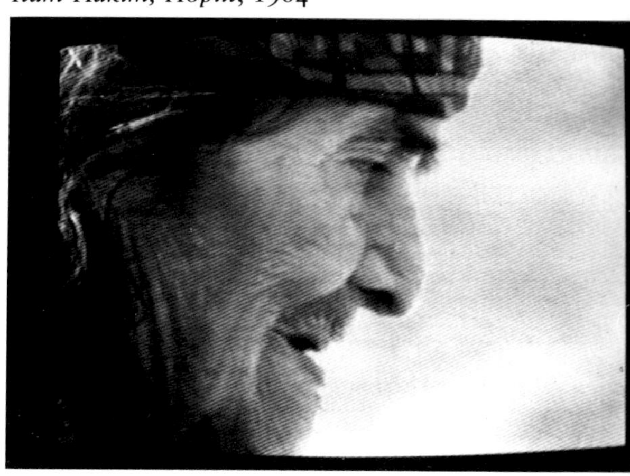

the children were returned to their beloved sandstone and expanses of blue sky; again the place soaked them in, and they were reunited with what continues and what has always continued. Victor Masayesva, Jr.'s two videos, *Itam Hakim, Hopiit* and *Ritual Clowns,* reveal that the subtle but pervasive power of communal consciousness, perfected over thousands of years at Hopi, is undiminished. In Victor Masayesva's hands, video is made to serve Hopi consciousness and to see with Hopi eyes.

Pueblo cultures seek to include rather than to exclude. The Pueblo impulse is to accept and incorporate what works, because human survival in the southwestern climate is so arduous and risky. Before the Europeans appeared, the cultures of the Americas had vast networks of trade and commerce; during times of famine, trade partners sent food. Guatemalan macaw feathers went to Taos, and Minnesota pipestones to Honduras.

Europeans were shocked at the speed and ease with which Native Americans synthesized, then incorporated, what was alien and new. Mexican Indians had embraced Jesus, Mary, Joseph, and the saints almost at once; the Indians had happily set the Christian gods on their altars to join the legions of older American spirits and gods. The Europeans completely misread the inclusivity of the Native American worldview; instead Europeans were disgusted by what they perceived to be weakness and disloyalty by the Indians to their Indian gods. For Europeans, it was quite unimaginable that Quetzalcoatl might ever share the altar with Jesus.

Euro-Americans project their own fears and values in their perception of a "conflict" between Hopi videomakers and Hopi basket-weavers. Hopi basketmakers reassure the Euro-Americans that, while not extinct, Native Americans are not truly part of American society. The Hopi with the video camera is frightening for a number of reasons. Euro-Americans desperately need to believe the indigenous people and cultures which were destroyed were somehow less than human; Hopi videomakers are proof to the contrary.

The Hopi with a video camera is an omen of a time in the future which all Euro-Americans unconsciously dread: the time when the indigenous people of the Americas will retake their land. Euro-Americans distract themselves by whether a "real" or "traditional" or "authentic" Hopi would, should, or could work with video. (Get those Hopis back to their basket making!)

Thus Euro-Americans desperately try to deny what has already begun, that inexorable force which has already been set loose in the Americas. Hopi, Aztec, Maya, Inca—the people who would not die, the people who do not change because they are always changing. The Hopi with the video camera announces the twilight of Eurocentric America.

Pueblo people today are quite sophisticated about film and video technology. Like all human beings they are concerned with their continued survival as the people *they believe themselves to be.* What is essential to all Pueblo people is that generation after generation will continue to remember and to tell one another who they are, who they have been, and who they may become.

Thus Pueblo narratives are not mere bedtime stories or light entertainment; through the narratives Pueblos have for thousands of years maintained and transmitted their entire culture—all strategies and beliefs necessary to Pueblo survival are not written, but remembered and repeated, generation after generation. Even the most ordinary deer-hunting story is dense with information, from stalking techniques to weather forecasting and the correct rituals to be performed in honor of the dead deer. In short, the stories and reminiscences which enliven all Pueblo social gatherings are densely encoded with expression and information.

Thus when the U.S. government began to forcibly remove Pueblo children to distant boarding schools in the 1890s, the Pueblo people faced a great crisis. Like the slaughter of the buffalo, the removal of native American children to boarding schools was a calculated act of cultural genocide. How would the children hear and see, how would the children learn and remember, what Pueblo people, what Hopis for thousands of years, had known and remembered together?

The Psychoids of Oppression and a Faith in Healing: The Life and Work of W. Eugene Smith
By A. D. Coleman

Some might think that 1989 was the year Gene Smith came back to haunt us. I prefer to think he never left. Like Banquo's ghost, he has unfinished business to resolve. For among the many things Smith embodied was the uneasy conscience of photojournalism and of photography itself, which neither can nor should ever be laid to rest.

In any event, with the 1989 double whammy of the broadcast premiere of Kirk Morris's biographical docudrama, "W. Eugene Smith: Photography Made Difficult," over PBS nationwide, and the virtually simultaneous publication of *W. Eugene Smith: Shadow and Substance* (McGraw-Hill, $29.95 hardbound), Jim Hughes's long-awaited biography, the question of Smith is raised anew.

Both these ambitious projects—which were separately conceived and executed—are, inevitably, flawed; Smith was a larger-than-life entity who ultimately evades capture in prose or reenactment. It's noteworthy that both projects are driven to epic scale in their attempts to encompass him (the Morris film is 90 minutes long rather than the usual hour allotted to such profiles, and the published version of Hughes's book, a dense 550 pages, was carved from a manuscript at least twice that size). This is appropriate not only because Smith's life was exceedingly complex and tormented, but because he remains one of the medium's few epic poets—and, arguably, its greatest.

Photography has had fine lyric poets by the score—Helen Levitt, Henri Cartier-Bresson, dozens more we could name offhand. The ranks of those who even attempted to work on an epic scale are far thinner, and very few of them succeeded: Robert Frank, Edward Weston, Dorothea Lange, Walker Evans are some. Often, though not always, their success depended on some form of collaboration, as was the case with much of Smith's work, especially his magnum opus, *Minamata,* which owes so much to his wife Aileen. It may be that photography lends itself more readily to the lyric than to the epic. Alternatively, it may simply be easier to craft chamber music than to construct a symphony. Whatever the case, Smith was one of that handful capable of conceptualizing photographic works with the emotional resonance, dramatic richness, and narrative sweep required by the form to which he was drawn.

No nihilist ever wrote an epic. Epic poets, as a type, are necessarily romantics, storytellers who assume that life has meaning and makes sense—or, at least, that it *should,* and can by superhuman effort (the sometimes triumphant but more often tragic overreaching known as hubris) be made to do so. The themes and issues one grapples with in this form are the big ones—life, death, madness, war, loss, the struggles between love and hate, good and evil.

These were the concerns that obsessed Smith, apparently from his adolescence on; reconciling this essentially philosophic and artistic inquiry with the photographic image's relationship to actuality, with photojournalism's obligation to report as well as to inform, and with the intractabilities and practical demands of the then-available mass-circulation distribution networks for informational imagery was the dilemma that preoccupied him once he decided, while still in his teens, to make photojournalism his profession.

Those conflicts—creatively provocative though ultimately irreconcilable—were the goads that spurred Smith through his working life. The tensions between his theoretical and practical concerns as a poet on one hand and a journalist on the other were productive, yet he seems never to have been able simply to accept and live with the fundamental incompatibility. As Hughes makes agonizingly clear, he took the resulting frustrations out on himself—through overwork, an inability to effect closure in almost every area, general recklessness, and habitual substance abuse. And he soon became a classic manic-depressive alcoholic with a positive genius for identifying and exploiting codependent tendencies in those he encountered, especially young women.

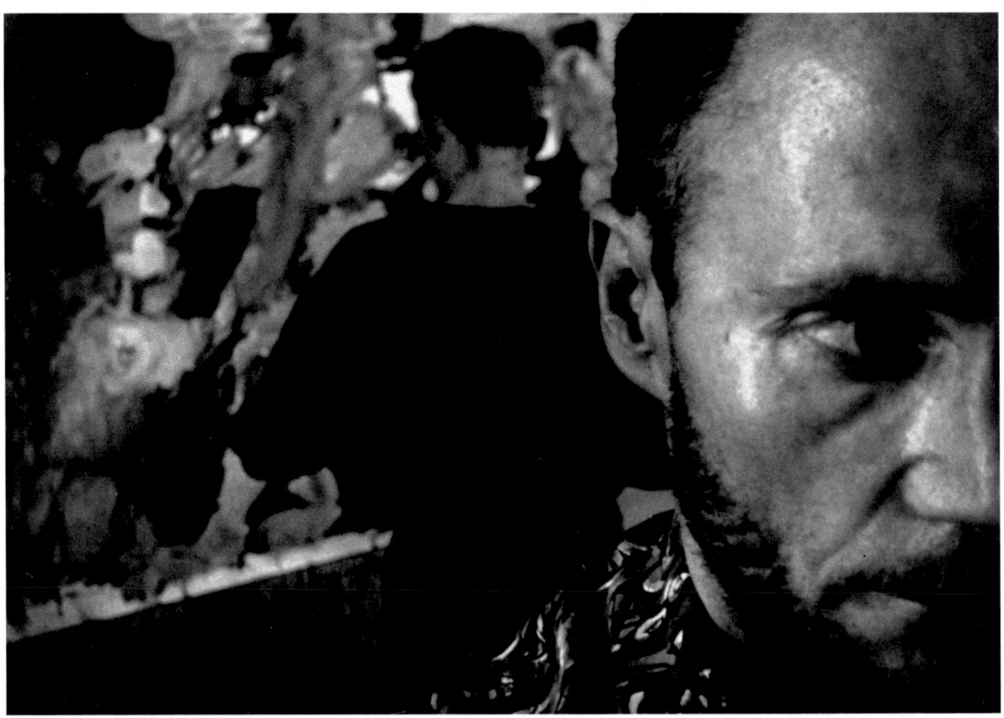

W. Eugene Smith, *The Loft from the Inside In* (self-portrait with Dave Young), c. 1957.

What Hughes attempts in his painstakingly researched account—as indicated by the book's subtitle, "The Life and Work of an American Photographer"—is itself a melding of two less-than-harmonious forms, critical biography and psychobiography. He is not wholly successful at either. Yet there is something oddly Smith-like in this method, as well as a curious symmetry in Hughes' striving to tell an epic version of an epic storyteller's story.

In fact, given his own long association with Smith (Hughes published the first U.S. version of the Minamata story in *Camera 35*, turning over full editorial control of an unprecedented 24 pages to Gene and Aileen), and this book's decade-plus gestation period, one can't help but suspect not only identification and empathy between author and subject but also parallels of personality, as if in order to complete this book Hughes had to confront and exorcise the Smith in himself, or vice versa.

Hughes is at his best in unraveling the knots and snarls of Smith's personal and professional history. Piecing this patchwork quilt together from assorted public and published sources, the countless interviews he and his wife and collaborator Evelyn conducted, and the massive archive Smith accumulated around himself (he shipped 44,000 pounds of stuff to the Center for Creative Photography in Tucson a few years before his death), Hughes provides an engrossing and no doubt accurate account of the quality of Smith's workaday life and personal environments.

In skeletal and/or rumor form, this is familiar. Hughes's accomplishment in this area is to sort out reality from myth (in Smith's case, the former was often the weirder), providing documentation substantial enough to be utterly convincing yet not so obtrusive as to bog down the narrative. Indeed, he maintains a remarkable consistency of tone throughout, rarely allowing his own emotions to intrude, even when discussing his own professional and personal involvement with the photographer.

Yet the book is nonetheless heavy going—because Smith himself was. Notwithstanding Hughes's evenhandedness and the distancing effect of print, by halfway through the book one feels oneself sinking into the miasma that was Smith's psyche and, by extension, his life. The biographer's thesis is that Smith never recovered from the trauma of the Depression-era suicide of his father, nor ever freed himself from the almost lifelong domination of his mother. Certainly in his own life Smith seems to have set out to replicate, in slow motion, his father's slide into bankruptcy and suicide. And the women he chose to love, always desperately, were never his equals in life experience or professional stature; instead, he found a series of child brides too inexperienced to keep him from infantile acting out, each of them finally growing up enough to strike out on their own—thereby abandoning him in their process of individuation.

Patently, Smith brought much of the grief of his life—professional as well as personal—upon himself. He knew this, and practiced an endless, preemptive self-flagellation to rationalize it. Even as a reader, there is only so much of this one can take; by the point in 1965 where Smith, who had a hard enough time completing his own essays even on his own schedule, undertakes the planning and editorship of a national monthly magazine, one can only echo the wisdom of Dirty Harry: "A man's got to know his limitations."

And yet . . . and yet, there is the work. For out of the disaster and the shambles of this life there emerged some of most important imagery—and some of most brilliantly redacted work in extended form—of photography to date. Imagery that resonated around the world; imagery that (perhaps due to Smith's perpetual entrapment in failure, defeat, isolation, and pain) renders and evokes the psychoids of oppression more articulately than any that preceded his.

"Where the accepted approach in photojournalism . . . had been for the photographer to put himself in the reader's place, Gene had found a way to put himself in his subjects' place," as Hughes points out. "My people have always been those people trapped in a corner," Smith himself said; and, later, "I am of the fellowship of those who bear the mark of pain." In that empathy with the trapped and damaged—in whom, doubtless, he saw himself—lies the source of his faith in the possibility of healing, so central to so much of his finest work: "Country Doctor," "Nurse Midwife," the Albert Schweitzer essay and, of course, the Minamata story.

It is to Hughes's credit that the work does not play second fiddle to the barely controlled dementia of Smith's personal and professional circumstances. His life was full of the stuff that stokes the gossip mills—brushes with death, clandestine affairs, an illegitimate child. Hughes tackles all of this head-on. Yet the urge the book generates, at its conclusion, is not for the pursuit of more juicy tidbits, but for the replenishing encounter with the work itself, which is where Smith put the best of himself.

Hughes allows Smith to paint himself, through words and deeds, and because Smith was articulate and prolific this method succeeds. It does not work so well with the book's other protagonists, who are presented only in their interactions with the photographer and are rarely described, even in the most elementary physical terms. Consequently, they come off as one-dimensional beings, foils for Smith's careening passage through life, rather than being fleshed-out characters in their own right.

I have other complaints as well. Smith's involvement with music is made clear, but an extended discussion of the influence of music on his conception of photography is missing. And, while every biography leaves things out, the fact that no mention whatsoever is made of his friendship with Robert Frank is striking. Yet, weighed against what Hughes has accomplished here, these are minor cavils; what he has given us is the shape of the man's life, in a form that rings true.

"Writing a biography," the film critic P. Adams Sitney has said, "is a process of falling out of love with your subject." Certainly, by the end of this one, the reader has fallen out of love with Smith. His death in Tucson, Arizona, in 1978, at the age of 59—nominally from a cerebral hemmorhage, though in truth he died, as someone once said of Charlie Parker, "from everything"—comes as a relief. It must have been such for all those who cared for and were involved with him—even, perhaps especially, for the man himself, an "authentic genius" (according to psychiatrist Nathan Kline) who, not by choice but chased by his own Furies, spent an eternity in hell during his time here on earth and devoted himself to speaking to and for the mute among the damned.

The South, Inside and Out
By Alice Rose George

A World Unsuspected: Portraits of Southern Childhood, edited and with an introduction by Alex Harris. Published by the Center for Documentary Photography, Duke University, and the University of North Carolina Press, Chapel Hill and London, 1988 ($16.95 hardcover).

Encyclopedia of Southern Culture, edited by Charles Reagan Wilson and William Ferris. Published by the University of North Carolina Press, Chapel Hill, 1989 ($59.95 hardcover).

No one is shouting "The South will rise again." At last the American South has become life-size, enhanced by its myths, not overcome by them, no longer nearly destroyed by the fantasy of what it was and what it might have been. The passage of time has healed the wounds.

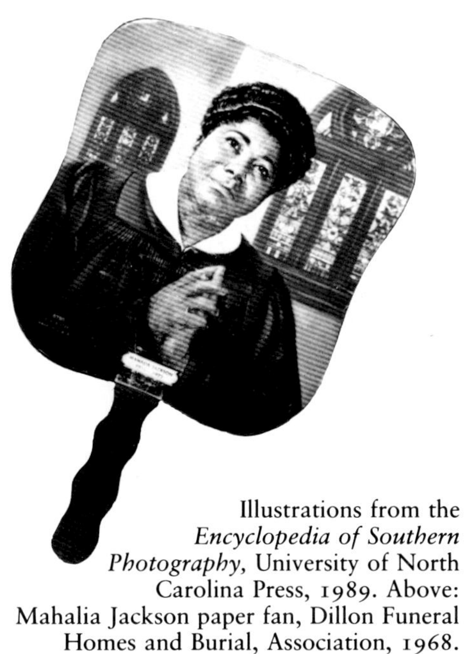

Illustrations from the *Encyclopedia of Southern Photography,* University of North Carolina Press, 1989. Above: Mahalia Jackson paper fan, Dillon Funeral Homes and Burial, Association, 1968.

Time, and exorcism by the word. Writing has provided the means by which the South could preserve its past without being destroyed by it. Without losing its uniqueness, the South has begun to see itself as part of the contemporary world. It wants to progress, to turn its back on past inequality and poverty; but, just as strongly, it wants to retain its Southernness. These two goals are not obviously compatible, but the South thrives on contradiction.

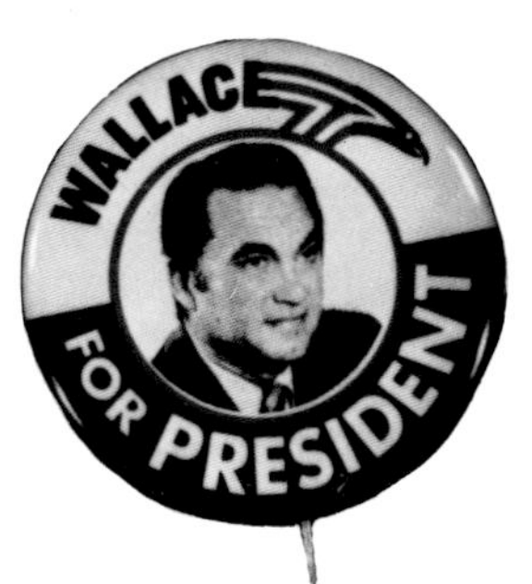

George Wallace campaign button.

Now we can look back with a pride that is not vanity, that does not hide a shame or sense of inferiority. I say "we" because I am one of those who, though long gone from the area, will always be Southern—a statement common to those born in the South but no longer living there. We have come to know what is good in us and what is bad. After knowing comes acceptance. There is a strong sense of identity in being Southern. Its foundation is both personal, strongly resting on the family, the county, the state; and formal, in its adherence to a tradition of strong social structures.

The Encyclopedia of Southern Culture and *A World Unsuspected* reflect the new maturity of the South. One, as its name suggests, is a serious documentation of the region. In contrast to this comprehensive analysis, the other book is a microscopic view; writers tell personal histories of childhood, guided and illustrated by family pictures. The strong Southern sense of identity is exhibited in both.

The Encyclopedia is massive, 1,634 pages. It evolved from work at the University of Mississippi's Center for the Study of Southern Culture and defines the South in terms of culture as expressed by T. S. Eliot in *Notes toward the Definition of Culture,* "all the characteristic activities and interests of a people." Twenty-four chapters, beginning with Agriculture and ending with Women's Life—and in between Violence, Mythic South, Black Life, Environment, Language, Literature and Law, to name a few—open with essays by an expert in the field. Each explores the general and the specific—personalities, dead and alive, codes of social behavior, folklore, dialects, dress, resources, money, politics, etc. Simply put, the encyclopedia tells you anything you want to know about the South. It is easy to use and entertaining, as well as informative. The editors, Charles Reagan Wilson and William Ferris, have created their own monument to the South. It is not a sentimental tirade; it is an act of remembrance with a cool eye on today.

The oral tradition of the South is universally acknowledged. It is out of this tradition that the Southern writer grew. The family is a prime source of storytelling, and a primary subject for most writers. The isolation that kept parts of the South backwards to the rest of the world created from within a culture based on language. Alex Harris has asked eleven Southern writers to use family photographs "as a catalyst for memory, to tell the true story of their childhoods." *A World Unsuspected* is the result.

On their own, the photographs rarely do what good photographs can—hold in balance what is known and what is unknown so that the mind creates a truth from the stimuli of visual relationships. Some snapshots here might arrest attention even without knowing the stories behind them, but in general the pictures are "fun" to look at only in relation to the story. Fortunately, these writers tell good stories, so we are not bored as we might be looking at some family photo albums.

It would seem irrelevant whether or not they are reporting reality or are acts of the imagination. But the pictures turn these stories into documents; without them it would be a different collection altogether. They become a verification of the word. So, we read differently. And we look differently—because the pictures, though less artful than the words, are about these specific people and things. It is as though we were sitting on a porch hearing real stories about people and places we knew—or nearly knew—and were ourselves a part of the oral tradition.

We travel all over the South—and North, being Southerners still. There is Sheila Bosworth's wonderful account of her New Orleans family; Bobbie Ann Mason's rock 'n' roll obsessions (re Elvis: "I knew he had dreamed the same dreams"); James Alan McPherson's coming to accept his father (in the end, "He loved electricity, loved to play with it, and must have found some connection with God within the mysteries of that invisible flow"); Robb Forman Dew's Baton Rouge girlhood ("I had a wonderful personality until I was about fourteen when I was simply too tired to have it anymore"); Ellease Southerland's Northern-born, Southern-feeling vivid tale of poverty, loss, love, and joy—the whole family story. Dave Smith, Barry Hannah, Josephine Humphreys, Padgett Powell, Al Young are the other, equally good storytellers.

These stories are distinctly Southern, but they do not feel alien to the American experience. The South has finally become a part of the Union. This is a relief. But no Southerner I know would ever give up the passion for being different, for being Southern. *The Encyclopedia of Southern Culture* seems to mark a past and a present from which the future can take off. It seeks to define and preserve without being narrow. *A World Unsuspected* confirms the best of Southern tradition.

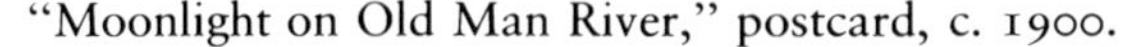

"Moonlight on Old Man River," postcard, c. 1900.

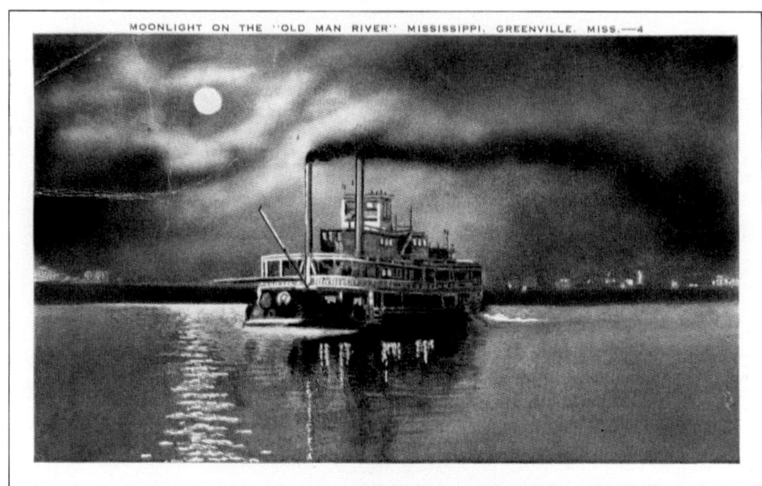

CONTRIBUTORS

OMAR BADSHA, a photographer, teacher, and writer, is the director of the Documentary Photography Project at the University of Cape Town, and a founding member of the photographers' collective Afrapix.

MEGAN BIESELE is the project director of the JU/WA Bushman Development Foundation, P.O. Box 9026, Windhoek, Namibia, and an adjunct professor of Anthropology at Rice University, Houston, Texas.

A. D. COLEMAN is photography critic for the *New York Observer* and the author of *Light Readings: A Photography Critic's Writings, 1968–1978* (Oxford University Press, 1979).

WENDY EWALD'S photographs made with Appalachian children were featured in *Aperture* 100; most recently she has worked with children in a village in India.

PHYLLIS GALEMBO is an associate professor at the State University of New York at Albany. This work is from a book entitled *Divine Interpretation: From Benin to Bahia*, to be published by University of New Mexico Press in 1991. She has received two Visual Artist Project grants from the New York State Council on the Arts.

MARC GARANGER lives in Paris and is the author of *Femmes Algériennes 1960* (Contrejour, 1982) and *La guerre d'Algérie* (Editions de Seuil, 1984), among other titles.

ALICE ROSE GEORGE is a poet and former publisher of *Granta*.

DAVID LEWIS worked in the South African Trade Union Movement for fifteen years, and is currently a lecturer in the Department of Economic History at the University of Cape Town.

ROGER MEINTJIES is a resident of Cape Town, South Africa, and is currently working in Mozambique photographing the process of agricultural reconstruction and documenting the reconstruction of a communal village.

SUSAN MORGAN lives in Brooklyn, New York, and Edinburgh, Scotland, and writes frequently about the arts for *Artpaper* and *Interview*.

CAROLE NAGGAR is a poet and American editor for *Camera International*.

KAROLINE POSTEL-VINAY is currently working in Tokyo for the Musée du Louvre, and is doing research in sociology at the École des Hautes Etudes en Sciences Sociales, Paris. She has also written for *Le Monde Diplomatique* and *Dynasteurs*, the monthly magazine of *Les Échos*.

ELAINE REICHEK is an artist represented by the Carlo Lamagna Gallery, New York.

NAN RICHARDSON is a writer who lives in New York, and is a former editor of *Aperture*.

LESLIE MARMON SILKO is a writer from Laguna Pueblo in New Mexico. She lives in Tucson, where she is completing a novel entitled *Almanac of the Dead*.

ROBERT FARRIS THOMPSON is professor of the history of art at Yale University. He is currently preparing a book, *New York: The Secret African City*, for Pantheon Press.

EDIN VELEZ has worked with video as an experimental art form since 1969. He is also currently designing and constructing unique pop-up books.

ELIZABETH WEATHERFORD heads the Film and Video Center of the Museum of the American Indian and is coauthor of the annotated catalogue, *Native Americans on Film and Video*. She is also on the humanities faculty of the School of Visual Arts, New York.

PAUL WEINBERG is a photographer in Johannesburg, South Africa, and is a founding member of Afrapix. A book of his photographs from Bushmanland, entitled *Shaken Roots*, is in preparation.

ACKNOWLEDGEMENTS

For their welcome advice and timely assistance, we would like to thank many people who helped with this issue, and in particular Alex Harris, Jay Ruby, Susan Jonas, Darrill Bazzy, Margaret Sartor, Sue Cabazas, and Jaine Roberts.

The World's Reality Conference was hosted through the generosity of the Esalen Institute. Founded in 1962 by Michael Murphy, who remains a guiding force of the Institute, Esalen continues its tradition of broadening life dimensions for a significant number of people every year through its superb facilities on the Big Sur Coast. Steve Donovan is the President; Nancy Lunney, the Director of Programs, helped to ensure the success of the conference.

CREDITS

Unless otherwise noted, all photographs are courtesy of and copyright by the artists.

Cover photocollage by Elaine Reichek, 60" x 45 1/2", courtesy of the Arthur and Carol Goldberg Collection; pp. 3–11 photographs by Marc Garanger; pp. 12–19 photographs by Roger Meintjies, courtesy of Afrapix; p. 21 photograph by Javier Reyes, courtesy of Wendy Ewald; p. 22 photograph by Alirio Casa, courtesy of Wendy Ewald; p. 23 photograph by Luis Arturo Gonzalez, courtesy of Wendy Ewald; p. 24 photograph by Dalida Reyes, courtesy of Wendy Ewald; p. 25 photograph by Diamel Vargas, courtesy of Wendy Ewald; pp. 26–27 photocollage by Elaine Reichek, 65" x 70", courtesy of Carlo Lamagna Gallery; p. 28 photocollage by Elaine Reichek, courtesy of Carlo Lamagna Gallery; p. 29 photocollage by Elaine Reichek, 61" x 47", courtesy of Carlo Lamagna Gallery; pp. 30–31 photocollage by Elaine Reichek, 47" x 66", courtesy of Prudential Insurance Company; pp. 32–40 photographs by Phyllis Galembo; pp. 42–43 photograph by Ricardo Block; p. 45 photograph by Eugene Richards; p. 46 (left) photograph by Robert Levy; p. 46 (right) photograph by Pablo Ortiz Monasterio; p. 47 still from "First Contact," by Bob Connolly and Robin Anderson; p. 48 photograph by Marilyn Bridges; p. 49 video stills from "I Do Not Know What It Is I Am Like," by Bill Viola, stills by Kiva Perov; p. 50 photographs by John Marshall, courtesy of The Marshall Family Collection and D.E.R. Productions; p. 51 video stills from "N!ai, The Story of a !Kung Woman," a film by John Marshall and D.E.R. Productions; p. 53–56 photographs by Paul Weinberg; pp. 58–59 video still from "Video in the Villages," by Vincent Carelli, courtesy of the Museum of the American Indian; pp. 60–61 video stills from "Magic in the Sky," by Peter Raymont, courtesy of Investigative Productions; pp. 63–64 photographs by Omar Badsha; pp. 66–71 video stills from "Meaning of the Interval," by Edin Velez, stills by Ethel Velez; p. 72 (left) video still from "Ritual Clowns," (right) video still from "Itam Hakim, Hopiit," by Victor Masayesva, Jr.; p. 74 photograph by W. Eugene Smith, courtesy of Jim Hughes, copyright heirs of W. Eugene Smith; pp. 75–76 illustrations from the *Encyclopedia of Southern Culture,* published by the University of North Carolina Press.

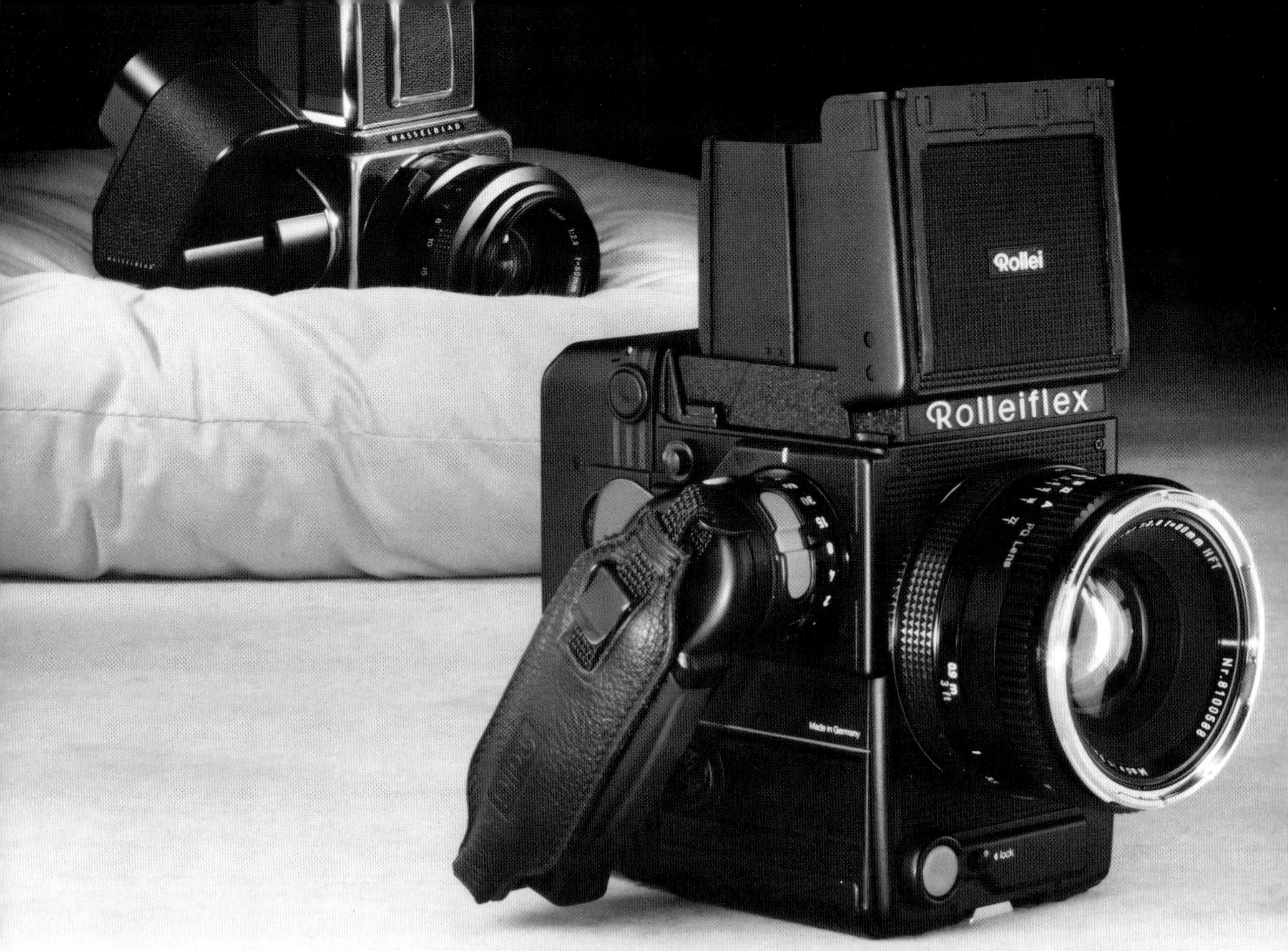

While Hasselblad has slept, Rollei has turned dreams into reality.

Hasselblad® has made essentially the same wonderful cameras for decades. Yet, technological advances have made much higher medium-format performance possible.

Rollei has turned these possibilities into realities and embodied them in the 6000 series cameras, extremely advanced Zeiss and Schneider lenses, and accessories that perform a vaster scope of tasks: with greater speed, accuracy, control and ease-of-use.

While Hasselblad has evolved dedicated flash and such, Rollei – in the new 6008 model – has introduced 13 medium-format "firsts." For superb accuracy, pick your spots: center weighted multi-zone, multi-spot, or tight-spot readings covering under 1%! Save time when you select auto-bracketing: ± 2/3 stop automatically. For situation versatility, switch "modes operandi": Shutter Priority AE mode; Aperture Priority AE mode; and Programmed AE mode; plus Manual Metering. For more exacting control, the leaf shutter adjusts from 30 to 1/500 stops in 1/3 stop increments; with 2 increments beyond 1/500! Now see all and know all: all vital data is numerically displayed within your view yet not in the "live" screen viewing area.

Discover the benefits of auto ISO speed-settings; exposure compensation from − 4 2/3 to + 2 stops; open aperture metering; 2 frames/second motor drive; a removable action-grip for single hand operation. And more. New Rollei PQ lenses from Zeiss and Schneider (including 80mm 2.0 and 180mm 2.8 lenses!) make a total of 19 Rollei lenses. And every accessory (some enabling photographic "wizardry") is fully compatible between 6006 and 6008 models (except, alas, the neckstrap).

The stuff of dreams is ready to be put in your hands. Don't sleep on it – explore the possibilities at your Rollei dealer.

ZEISS West Germany

Rollei fototechnic

We're looking at things from your point of view.

hp Marketing Corp.
16 Chapin Rd., Pine Brook, NJ 07058, 201/808-9010

Hasselblad is a registered trademark of Victor Hasselblad Inc.

Linhof's World Views.

Linhof's yaw-free views.

The Kardan Master GTL and Kardan GT, with telescoping rails and tri-axial movement, yield yaw-free indirect as well as our traditional yaw-free direct displacements. Thus these large-format cameras are "yaw-free-er" than anyone's. And they are stable even under extreme extensions (8 x 10 with long bellows fully extended). 4x5, 5x7, and 8x10 models, with conversion and reducing kits to expedite format-changing are available. These are the most technically perfect view cameras you will see.

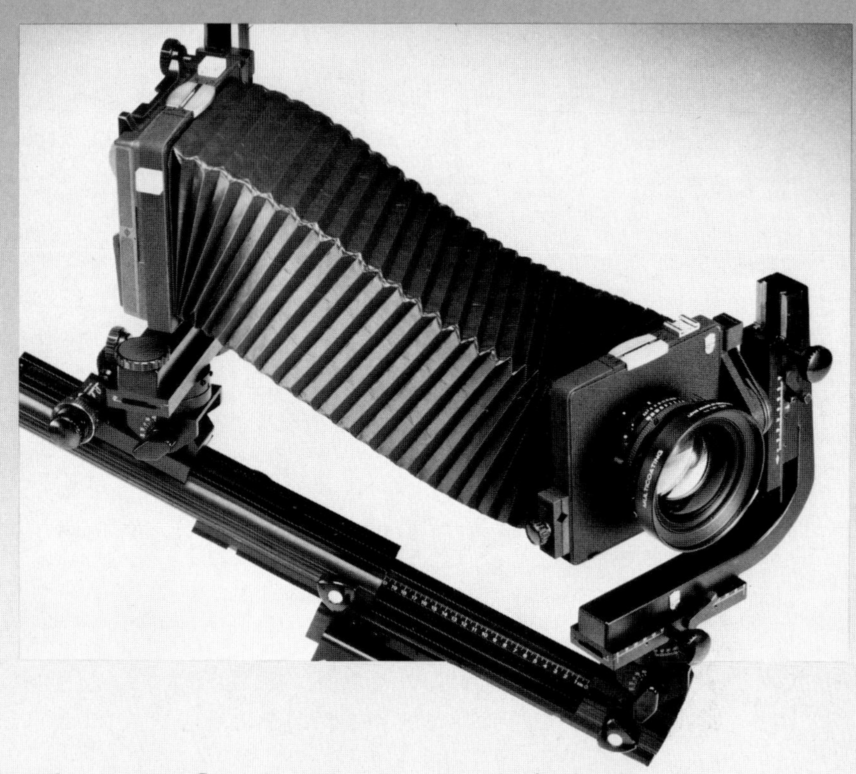

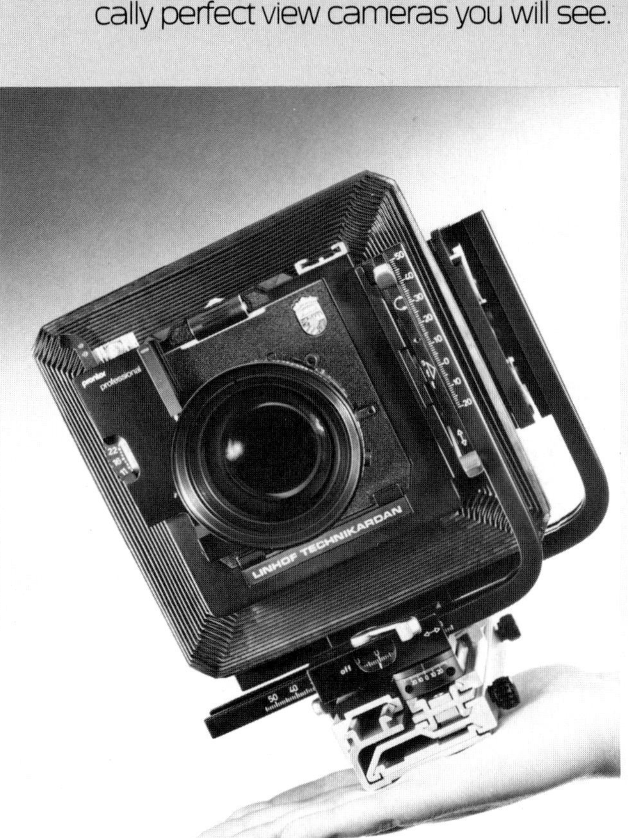

Linhof's large-format to go views.

The Linhof Technikardan 45 closes to only 8.5"x 10"x 4" (book size)—yet opens to 19" and uses lenses from 47mm to 600mm. It's a true large-format that goes outdoors and indoors. Rise, shift, swings and tilts are flawlessly performed. A unique Prontor shutter control allows aperture adjusting/reading from **behind** the camera. No fancy footwork required. And the TK 45 weighs only 6.5 pounds. Its smaller sister, the TK 23, weighs even less. The Technikardans are small in size but big in performance. See for yourself.

Linhof's widest views.

For large-format's exacting quality plus the convenience of roll film in a hand-held camera, Linhof's Technorama 617S and 612PC II are revelations. The travel/scenic, architectural, interior and industrial images they capture are breathtakingly unique. Both have an integrated spirit-level for exact camera positioning; brightline viewfinder with cross hairs; exposure times from 1 to 1/500 second and B; aperture settings from f5.6 to f45 in ½-stop increments; and more.

The 617S yields superbly detailed 87° shots in a film area 3 times larger than 2¼x 2¼; using a Schneider Super Angulon 5.6 90mm lens in precision helical focusing mount. The 612PC II has 2 interchangeable lenses, a 5.6 65mm and 5.6 135mm; a built-in lens pre-shift for perspective control; and takes up to 86 images twice as large as 2¼x 2¼. Both cameras give wide, wide views that are distortion-free with straight and no converging lines.

Consider Linhof's views at any authorized Linhof dealer.

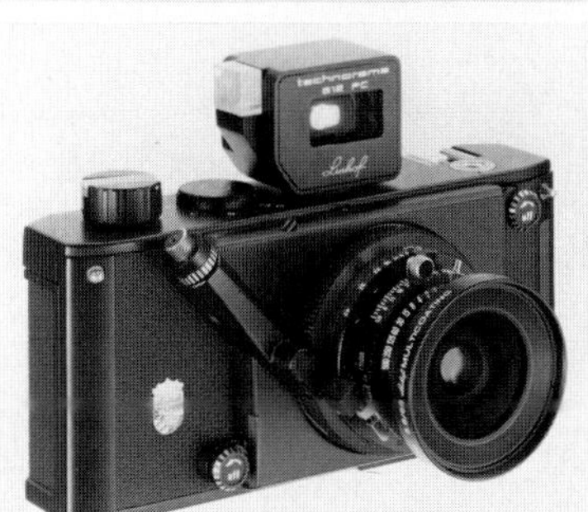

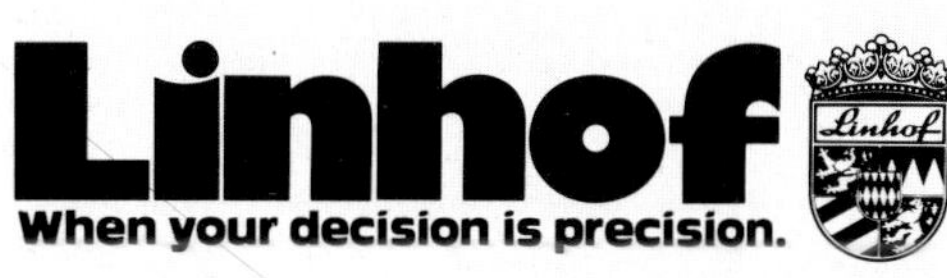

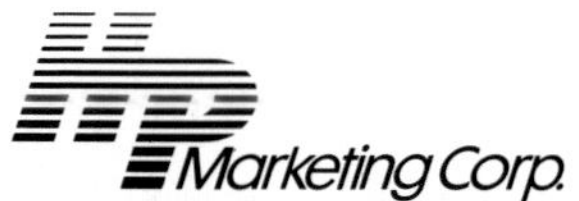

16 Chapin Rd., Pine Brook, NJ 07058, 201/808-9010

In Canada available through: Daymen Photo Marketing Ltd., Scarborough, Ontario M1V2J9